Essentials of Pricing Analytics

This book provides a broad introduction to the field of pricing as a tactical function in the daily operations of the firm and a toolbox for implementing and solving a wide range of pricing problems.

Beyond the theoretical perspectives offered by most textbooks in the field, *Essentials of Pricing Analytics* supplements the concepts and models covered by demonstrating practical implementations using the highly accessible Excel software, analytical tools, real-life examples and global case studies. The book covers topics on fundamental pricing theory, break-even analysis, price sensitivity, empirical estimations of price–response functions, price optimization, markdown optimization, hedonic pricing, revenue management, the use of big data, simulation, and conjoint analysis in pricing decisions, and ethical and legal considerations.

This is a uniquely accessible and practical text for advanced undergraduate, MBA and postgraduate students of pricing strategy, entrepreneurship and small business management, marketing strategy, sales and operations. It is also important reading for practitioners looking for accessible methods to implement pricing strategy and maximize profits.

Online resources include Excel templates and PowerPoint slides for each chapter.

Erik Haugom is Professor in Business Administration at Inland Norway University of Applied Sciences, Norway.

"A refreshingly new approach to the teaching of pricing from a very practical point of view."

Nicholas Perdikis, *Professor of International business, Aberystwyth Business School, Aberystwyth University, Wales, UK*

"This book explains the impact of pricing on companies' profit in a highly accessible way. Excel examples help readers to further deepen their understanding of these topics. I highly recommend this book to anybody who wants to learn the basics of pricing analytics in a very short time."

Peter Molnar, *Associate Professor at University of Stavanger, Norway*

"More and more businesses are embracing analytics. But not everyone can afford a price analytics software. This book is a good way to get started, learn, and practice the pricing fundamentals. The 'cookbook' approach breaks down the barriers to getting started. Now every business professional can start answering real pricing questions by using a tool they are familiar with."

Stephan M. Liozu, *Chief Value Officer of Thales Group*

"*Essentials of Pricing Analytics* is a valuable and original contribution to the pricing literature. Managers and academics will appreciate up-to-date tools that enable them to estimate demand curves, optimize prices and increase profits. Highly recommended."

Andreas Hinterhuber, *Associate Professor of Marketing, Ca' Foscari University of Venice, Italy*

Essentials of Pricing Analytics

Tools and Implementation with Excel

Erik Haugom

LONDON AND NEW YORK

First published 2021
by Routledge
2 Park Square, Milton Park, Abingdon, Oxon OX14 4RN

and by Routledge
52 Vanderbilt Avenue, New York, NY 10017

Routledge is an imprint of the Taylor & Francis Group, an informa business

© 2021 Erik Haugom

The right of Erik Haugom to be identified as author of this work has been asserted by him in accordance with sections 77 and 78 of the Copyright, Designs and Patents Act 1988.

All rights reserved. No part of this book may be reprinted or reproduced or utilised in any form or by any electronic, mechanical, or other means, now known or hereafter invented, including photocopying and recording, or in any information storage or retrieval system, without permission in writing from the publishers.

Trademark notice: Product or corporate names may be trademarks or registered trademarks, and are used only for identification and explanation without intent to infringe.

British Library Cataloguing-in-Publication Data
A catalogue record for this book is available from the British Library

Library of Congress Cataloging-in-Publication Data
Names: Haugom, Erik, 1982– author.
Title: Essentials of pricing analytics: tools and implementation with excel/Erik Haugom.
Description: New York: Routledge, 2021. | Includes bibliographical references and index.
Identifiers: LCCN 2020026974 (print) | LCCN 2020026975 (ebook) |
ISBN 9780367363222 (hardback) | ISBN 9780367363239 (paperback) |
ISBN 9780429345319 (ebook)
Subjects: LCSH: Pricing. | Pricing–Computer programs. |
Microsoft Excel (Computer file)
Classification: LCC HF5416.5 .H378 2021 (print) |
LCC HF5416.5 (ebook) | DDC 658.8/160285554–dc23
LC record available at https://lccn.loc.gov/2020026974
LC ebook record available at https://lccn.loc.gov/2020026975

Figures 1.4, 9.3 and 9.5 are adapted from *Pricing and Revenue Optimization* by Robert L. Phillips. Copyright © 2005 by the Board of Trustees of the Leland Stanford Jr. University. All rights reserved. Used by permission of the publisher, Stanford University Press, sup.org

ISBN: 978-0-367-36322-2 (hbk)
ISBN: 978-0-367-36323-9 (pbk)
ISBN: 978-0-429-34531-9 (ebk)

Typeset in Times New Roman
by Newgen Publishing UK

Visit the eResources: www.routledge.com/9780367363239

To Alexander and Leon

Contents

About the contributors viii
Preface ix

1	Introduction	1
2	Fundamentals of price theory	12
3	Segmentation and price differentiation	36
4	Break-even analysis	49
5	Price sensitivity and willingness to pay	64
6	Empirical estimations of price–response functions	82
7	Price optimization	105
8	Case study: Optimal prices of movie theater tickets	128
9	Markdown optimization	154
10	The hedonic pricing model	169
11	Revenue management	178
12	Big Data and pricing analytics	188
13	Monte Carlo simulation for pricing decisions	218
14	Conjoint analysis for pricing decisions	245
15	Acceptance, ethics, and the law	264

Bibliography 274
Index 277

About the contributors

Author biography

Erik Haugom holds a PhD in Managerial Economics, Finance and Operations from the Norwegian University of Science and Technology and an MSc in Business Administration from Copenhagen Business School. His employment experience includes positions as a taxi driver in Lillehammer, child welfare, and research planner at Omnicom Media Group. Today he is employed as a Professor in Business Administration at Inland Norway University of Applied Sciences. He is also project manager of the ongoing research project, Innovative Pricing Approaches in the Alpine Skiing Industry. His special fields of interest include energy price and volatility modelling and forecasting, risk analysis, risk management, demand and price analyses, and econometric modelling and forecasting in general.

Contributor biography

Andrew Musau is a senior research fellow at the Inland Norway University of Applied Sciences and a statistical consultant for the social sciences research institute Agderforskning. He obtained his PhD in Economics and Management from the University of Trento. His research interests are in behavioural and experimental economics, energy economics and macroeconomics.

Gudbrand Lien has a dr. oecon (PhD) in finance and a cand. oecon. degree in business administration from the Norwegian School of Economics (NHH), and a cand. agric. degree in agricultural economics from the Norwegian University of Life Sciences. He is currently a Professor in Business Administration at Inland Norway University of Applied Sciences. His main fields of research have been within energy finance, energy economics, agricultural economics, quantitative innovation studies, and econometric modelling in general.

Preface

Essentials of Pricing Analytics – Tools and Implementations with Excel is written for academics and practitioners who want a "cookbook approach" to learning and understanding pricing analytics. The book is an introductory text to pricing analytics and offers the basic theoretical foundation needed to understand the numerical examples better.

Most of the material in this book is at the introductory level and the majority of readers should be able to follow the examples without any prior knowledge of the field of pricing analytics. It is an advantage to have some prior knowledge of microeconomic theory, or at least a strong interest in quantitative analysis in general. Some of the topics covered are at a more advanced level. An example is the chapter on conjoint analysis for pricing decisions.

I would like to thank the many people who have contributed to improving this text. These include Steinar Veka, Gudbrand Lien, Iveta Malasevska, Sophia Levine, Emmie Shand, Louise Bolotin and three anonymous reviewers.

I would also like to thank students of the course, Pricing and Revenue Management, at the Inland Norway University of Applied Sciences for their valuable feedback on earlier versions of the manuscript.

Finally, I send very special and warm thanks to Andrew Musau, who has contributed with writing and editing parts of the manuscript.

Lillehammer, 2020

Chapter 1
Introduction

In this first chapter, the following topics will be covered:

- The purpose of the book.
- The impact of price management on profit.
- Pricing analytics.
- Who can use pricing analytics.
- Alternative approaches to pricing.

1.1 The purpose of the book

The purpose of this book is to provide a broad introduction to the field of pricing analytics with a special focus on how the various models can be implemented in Excel. My main goal is that you as a reader can be helpful to a current or future manager when they want answers to specific questions related to the use of pricing as a tactical or operational function from day to day. Examples of such questions, which I want you to be able to answer, include:

- Do we have an opportunity to use price as a tool to increase operating profits at all in this company?
- What is the impact on operating profits from price improvements compared to improvements in costs?
- What change in sales volume is required for a 5% price increase to break even?
- What is the break-even sales change for a range of price changes?
- How can we determine the uncertainty associated with a volume change stemming from a specific price change?
- How can we estimate our customers' willingness to pay from historical transactions or empirical data?
- How can we use information about our customers' willingness to pay to form price–response functions and subsequently adjust the price to maximize profits?
- How can we sell the same product or service to different buyers at different prices to increase profits?
- How can we dynamically adjust, and possibly mark down, the price to maximize profits?
- How can we make use of big data to make better pricing decisions?

2   Introduction

- What would make our customers accept a new pricing scheme?
- What are the ethical and legal aspects we should be aware of before implementing new pricing schemes?

More generally, the focus will be on introducing you to a range of basic techniques that are useful in many practical business situations, rather than on the technical nuances of algorithms. By following the instructions in the book, you should be able to reproduce all the examples and/or exercises using Microsoft Excel. If you are not familiar with Microsoft Excel, you should spend some time in the beginning to familiarize yourself with the interface and some basic formulas for doing simple calculations in a spreadsheet. The book is accompanied by Excel files containing both the examples and solutions to the problems at the end of each chapter.

1.2 The impact of price management on profit

To illustrate how changing the price can affect the profit, consider the following model that computes the total profit accruing from the number of items sold, v:

$$Z = pv - c_v v - c_f \tag{1.1}$$

In this model Z is the total profit, p is the price, c_v is the variable unit costs, v is the volume, that is; the number of items sold, and c_f is the fixed costs. The first term (pv) in Equation (1.1) constitutes the revenues, while the two latter terms reflect the total costs.

A local coffee shop has done a market survey of consumers' preferences related to regular black coffee. The survey indicates that setting a price of $1 per cup will lead to a demand of 100 cups per day. Increasing the price to $2 reduces demand by 40 cups/day. It turns out that the variable unit costs associated with producing one cup of coffee are $0.50 and the fixed costs are $20 (this will not affect the solution; why?). What price should the local coffee shop charge per cup of coffee to achieve the highest profit?

To help the manager of the coffee shop with this problem, we can calculate the total profit using Equation (1.1) and check which of the two price levels induces the highest profit. This problem is small enough to be solved with pencil and paper. However, as this book makes extensive use of Microsoft® Excel, we shall do the calculations needed to advise the manager on what price that maximizes the profit from selling coffee in an Excel spreadsheet. Another reason for implementing the problem in Excel right away is that we can adjust the calculations quickly once new information arrives. And soon enough the problems we want to solve get so big that just using pencil and paper would be a very tedious task.

The results of the Excel calculations are illustrated in Figure 1.1 and show that charging a price of $2 is most profitable. By charging a price of $2 instead of $1, the total profit ends up at $70 instead of $30 even though the sales volume is 40 cups lower per day at the high price level. Even though this example is simple, it illustrates the major impact price can have on demand and profit. Without doing the survey, and the subsequent analysis, the manager could wrongly believe that a price of $1 induces the highest profit.

	A	B	C	D
1				
2	COMPUTING TOTAL PROFIT FROM SELLING COFFEE			
3				
4	Price	Demand	Profit (Z)	Formula
5	$1.00	100	30	=A5*B5-0.5*B5-20
6	$2.00	60	70	=A6*B6-0.5*B6-20

Figure 1.1 Implementation of the profit function for two price/demand combinations in Excel.

However, it is important to note already at this stage that there could be several other good reasons for setting a price of $1 to achieve a demand of 100 cups, even though this price in isolation induce a lower profit compared to setting a price of $2. One such reason could be that the coffee shop sells other items, such as cookies, and that this bundling aspect justifies a lower profit on the coffee.

Another aspect worth mentioning is the potential bias occurring in a survey where we ask about the customers' intended behavior instead of measuring their real actions. It turns out that there rarely is a 100% match between stated purchase preferences and real purchase behavior.

The manager of the coffee shop is somewhat concerned about this potential bias and decides to run a simple price experiment. For four consecutive weeks the price is adjusted by $1 per week. The price/demand data for the four weeks are handed over to us and are presented in Table 1.1

This time we decide to impress the manager even more with our Excel skills and choose to first depict the relation between the various price levels and the corresponding demand. This is presented in Figure 1.2. The dots in this figure represent the quantity demanded (Y-axis) at each price level, which is referred to as a *price–response function* in pricing analytics. As the data points are discrete, we refer to it as a *discrete price–response function*. A price–response function specifies the quantity of coffee cups demanded at various price levels for this particular coffee shop and therefore contrasts with the market demand curve for coffee. An illustration of the price–response function will help the manager to understand how the quantity of coffee demanded varies by price for her own shop. The information in this graph can also indirectly be used to imagine how a continuous price–response function may look. This will become clear in later chapters.

The objective now, though, is still to set the price that will maximize the total profit accruing from selling coffee. Hence, we should make it easy for the manager to make the correct decision based on the data we have at hand. To do so, we can calculate the profit

Table 1.1 The price experiment results for the coffee shop

Week	Price	Demand
1	$1.00	121
2	$2.00	84
3	$3.00	42
4	$4.00	12

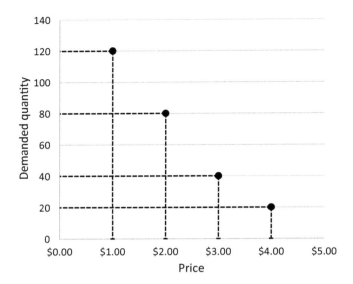

Figure 1.2 A discrete price–response function for coffee based on the data given in the text.

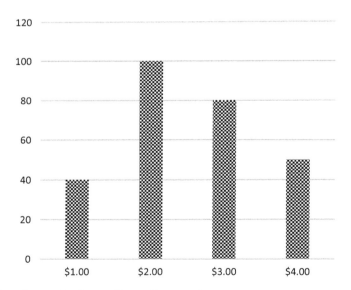

Figure 1.3 Total profit accruing from selling coffee at various prices.

using the same formula as in Figure 1.1 and then create a graph that shows the results. This is done in Figure 1.3.

The graph clearly shows that charging a price of $2 induces the highest profit. In fact, the difference between the optimal price and the next-best price in this example is as much as 25%. The impact from improved price management on operating profit has also been documented in published research. Marn and Rosiello (1992) found that improved price management has the biggest financial impact on operating profit when compared with variables such as variable costs, sales volume, and fixed costs. Therefore, being good at pricing analytics seems like a good investment.

Another key lesson to learn from the above example is that the revenue part of the profit function consists of two elements: One price element and one quantity element. The coffee shop is doing a trade-off between selling more cups at a lower price versus selling fewer cups at a higher price. What price level that will induce the highest profit depends on the sizes of the price and quantity elements when moving from one price level to another. This is linked to the characteristics of the market the coffee shop operates in and the preferences the customers have for the coffee sold at this particular coffee shop. These characteristics will always be reflected in the price–response function. We shall examine this in detail in later chapters.

In the above example we have performed *pricing analytics* to help the coffee shop manager to make a *pricing decision*. But what exactly is pricing analytics? As the title of the book includes these words, we should devote a section to defining it.

1.3 Pricing analytics

Put simply, we can say that *pricing analytics* is all about transforming data of some sort into insight for making better *pricing decisions*. Pricing analytics is usually concerned with the *short-term*, tactical or operational, part of pricing, in contrast to strategic pricing, which is more related to the *long-term* pricing decisions on how value should be created and captured.[1]

In the coffee shop example, the data we used were information about price levels and corresponding demand, and the costs associated with producing coffee. These data were then transformed into calculations of profit levels, which in turn could be put forward to the management when deciding what price to set for one cup of coffee. The analytical methods used can vary from very simple descriptive analysis to advanced dynamic optimization. We shall introduce you to a range of techniques later in this book.

In the coffee example there was only one product: Black coffee. This product was offered only at the coffee shop and we did not distinguish between various customer types. In practice, however, the coffee shop probably offers multiple coffee types (e.g., café latte, cappuccino, espresso, etc.). It may also sell the various coffee types through different sales channels (e.g., at the coffee shop, home delivery in a thermo cup, at the local sport stadium during home games, etc.). Finally, it would be possible to differentiate between various customer types based on some simple characteristics (e.g., students, retirees, frequent buyers, etc.).

The three dimensions (product/service type, sales channel, and customer type/segment) can be illustrated in what Phillips (2005) refers to as a *pricing and revenue optimization (PRO) cube*. Such a cube is presented in Figure 1.4. The aim of pricing analytics is always to find the right price for each of the *relevant* elements of the cube, and to update these prices over time. We emphasize *relevant* because some of the elements in the cube may be empty (e.g., only black coffee is offered for home delivery), or some elements may be constrained by factors outside our control. In theory, each element of the cube could have its own unique demand characteristics, which in turn would lead to unique

6 Introduction

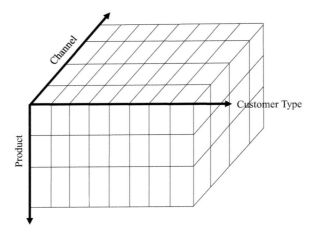

Figure 1.4 Dimensions of the pricing and revenue optimization cube. Source: Phillips (2005, Figure 2.4, p.27: The PRO cube). Reproduced by permission of the publisher, Stanford University Press. The gridlines are not included in the original version of the figure, but added for this publication.

optimal (profit-maximizing) prices. Additionally, market conditions change rapidly, and the right price today could be wrong tomorrow.

Pricing analytics as a continuous process

Because of the very rapidly changing conditions in most markets, pricing analytics can be considered a continuous process where new information must be incorporated in the analysis as soon as it arrives. A simplification of such a process is illustrated in Figure 1.5. The pricing analyst first receives the raw price/demand data, then builds a model that aims to optimize the price. The model is then solved, and the suggested price level is implemented. After having executed a given pricing scheme, the performance is monitored and evaluated, and the models are updated using the latest information. In today's e-commerce, such updates may be done automatically, at a very high frequency in some cases.

In practice, the pricing process depicted in Figure 1.5 must be carried out for each element of the pricing cube and the analysis may also consider restrictions or dependencies occurring between the various elements. It is, however, always convenient to start simple and then expand the model and process of optimizing prices for the whole portfolio of products or services once we understand the important aspects of the key elements involved. We shall therefore start by looking at single products or services when we perform pricing analytics in the subsequent chapters.

1.4 Who can use pricing analytics?

Pricing analytics as a tactical and operational function has been derived mainly from the field of management science, and the use of quantitative techniques to set prices in

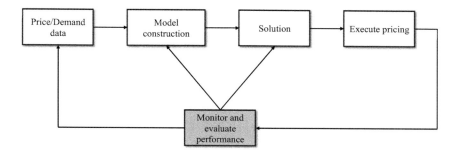

Figure 1.5 Pricing analytics as a continuous process.

complex and dynamic environments is relatively new (Phillips, 2005).[2] The passenger airline industry was one of the first industries to systematically apply these techniques to increase profitability. Today, pricing analytics is used everywhere. The only requirement is that you have a product or service that is offered in a market.[3] However, it turns out that many of the techniques are particularly applicable in the service industry. The main reasons for this are that service providers usually have fixed capacity with low costs of marginal sales and high fixed costs. Hence, price can be used to form demand to exploit existing capacity. Therefore, many of the examples used in this book will stem from the service industry.

1.5 Alternative approaches to pricing

From Equation (1.1) we understand that pricing analytics incorporates costs and customer demand (defined as *volume* in the equation) to find the profit-maximizing price. Later in the book we shall also see that the competitive environment is indirectly accounted for in the techniques we use to find the optimal prices. Other approaches to pricing tend to emphasize either costs, customers, or competitors when determining the price.

Examples of such alternative approaches include (but are not limited to):

- *Cost-plus pricing*: Calculating costs and adding a margin to the costs when setting the price.
- *Market-based pricing*: Setting prices based on our competitors' actions.
- *Customer-driven pricing*: Places the customer at the center of the pricing decision.
- *Value-based pricing*: Setting the price based on estimates of how customers value the firm's product or service.

When applying pricing analytics, we try to incorporate all these aspects with the objective of maximizing operating profits. However, it is important to note that the process of setting the right price in both the short and long-term is a very complex task that involves many departments and people. Therefore, we must make some simplifying assumptions when building the analytical models.

1.6 Summary

- The purpose of this book is to provide a broad introduction to the field of pricing analytics with a special focus on how the various models can be implemented in Excel.
- Price management has a major impact on operating profit.
- Pricing analytics is all about transforming data of some sort into insight for making better pricing decisions.
- All companies having a product or service that is offered in a market can apply pricing analytics, but many of the techniques are particularly applicable in the service industry.
- Alternative approaches to pricing are: (1) Cost-based, (2) market-based, (3) customer-driven, and (4) value-based.

1.7 Problems

1. The ice cream shop *Icy* has just completed a market survey examining expected demand at various price levels for one of their products – Icy Cool. The data are summarized in the table below:

	A	B	C
1	RESULT OF MARKET SURVEY		
2	FOR ICY COOL		
3			
4	Price ($)	Demand	Profit
5	0.5	500	
6	1	300	
7	1.5	100	
8	2	50	
9	2.5	20	

You also know that the variable unit costs associated with producing this ice cream type amount to $0.25 and that the fixed costs are $100. Your job is to calculate the total profit for each price/demand combination and give your advice to the manager of *Icy* about what price to set for this product.

2. In the same market survey, *Icy* examined the expected demand for another ice cream type. The data for this product is given below:

	A	B	C
1	RESULT OF MARKET SURVEY		
2	FOR ICY HOT		
3			
4	Price ($)	Demand	Profit
5	0.5	200	
6	1	180	
7	1.5	170	
8	2	150	
9	2.5	100	

The variable unit costs for this ice cream type is $0.45 and the fixed costs are still $100. What price would you recommend setting for this ice cream type?

3. Fill in as many element names as possible in the figure given below: You can, for example, insert numbers in the boxes and list them next to the figure: e.g., 1. Black coffee, sold in a physical coffee shop to customers with a student ID card.

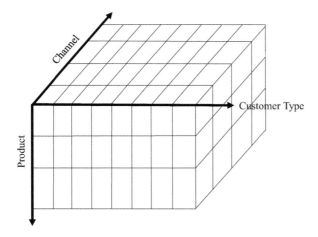

4. *Back to Icy:* It turns out that you can also sell Icy Hot at the local sport stadium during home games. You have been given information about the (average) expected demand at the various price levels during home games (see table below).

The variable unit costs are $0.65 and the fixed costs are $50. This time you shall create a simple spreadsheet model where you include the variable unit costs and fixed costs in separate cells. Then you shall illustrate in a graph how the profit varies according to the price level (similar to that presented in Figure 1.3). What price should *Icy* charge for *Icy Hot* at the sport stadium during home games to maximize (expected) profit?

Price ($)	Demand
0.5	600
1	500
1.5	450
2	390
2.5	350
3	250
3.5	150
4	50

5. Various approaches to pricing are presented below. Determine what the actual price set by the firm will be in each case and specify what kind of pricing approach that is used in each case.
   a. The variable unit costs associated with producing an item are $15. The company adds a surcharge equal to 60% of the variable unit costs to determine the price.
   b. Three competitors of a company quote the following prices for a widget: A, $15; B, $20; C, $22. Our price is set such that it is consistently 10% below the average of these three main competitors.
   c. The relationship between the price and the demanded quantity of a widget a firm produces is illustrated in the figure below. Set the price such that the firm guarantees a sale of 5,000 units of the product in the next month.

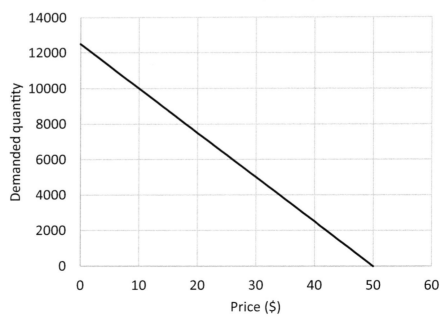

Price and demanded quantity for a widget

d. The following data relates to a survey measuring the perceived value of a service. Determine the price charged for the service, given that price is at 5% below the perceived value.

Customer	Perceived value
1	19
2	19
3	19
4	12
5	15
6	17
7	15
8	18
9	15
10	13

6. What is pricing analytics?
7. What are the most crucial steps involved in the pricing analytics process?

Notes

1 This is a simplification for expository purposes. Nagle et al. (2011) provide a comprehensive examination of the term strategic pricing. Interested readers should consult their book to gain a deeper understanding of this concept.
2 The theoretical foundation, mostly derived from the field of economics, has been around for a long time.
3 And in the absence of perfect competition. We shall return to the various market structures in Chapter 2.

Chapter 2

Fundamentals of price theory

In the last chapter we saw how the key to setting an optimal price is information about the price–demand relationship. The coffee shop had to know the quantity demanded at various price levels. Before going deeper into how firms should set, and adjust, the prices of their products or services to maximize profit, we present the fundamentals of the classical economic theory involved to explain the shape of price–response functions. Remember the difference between the market demand function and the price–response function? The distinction is important as it is the quantity demanded for your particular product or service that matters when optimizing the prices of these, not the quantity demanded of this product or service category in the whole market. Hence, when we illustrate the theoretical concepts, the focus will be on *one element of the PRO cube at the time.*

The chapter covers the following topics:

- Consumer preferences and the link to price–response functions:
  - Indifference curves;
  - Budget lines;
  - Utility maximization;
  - The link between price changes, the budget line and the price–response function;
  - Consumer surplus.
- Costs that matter in pricing decisions.
- An example of where the objective is to decide the optimal price and quantity.
- The role of pricing under various market structures.

Discussion in this chapter is limited to the fundamental theoretical concepts needed to perform pricing analytics. Readers interested in a deeper understanding should consult a textbook in microeconomics.

2.1 Consumer preferences and price–response functions

To fully understand the shape of price–response functions, and how they may change with the price of competing products or services, we need a model of consumers' behavioral choices. The *theory of consumer behavior* can be used to understand the relationship between consumers' limited income and their consumption of various goods and services. This theory is thoroughly covered in most textbooks in microeconomics and a detailed description is beyond the scope of this textbook. Here, the focus will be on illustrating the fundamentals of the theory in a pricing analytics framework.[1] We shall do this by presenting the decision problem of an economic agent wanting to maximize her utility from consuming black coffee while visiting the city center during a given week. We start by illustrating the consumers' preferences graphically. Then we include the budget constraint[2] and show how this is linked to the prices and consumption of black coffee in Shop X and Shop Y. Finally, we show the link between price changes and consumption changes when the consumer allocates her income between black coffee sold in Shop X and Shop Y, respectively. That is, we show how the shape of the price–response function is formed.

Indifference curves, budget lines, and the utility maximization problem

The classical model of consumer choice assumes that consumers have preferences for specific products or services. In the case of regular black coffee bought in the city center, this means that a potential consumer will either (1) prefer regular black coffee sold at Shop X, (2) prefer regular black coffee sold at Shop Y, or (3) be indifferent about the two.[3] The concept of indifference can be visualized in what is called an *indifference curve*. This is done in Figure 2.1. All the combinations of cups of coffee bought from Shop X and Shop Y along the curve give the consumer the same satisfaction (e.g., points A, B, and C). The combination in point D is clearly worse than any combination on the indifference curve and will not be chosen by any rational consumer. Any

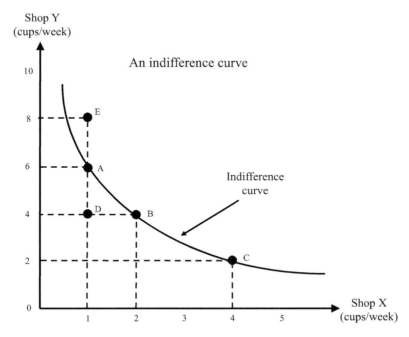

Figure 2.1 Illustration of an indifference curve. The consumer is indifferent about combinations of cups of black coffee bought in Shop X and Shop Y on the indifference curve.

14   Fundamentals of price theory

combination above the curve, for example point E, will be chosen over the combinations at or below the indifference curve. As the indifference curve presents combinations of two goods or services that induce the same level of satisfaction, they are often named iso-utility curves in the economic literature. Further, the term *market basket* refers to the combination of cups purchased at Shop X and Y. In general, a market basket could refer to the quantities of food, electronics, movie theater tickets and other goods and services that a consumer buys each week, month, or year. For expository purposes, we shall continue to look at a simple market basket consisting of specific quantities of two goods only; cups of black coffee bought in Shop X and Shop Y each week. Even though the product may seem the same (black coffee), it is not. Why? Because it is offered at two competing shops (X and Y). The use of the same product at different shops highlights the important difference between the market demand curve and the price–response function.

We now know that any market baskets (that is, combination of cups of black coffee bought from Shop X and Shop Y) on the indifference curve induce the same level of satisfaction for this specific consumer. But how many cups of black coffee will this consumer end up buying from Shop X and Shop Y per week? To answer this question, we first need information about the consumer's budget for regular black coffee per week, and the price of one cup bought at Shop X and Shop Y. In other words, we need the budget line.

The total budget the consumer has available to spend on black coffee, in the city center, is $10 per week. One cup of regular black coffee is priced at $2.00 at Shop X and $1.00 at Shop Y. This means that the budget constraint can be formulated as:

$$2.00X + 1.00Y + \leq 10 \tag{2.1}$$

To plot the budget line, we simply need to determine two points that are on the line and then draw a straight line through these points. This can be done by treating the constraint as an equation (which means that the consumer uses the total budget of $10, nothing less) and then calculate how many cups the consumer could buy at Shop X if buying all the cups there, and vice versa. We find the first point by letting $Y = 0$ and solving for X:

$$2.00X + 1.00(0) = 10$$
$$X = \frac{10}{2} = 5$$

This means that the consumer can buy five cups of black coffee sold at Shop X every week. Alternatively, the consumer can buy ten cups at Shop Y:

$$2.00(0) + 1.00Y = 10$$
$$Y = \frac{10}{1.00} = 10$$

Now we have two points and can draw a straight line connecting these. This is done in Figure 2.2 and the line is referred to as the *budget line*. All combinations of regular black

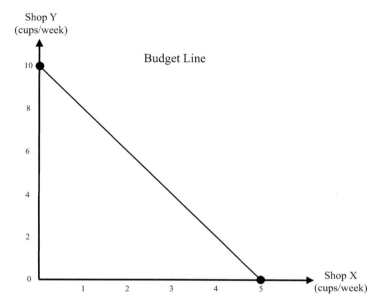

Figure 2.2 Illustration of the budget line. All combinations on the line spend the entire budget of $10.

coffee bought at Shop X and Shop Y on that line will spend the whole budget of $10 – before any price changes take place.

Note that when drawing this budget line, we assume that it is possible to buy fractions of cups of coffee. This is rarely possible in practice, of course, but it makes the illustration of the theoretical concepts much easier.

However, we *still* do not know how many cups of regular black coffee the consumer will buy at Shop X and Shop Y per week. To figure this out, we need to combine the information provided by the indifference curve and the budget line. Figure 2.3 combines the indifference curve from Figure 2.1 (the indifference curve is now labeled I_1 in Figure 2.3) with the budget line presented in Figure 2.2. All the combinations at, or below, the budget line, are affordable by the consumer; for example, point A or point B. At point A (four cups bought at Shop X and two cups bought at Shop Y), the entire budget is used. We see this because the point is on the budget line. At point B (two cups bought at Shop X and four cups bought at Shop Y) the consumer spends only $8 ($2×2+$1×4 = 8). As the two points are on the same indifference curve, they yield the same level of satisfaction and the consumer would be indifferent between the two points A and B. However, the consumer can do better. Because of the assumption that *more is better than less* the consumer will always strive to achieve a higher level of satisfaction. This is illustrated with a new indifference curve, I_2. All market baskets on this new indifference curve generate a higher level of satisfaction to the consumer. The question then is, can she afford any of these market baskets? The answer is only one of the market baskets on indifference curve I_2 can be affordable, and that is the combination at point C (two cups bought at Shop X and six cups bought at Shop Y). At this point, it is

16 Fundamentals of price theory

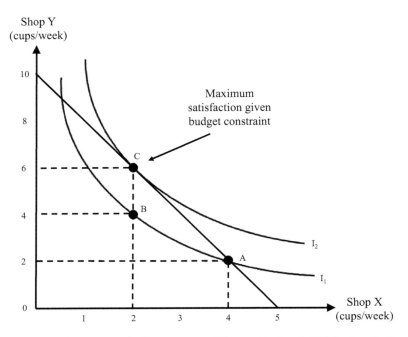

Figure 2.3 Maximum satisfaction given budget constraint. The total budget is $10 (budget line) and two indifference curves indicate a low- (I_1) and a high (I_2) level of utility.

impossible for the consumer to achieve a higher level of utility (satisfaction) given the budget constraint of $10 per week. In other words, the consumer has maximized her satisfaction by choosing point C.

So far, we have seen how the quantity demanded of black coffee for a given consumer can be found, given the shape of the indifference curve and the budget line. But we do not know how the quantity demanded varies with the price level at Shop X or Shop Y. That is, we do not know how the *price–response function* for black coffee for any of the two shops looks like. To make the link between indifference curves, budget lines, and price–response functions, we need to do one more thing: change the price for black coffee at one of the shops. We start by showing how the individual price–response function can be obtained and then show that the complete price–response function one of the coffee shops is facing is simply the sum of the demanded quantity by the individual consumers at every price level.

The link between price changes, the budget line and the price–response function

The left panel (a) of Figure 2.4 illustrates the effects on the budget line of a price increase from $1.00 to $1.50 for one cup of black coffee at Shop Y. The total weekly budget for black coffee for this consumer is still $10, but the increased price of coffee at Shop Y induces a new budget line. This new budget line is found using the same approach as for the original line, but now with the updated price level at Shop Y.

The number of cups bought at Shop X if buying zero cups at Shop Y is still five. Why? Because the price of coffee at Shop X has not changed:

$$2.00X + 1.50(0) = 10$$
$$X = \frac{10}{2} = 5$$

However, as the price at Shop Y has increased, the number of cups we can buy if spending the entire weekly coffee budget there must decrease:

$$2.00(0) + 1.50Y = 10$$
$$Y = \frac{10}{1.50} = 6.67$$

That is, because the price increased from $1.00 to $1.50, we can now only buy 6.67 cups of coffee at Shop Y per week. The new line is again found by drawing a straight line through the two points. This is done in panel (a) of Figure 2.4. We can clearly see that the price increase at Shop Y changes the potential market baskets the consumer can choose. To further illustrate this, we include indifference curves that trace out the market baskets that maximize the satisfaction at the two price levels (panel (b) of Figure 2.4). Before the price change, the consumer would choose a market basket consisting of one cup bought at Shop X and eight cups at Shop Y (point A). After the price increase, the consumer achieves maximum satisfaction by consuming two cups at Shop X and four cups at Shop Y.

We now have two discrete points of both price ($1.00 and $1.50) and quantity demanded (eight and four) at Shop Y, and could have plotted these in a diagram to obtain an estimate of a linear price–response function. However, to better illustrate how the individual price–response function is formed, let us do one more price change. This

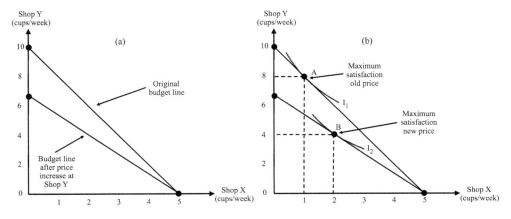

Figure 2.4 Effects of a price increase at Shop Y on the budget line (a) and preferred market basket (b).

18 Fundamentals of price theory

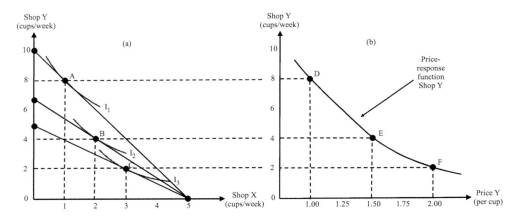

Figure 2.5 Effects of a price increase at Shop Y on budget line (a) and the corresponding (individual) price–response function (b).

time we increase the price of one cup bought at Shop Y to $2.00. Given the same total weekly budget of $10.00, the total number of cups we can buy at Shop Y is reduced to five (why?). In Figure 2.5, the new budget line is depicted together with the two budget lines from Figure 2.4. The indifference curves (I_1, I_2, I_3) are included to show the utility maximizing market baskets at the three price levels (points A, B, and C, respectively). Panel (b) of Figure 2.5 illustrates the relation between demanded quantity and the price at Shop Y. Point D indicates that eight cups would be bought at Shop Y at a price level of $1.00. When the price increases to $1.50, the weekly demanded quantity from this consumer drops to four cups at Shop Y (point E). Increasing the price further at Shop Y induces another drop to two cups per week. Having quantity demanded on the Y-axis and price level on the X-axis, the points D, E, and F now form a discrete price–response function for this individual consumer. To make it continuous, we simply draw a line through these three points. In later chapters we shall learn various methods for drawing such a line.

If Shop X and Shop Y were competing in a market where there was only one consumer, the individual price–response function illustrated in Figure 2.5 would also be the complete price–response function Shop Y was facing. In practice, this is not likely though. The individual consumers' price–response functions need to be combined into a single aggregate price–response function, that is; the price–response function faced by Shop Y. To illustrate the concept, it is enough to look at a simple example where we have two consumers instead of one. Table 2.1 does this. Consumer #1 in this table is the one whose demanded quantity at each price level is depicted in Figure 2.5. Consumer #2 is new and her demanded quantity at each price level is also given in Table 2.1. If these are the only two customers in Shop Y's market, we find the total quantity demanded at each price level by aggregating the demand of the two individuals. This is done in the rightmost column of Table 2.1. The concept of aggregating the individual demand can also be illustrated visually, as shown in Figure 2.6.

In the left panel of Figure 2.6 we see that the individual demands are simply stacked on top of each other. The total demanded quantity is then just the sum of these two.

Table 2.1 Aggregating demand from individual consumers

Price	Consumer #1	Consumer #2	Total
$1.00	8	10	18
$1.50	4	8	12
$2.00	2	6	8

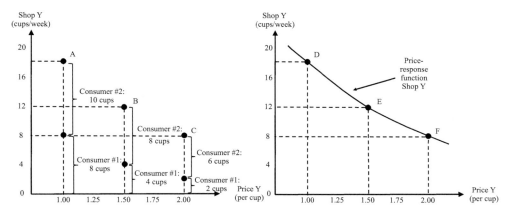

Figure 2.6 Aggregating the individual demand of consumer #1 and consumer #2 from Table 2.1. Panel (a) shows quantity demanded by the individual consumers while panel (b) illustrates the new, aggregated, price–response function for Shop Y. For expository purposes, the budget line and indifference curves are dropped in this figure.

For expository purposes the budget line and indifference curves are dropped in panel (a) of this figure. In panel (b) the corresponding total demanded quantity is illustrated together with the price–response function for Shop Y.

Consumer surplus

When having the aggregate price–response function available, and if knowing the actual price charged by Shop Y, we can also calculate what the economic literature refers to as the *consumer surplus*. At the individual level, the consumer surplus is defined as the difference between the maximum amount a given consumer is willing to pay for the good or service, and the price. It is important to note that this is the consumer surplus if consuming *one unit only*. As an example, if consumer #1 above has a maximum willingness to pay of $2.25 for one cup of coffee and the price is $1.00, the consumer surplus would be $1.25 if consuming only one cup. However, we know that in many cases consumers have individual price–response functions showing the relation between quantity demanded and price. Hence, also at the individual level, the consumer surplus is the difference between the price–response function for *that* consumer and the price charged for one unit. This concept is illustrated in Figure 2.7.

20 Fundamentals of price theory

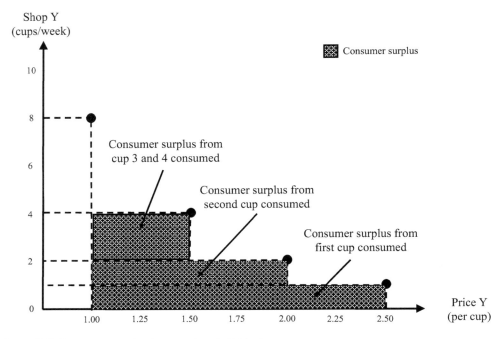

Figure 2.7 Consumer surplus for one given individual.

From this figure we see that for the first cup of coffee consumed the consumer surplus is the difference between the maximum willingness to pay for the first cup, $2.50, and the price of $1.00, which is equal to $1.50. For the second cup consumed the willingness to pay is reduced to $2.00 and the consumer surplus for that cup is therefore $1.00. For the next two cups the willingness to pay is $1.50 per cup (for both cups). Hence, the consumer surplus for these two cups also equals $1.00 ($2x(\$1.50-\$1.00)$). At a price of $1.00 per cup, this consumer is demanding a total of eight cups. However, for the last four cups, the willingness to pay is equal to the price and the consumer surplus for these cups is therefore zero. The total consumer surplus for this consumer can be found by adding the surpluses for all cups of coffee purchased:

$$1\times(\$2.50-\$1.00)+1\times(\$2.00-\$1.00)+2\times(\$1.50-\$1.00)=\$3.50$$

The concept of consumer surplus can easily be aggregated to reflect the total consumer surplus of the customers of Shop Y. To illustrate, consider Figure 2.8 which depicts one possible version of the aggregate price–response function Shop Y is facing. Note that the quantity demanded (Y-axis) is now in 1,000s of cups. The price charged by Shop Y for one cup of black coffee is still $1.00. The price–response function shows that the maximum willingness to pay for one cup of black coffee among all Shop Y's customers is $3.00 (the point where the price–response function crosses the X-axis) and that a total of 8,000 cups is demanded at a price of $1.00 per cup. The aggregated difference between price and the

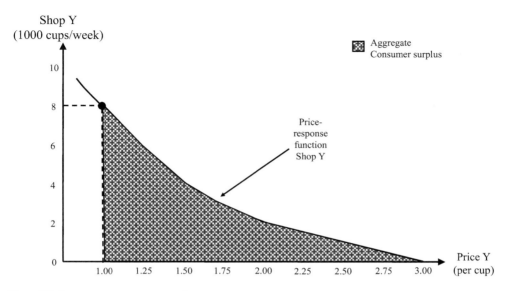

Figure 2.8 Aggregate consumer surplus.

consumer's willingness to pay will thus be reflected in the area below the price–response function and above the price level charged by Shop Y for one cup. We shall return to how businesses can use price differentiation to keep more of the aggregate consumer surplus in the next chapter.

We now have a basic understanding of the fundamental economic theory involved in explaining how price–response functions are formed. Companies wanting to maximize their total profit accruing from selling a given product or service also needs a thorough understanding of their own costs associated with producing, or offering, the product or service to the market. As costs are crucial inputs in any optimization model aimed at finding the profit-maximizing price, we devote the next section to gaining a better understanding of the costs that matter in pricing decisions.

2.2 Costs that matter in pricing decisions

Put simply; the costs that really matters to a pricing and revenue manager are the incremental costs associated with one additional unit sold of the product or service offered. If the revenue from selling that unit exceeds the costs, we should offer it to the market. If the opposite is true, we should not offer it to the market. This concept of *marginal costs and revenues* lies at the heart of all pricing decisions. To calculate the marginal costs (MC), we need to know what the total cost function looks like. In Equation (1.1) in Chapter 1 the profit function was presented. The last two terms in this equation represent the total costs accruing from the number of items produced of the product or service of interest:

$$TC = c_v v + c_f \tag{2.2}$$

where v is the number of items produced (or alternatively sold, i.e. the volume), c_v is the *variable unit costs* and c_f is the *fixed costs*. We shall describe these cost components next and link them to the concept of MC.

Fixed costs (c_f)

In the short term, the fixed costs (c_f) do not vary with the level of output. Consider again a given coffee shop. To keep the shop open it needs: (1) electricity for heating/cooling, (2) insurance, (3) maintenance of buildings and inventory, and (4) a minimum number of employees just to keep the shop open. All these costs run, even if there are zero customers on a given day. Hence, going from zero to one customer induces no change in the fixed costs. If the costs associated with keeping the shop open and running were all *fixed*, the MC associated with one extra customer would be zero.

Variable costs (c_v)

Variable costs (c_v) vary with output. The easiest example is costs associated with raw materials used to produce the final product. Examples of variable costs for the coffee shop are costs related to the electricity used to keep the various coffee machines running and, obviously, the coffee, milk, sugar, and other raw materials going into the final products they sell. The total variable costs are given by the level of the output (volume) times the c_v per unit (number of cups sold in the coffee shop example).

Fixed, variable, or sunk costs?

Whether a given cost is fixed or variable depends on the time horizon used. In the very long run, nearly all costs are variable. The coffee shop, for example, could decide to reduce or increase the general level of activity in the shop by shutting down and restarting specific coffee machines. In this case, the number of employees needed to keep the shop open would vary. The same goes for electricity and potentially also insurance and maintenance. However, decisions about how many different coffee machines, and hence what menu is available to customers, should not be made on a day-to-day basis. These decisions need to be part of a longer-term plan. Even though the fixed costs can vary, they are not usually referred to as variable costs, but rather incremental fixed costs. The idea is that the fixed costs are fixed within some general levels of activity. The coffee shop, for example, could have a general staff level of five for from 0 to 1,000 daily customers. For higher levels of daily visitors than this, an additional five employees must be hired to keep customers sufficiently satisfied.

The labeling of fixed, incremental fixed, or variable costs is not that important if the price managers have accurate descriptions of the total costs (TC) function. What is important, though, is to leave out costs that have no impact on pricing decisions at all. Expenditures related to getting the business up and running in the first place are examples of such costs that should be left out of the TC function. These are referred to as *sunk costs* in the literature, because they cannot be recovered in any way when they have been incurred. For the coffee shop, an expenditure of $10,000 for a new and very fancy coffee machine is an example of a sunk cost. Once the decision is made to invest in

Fundamentals of price theory 23

the new machine, these costs cannot be recovered and should be ignored in any forward-looking operational decision, including pricing decisions. Most of the fixed costs, on the other hand, can be avoided if the coffee shop shuts down the coffee machines, the lights, and the heating/cooling, and closes the door. In most cases, the fixed costs are not relevant in pricing decisions. The reason why, and the exceptions, will become clear when we define MC next.

Marginal costs

The MC is the change in the TC function when increasing output with one unit. Formally, this can be expressed like this:

$$MC = \frac{\Delta TC}{\Delta Q} \tag{2.3}$$

The MC is the increase in costs associated with expanding output with one unit. Hence, $\Delta Q = 1$. In the economic literature the quantity given in Equation (2.3) is sometimes referred to as *incremental costs*. One could argue that VC could have been used instead of TC in the numerator. Why? Because fixed costs are fixed and will induce no change in TC if output is expanded whatsoever. But remember that fixed costs could be incremental. In this case, the use of VC in the numerator would simply be wrong. To further illustrate this, consider Figure 2.9.

In this figure, three possible shapes of total cost curves (left panel) and corresponding marginal costs (right panel) are illustrated. In the upper panel, we have fixed costs of $4,000.000 and variable unit costs that are constant for all output levels. By examining the slope of the TC function, we can easily calculate the variable unit costs. The TC increase from $4 to $6 when output is increased from 0 to 2,000 units. This means that the variable unit cost is $(6'' - 4'')/2,000 = 1,000$. In this case, the MC associated with selling one more unit of the product or service of interest will induce a MC of $1,000 for all output levels. This is reflected in the upper right panel. Hence, the revenues must exceed this number if the company is to profit from selling it. The fixed costs can be ignored in the pricing decision here, because they do not alter the basic shape of the TC function – they are constant across all output levels.

The middle panel of Figure 2.9 illustrates a situation with incremental fixed costs and constant variable unit costs. For output levels between 0 and 2,000 units, the fixed costs are $2,000.000. An output level higher than this (2,000+ units) induces some additional fixed costs of $2,000.000. As the variable unit costs are constant across all output levels, the slope of the TC function does not change anywhere, except for the one vertical jump where the fixed costs reach the higher level. However, as the TC function makes a jump at 2,000 units, the profit function will experience a kink at the same output level. This means that the fixed costs cannot be ignored in the pricing decision. In this case, the full TC function should be specified (maybe with an =IF-function) and used when searching for the optimal price.

The lower panel of Figure 2.9 illustrates a situation with fixed costs of $4,000.000 and variable unit costs that vary with output level. For low levels of output the variable unit

24 Fundamentals of price theory

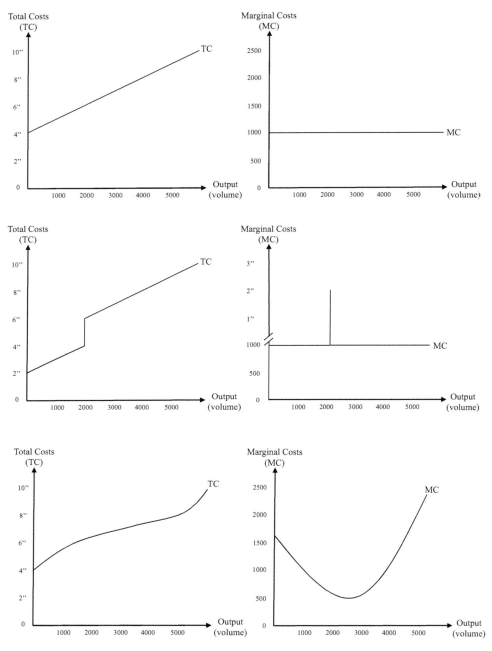

Figure 2.9 Possible shapes of total cost curves. Total costs (TC) in left panel and corresponding marginal costs (MC) in right panel. Upper panel: fixed costs of $4,000.000 and constant variable costs of $1,000.00 per unit across all output levels. Middle panel: fixed costs of $2,000.000 for output levels between 0 and 2,000, then the fixed costs increase by $2,000.000 for output levels of 2,000 or more. Constant variable costs of $1,000 per unit across all output levels. Lower panel: Fixed costs of $4,000.000 and variable unit costs that vary with output level.

costs are high (steep slope of TC function), then they decrease as the company becomes more efficient at higher production levels. At approximately 2,500 units of output, the variable unit costs increase again. This shape of the TC function is the most commonly used in economics textbooks to illustrate how the various cost curves for a firm may look like across output levels.

You should note that there are many other possible shapes of cost curves than those presented in Figure 2.9. In most cases you would probably have to do your own estimations based on information from various sources to accurately describe the TC function of the product or service you are building a pricing model for. It is beyond the scope of this book to go far into the details of estimating cost functions from accounting data and other relevant sources. We first and foremost focus on implementing an already estimated TC function. It is still important that you are aware of the importance of accurately describing the costs associated with producing/selling the product or service of interest to avoid unnecessary errors or omissions in the subsequent pricing analyses.

Next, we shall see how a firm can decide the optimal price based on information about the price–response function and the costs it faces. This will be illustrated with a simple example. In later chapters, we shall build on this insight to solve more complex problems.

2.3 Deciding optimal price and quantity – an example

A fundamental assumption in economic analyses of firms' decision-making is that they seek to maximize the profit accruing from selling the product or service of interest. In Chapter 1, the profit function was defined as:

$$Z = pv - c_v v - c_f \tag{2.4}$$

where p is the price v is the number of items sold (volume), and c_v and c_f are still the variable unit and fixed costs. The firm's objective is then to find the price for which this function is maximized. We shall illustrate how this can be done by walking through a simple example and link it to the topics of the previous two sections.

The golden rule that applies to any firm aiming for profit maximization is to set a price, or alternatively produce a quantity of the product or service of interest, such that the marginal revenue (MR) from selling one more unit equals MC. In less technical terms, this implies that in deciding whether to increase output by one more unit, the firm should produce an additional unit if it can increase its revenues by more than it costs to produce the unit. If the unit cost exceeds the additional revenue generated, production and subsequent sale of that unit should not be implemented. Consider the following table of two price levels and the number of units sold for a given company selling a widget:

Price	Units sold	Revenue
$10.25	10	$102.50
$10.00	11	$110.00

26 Fundamentals of price theory

What is the MR in this case? It is simple: by charging a price of $10.00 instead of $10.25 the company sells 11 units instead of ten units and earns an extra $7.50 ($110.00−$102.50). This MR consists of one *price element* and one *quantity element*. The quantity element consists of the extra revenue earned due to one more unit sold and equals $10.00 (10.00×1). The price element is calculated assuming that we sell all units at the lower price. In our case, this means that we lose $0.25 on the ten units that we previously could sell for $10.25 and thus the total price element is ($10.00 − $10.25) × 10 = −$2.50. Consequently, the total change in revenue is $7.50 ($10.00 − $2.50 = $7.50).

If the costs associated with increasing production/sales from ten to 11 units do not exceed $7.50, the company should lower the price to sell the additional unit. Furthermore, it should keep lowering the price until the MR is exactly equal to the MC. Why stop exactly there? Because if it lowers the price more than this the firm will start losing money on each item it sells when compared to the optimal (profit-maximizing) price.

The above example, expanded to include more prices and units sold, is given in Table 2.2 and Figure 2.10. We use fixed costs of $50.00 and variable unit costs of $1.00.

Table 2.2 Example marginal revenue, marginal costs and optimal produced quantity for the company selling the widget

Price	Units sold	Revenue	Marginal revenue	FC	VUC	TC	Marginal cost	Profit
12.50	1	12.50		50.00	1.00	51.00		−38.50
12.25	2	24.50	12.00	50.00	1.00	52.00	1.00	−27.50
12.00	3	36.00	11.50	50.00	1.00	53.00	1.00	−17.00
11.75	4	47.00	11.00	50.00	1.00	54.00	1.00	−7.00
11.50	5	57.50	10.50	50.00	1.00	55.00	1.00	2.50
11.25	6	67.50	10.00	50.00	1.00	56.00	1.00	11.50
11.00	7	77.00	9.50	50.00	1.00	57.00	1.00	20.00
10.75	8	86.00	9.00	50.00	1.00	58.00	1.00	28.00
10.50	9	94.50	8.50	50.00	1.00	59.00	1.00	35.50
10.25	10	102.50	8.00	50.00	1.00	60.00	1.00	42.50
10.00	11	110.00	7.50	50.00	1.00	61.00	1.00	49.00
9.75	12	117.00	7.00	50.00	1.00	62.00	1.00	55.00
9.50	13	123.50	6.50	50.00	1.00	63.00	1.00	60.50
9.25	14	129.50	6.00	50.00	1.00	64.00	1.00	65.50
9.00	15	135.00	5.50	50.00	1.00	65.00	1.00	70.00
8.75	16	140.00	5.00	50.00	1.00	66.00	1.00	74.00
8.50	17	144.50	4.50	50.00	1.00	67.00	1.00	77.50
8.25	18	148.50	4.00	50.00	1.00	68.00	1.00	80.50
8.00	19	152.00	3.50	50.00	1.00	69.00	1.00	83.00
7.75	20	155.00	3.00	50.00	1.00	70.00	1.00	85.00
7.50	21	157.50	2.50	50.00	1.00	71.00	1.00	86.50
7.25	22	159.50	2.00	50.00	1.00	72.00	1.00	87.50
7.00	23	161.00	1.50	50.00	1.00	73.00	1.00	88.00
6.75	24	162.00	1.00	50.00	1.00	74.00	1.00	88.00
6.50	25	162.50	0.50	50.00	1.00	75.00	1.00	87.50
6.25	26	162.50	0.00	50.00	1.00	76.00	1.00	86.50
6.00	27	162.00	−0.50	50.00	1.00	77.00	1.00	85.00
5.75	28	161.00	−1.00	50.00	1.00	78.00	1.00	83.00
5.50	29	159.50	−1.50	50.00	1.00	79.00	1.00	80.50
5.25	30	157.50	−2.00	50.00	1.00	80.00	1.00	77.50

Fundamentals of price theory 27

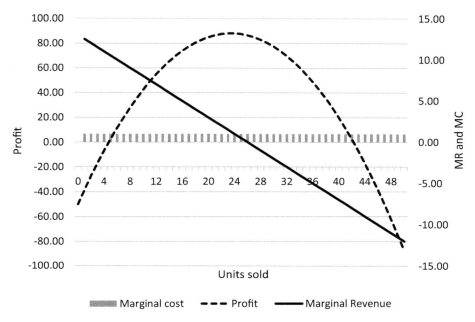

Figure 2.10 Graphical illustration of marginal revenue (MR), marginal cost (MC) and total profit as a function of units sold.

As we can see, the optimal price is found exactly where the MR equals the MC. The total demanded quantity when setting the price to $7.25 is 22 units, yielding a profit of $87.50. If lowering the price to $7.00 or $6.75, the demanded quantity increases to 23 and 24 cups, respectively. Both these prices yield a total profit of $88.00. This means that the optimal price is between $7.00 and $6.75. This is further confirmed when examining the MR. When increasing output from 22 to 23 units, the MR is $1.50 and exactly $1.00 when going from the 23 to 24 units sold. As the MC is $1.00 (fixed for all demand levels), we know that the optimal (profit-maximizing) price is between $7.00 and $6.75 as this is where the MR is exactly equal to the MC of $1.00. This can also be seen in Figure 2.10. The profit function (the short-dashed curve in the figure) reaches its maximum at 23/24 units where the MR (solid black line) is equal to the MC (gray bars). The exact optimal (profit-maximizing) price can also be found analytically. We shall show how this can be done in Chapter 7.

Note that in the microeconomic literature, the concepts of MR and MC are always related to the extra revenues or costs associated with *increasing output with one unit*. The decision problem is then essentially to figure out the optimal *quantity* to sell or produce, not the optimal *price*. Traditionally, the theoretical models focus on *how much should the firm produce to maximize profit*. From a price-setting perspective, however, it makes more sense to talk about MR as the extra revenue the firm could achieve from a small *price increase* instead of increase in output. The example we have just walked you through could just as easily have had a price focus. In Table 2.3 and Figure 2.11, the MR is calculated as the additional revenue the firm would achieve from increasing the price by $0.25 at the time. Even though the levels of MR are different compared to when

28 Fundamentals of price theory

Table 2.3 Example marginal revenue, marginal costs, and optimal price for the company selling the widget

Price	Units sold	Revenue	Marginal revenue	FC	VUC	TC	Marginal cost	Profit
5.00	31	155.00	3.00	50.00	1.00	81.00	-1.00	74.00
5.25	30	157.50	2.50	50.00	1.00	80.00	-1.00	77.50
5.50	29	159.50	2.00	50.00	1.00	79.00	-1.00	80.50
5.75	28	161.00	1.50	50.00	1.00	78.00	-1.00	83.00
6.00	27	162.00	1.00	50.00	1.00	77.00	-1.00	85.00
6.25	26	162.50	0.50	50.00	1.00	76.00	-1.00	86.50
6.50	25	162.50	0.00	50.00	1.00	75.00	-1.00	87.50
6.75	24	162.00	-0.50	50.00	1.00	74.00	-1.00	88.00
7.00	23	161.00	-1.00	50.00	1.00	73.00	-1.00	88.00
7.25	22	159.50	-1.50	50.00	1.00	72.00	-1.00	87.50
7.50	21	157.50	-2.00	50.00	1.00	71.00	-1.00	86.50
7.75	20	155.00	-2.50	50.00	1.00	70.00	-1.00	85.00
8.00	19	152.00	-3.00	50.00	1.00	69.00	-1.00	83.00
8.25	18	148.50	-3.50	50.00	1.00	68.00	-1.00	80.50
8.50	17	144.50	-4.00	50.00	1.00	67.00	-1.00	77.50
8.75	16	140.00	-4.50	50.00	1.00	66.00	-1.00	74.00
9.00	15	135.00	-5.00	50.00	1.00	65.00	-1.00	70.00
9.25	14	129.50	-5.50	50.00	1.00	64.00	-1.00	65.50
9.50	13	123.50	-6.00	50.00	1.00	63.00	-1.00	60.50

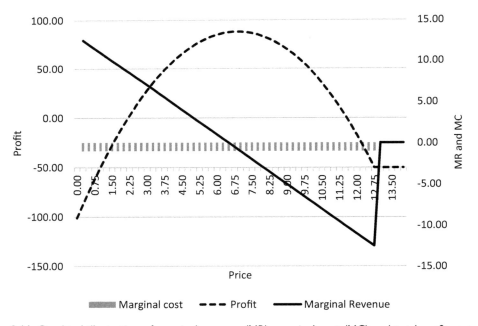

Figure 2.11 Graphical illustration of marginal revenue (MR), marginal cost (MC) and total profit as a function of units sold.

selling an additional unit, the conclusion is the same: set a price of between $6.75 and $7.00 to maximize profit. This price will again lead to a demanded quantity of 23 to 24 and a total profit of ~$88.00. Note the asymmetric shape of the profit function. When the price level reach $13.00 demands drop to zero. Increasing the price further induces no change in quantity demanded, and the revenues and variable costs are zero.

Optimal price in the case of incremental fixed costs

When the cost function consists of stepwise or incremental fixed costs for various output levels, the golden rule of setting the price such that MR=MC does not necessarily apply. The reason is that in such cases, the *shape* of the total cost and profit function will be altered and could, in turn, affect the optimal produced quantity (or alternatively the optimal price). To illustrate this, consider Figures 2.12 and 2.13 below. In both illustrations the widget producer experiences a jump in fixed costs when producing 12 units or more. In the first case (Figure 2.12), the fixed costs increase from $50.00 to $75.00. This is reflected in the figure in two ways. First, the MC when increasing output from 11 to 12 units is $26.00. Second, the profit function exhibits a distinct kink for the same output level. However, the maximum profit is still reached at an output of 23 to 24 units, which can be achieved by setting a price of between $6.75 and $7.00, as seen in the figure.

The situation in Figure 2.13 is different. In this case, the fixed costs jump from $50.00 to $100.00 when output increases from 11 to 12 units. The increase in the fixed costs is now so big that the previously found optimal output level (where MR=MC: ~23/24 units) induces a lower profit level compared with a production level of 11 units where the

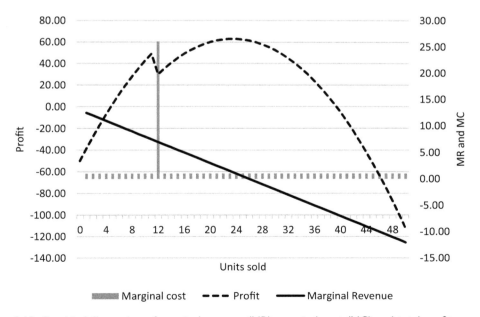

Figure 2.12 Graphical illustration of marginal revenue (MR), marginal cost (MC) and total profit as a function of units sold in the case of incremental fixed costs.

30 Fundamentals of price theory

additional incremental fixed costs can be avoided. The total profit the firm can achieve if producing 11 units, and if using the price/demand and variable cost information from Table 2.2, is:

$$\$10.00 \times 11 - \$1.00 \times 11 - \$100 = \$49$$

If still going for the quantity where MR=MC (~24), the total profit would be:

$$\$6.75 \times 24 - \$1.00 \times 24 - \$100 = \$38$$

that is, a reduction in total profit of approximately 22%. The lesson here is very clear: When facing incremental, or any sort of non-smooth cost functions, we have no guarantee that the profit is maximized when MR=MC. In such cases the analyst must compare profit levels at the various relevant output levels to set the profit-maximizing price. The relevant output levels to compare in these cases are the levels right before the new incremental fixed costs kick in and where MR=MC.

As briefly mentioned, the focus in microeconomic texts has historically been on choosing how much output the firm should produce to maximize profit, and not on choosing what price to set. To get a better understanding of why this is the case, we shall briefly examine the role of pricing under various market structures next.

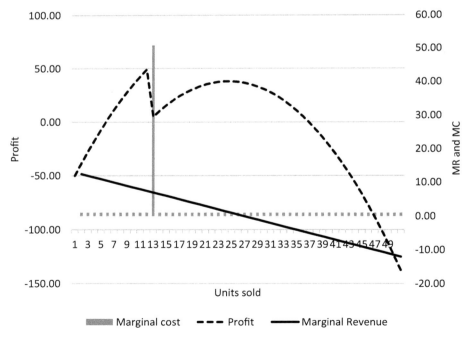

Figure 2.13 Graphical illustration of marginal revenue (MR), marginal cost (MC) and total profit as a function of units sold in the case of incremental fixed costs.

2.4 The role of pricing under various market structures

To what degree the firm can use price as a tool to generate higher profits depends on the market it competes in. Most textbooks in economics classify markets based on two things: (1) the characteristics of the good or service sold, and (2) the number of companies competing for the same customers. An example of such a classification is presented in Figure 2.14.

As Figure 2.14 shows, the only situations where no pricing decisions have to be made are when the goods or services sold by different firms are *homogeneous* and customers have no preferences for various brands. This means that the product or service sold by one firm can easily be substituted by the good or service sold by another firm. When many firms compete for the same customers, such market structure is referred to as *perfect competition*. Companies operating in markets with perfect competition have no pricing decisions. Why is this the case? The answer is that the relative output produced by a single firm is so small compared to the total market that it will not have any impact on the market price. The company must, under such circumstances, take the price as given and is therefore referred to as a *price taker*. This concept is illustrated in Figure 2.15. In this figure, output is given on the horizontal axis and price per unit on the vertical axis, as in standard economics texts. The demand curve faced by a firm operating in a market with perfect competition is a horizontal line at the market price, P^*.[4] When lowering the price to $P1$ you face the demand of the entire market and if you increase the price to $P2$ all your customers get the product or service you offer elsewhere and the quantity demanded from your business drops to zero. This makes sense. Why should any customers choose the high-priced product or service if they can buy an identical product or service at a lower price?

Perfect competition is a market structure that is seldom seen in practice. The most used examples of perfect competition in economics texts are agricultural products, but even wheat, milk, and eggs, which can be considered as homogeneous products, may still be differentiated in consumers' minds because of marketing activities. Hence, a price change will in most cases induce finite customer responses. This means that active pricing can be used as a tool to increase profits for most businesses around the world.

When only a few large companies compete for the same customers, and where the product or service sold is 'standard' (homogeneous), the market structure is referred to as an *oligopoly*. Strictly speaking, it is not correct to state that firms competing in such market structures have no pricing decisions. In fact, firms operating in oligopolistic market structures can face very complex decisions related to both output and prices. How complex these decisions are depends on the actions of the (few) competitors. In general,

CHARACTERISTICS OF GOODS OR SERVICES SOLD IN MARKET	NUMBER OF COMPANIES			
	ONE	FEW LARGE		MANY SMALL
HOMOGENEOUS: STANDARD GOODS. NO PREFERENCES.	MONOPOLY: ACTIVE PRICING DECISIONS	OLIGOPOLY: NO PRICING DECISIONS		PERFECT COMPETITION: NO PRICING DECISIONS
HETEROGENEOUS: DIFFERENTIATED (OR ASSUMED TO BE SO) GOODS. PREFERENCES.		DIFFERENTIATED OLIGOPOLY: ACTIVE PRICING DECISIONS		MONOPOLISTIC COMPETITION: ACTIVE PRICING DECISIONS

Figure 2.14 Examples of various market structures.

32 Fundamentals of price theory

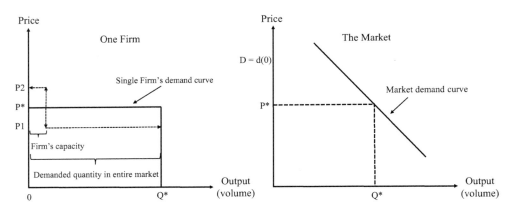

Figure 2.15 The relation between price and demand for a single firm (left panel) and the entire market (right panel) in the case of perfect competition.

such decisions require strategic thinking and involve game theory. Price-setting in the case of oligopolistic competition is beyond the scope of this book. Readers interested in the topic can consult any text in microeconomics.

A *monopoly* is a market structure where there is only one firm offering the product or service under consideration. In this case, the company is facing all the available demand in the market and can set the price it wants (if the market is not regulated). The price can be used to directly adjust the quantity sold. Monopolies can occur as a result of patents and regulations by governments.

In practice, most firms operate in markets that fall into a category somewhere between monopoly and perfect competition. The most common market structure in the industrialized world is *monopolistic competition*. This results from the effort of firms to induce preferences among customers for their product or service. When they succeed in doing this, they can set prices more freely compared with the more restrictive market structures that curtail competition. The pricing tools presented in this book assume that the firm faces finite customer responses. This means that the price–response function for a given product or service is downward-sloping and the firm can carry out pricing with monopoly-like market power. An important way of increasing profit in such cases is to charge different prices based on specific criteria of the customers or goods/services provided. This is known as *price discrimination* or *price differentiation* and is of high importance when it comes to making price-setting more profitable. Because of this, and because the concept is highly relevant when applying many of the pricing techniques presented later in this book, the next chapter is devoted to explaining the theoretical foundation and practical applications of price differentiation.

2.5 Summary

- Classical economic theory of consumer behavior can be used to understand the relationship between consumers' limited income and their consumption of various goods and services.

- We can use classical economic theory to show how the shapes of price–response functions are formed via budget lines and indifference curves.
- The consumer surplus is the sum of all the differences between individuals' maximum willingness to pay and the actual price for customers with a willingness to pay greater than the price.
- The costs that matter in pricing decisions are the marginal costs associated with increasing output by one unit.
- The profit-maximizing quantity and corresponding price are *almost always* at the point where MC equal MR. This holds across all market structures.
- The exception to the above rule is in the case of incremental fixed costs. In such cases, we have no guarantee that setting a price where MR=MC is optimal.
- Whether we can use price as a mechanism to increase profit depends on the structure of the market we are competing in. Generally, markets are categorized based on how homogeneous or heterogeneous the products or services in the market are and how many companies that compete in the market place.
- The most common market structure is *monopolistic competition*, which occurs when we have many small companies offering somewhat differentiated products (or at least products that are perceived to be differentiated by customers).
- A monopoly exists when we have only one company supplying a product or service. In this case, the company can set the exact price it wants.

2.6 Problems

1. Describe the terms indifference curve and budget line.
2. Consider the figure below. What combinations of bananas and bread would this rational consumer choose to consume? Are there any combinations of the two goods that the rational consumer would be indifferent to consuming?

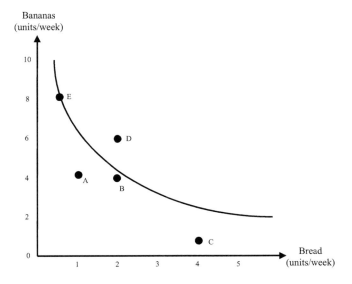

34 Fundamentals of price theory

3. Consider two products: X1 and X2. The price of X1 is $5 and the price of X2 is $10. The consumer has a total budget of $100 per month for these two products. Formulate the budget constraint.
4. Draw the budget line using the information in problem 3.
5. Illustrate how a price change of X1 from $5 to 10$ (in problem 3) affects the shape of the budget line.
6. Use the information in the table below to (1) calculate the aggregate demanded quantity and (2) illustrate this in a price–response function.

Price	Consumer #1	Consumer #2
$10.00	5	6
$20.00	2	5
$30.00	1	1

7. Consider the figure below. What area of this figure corresponds to the consumer surplus if the price is equal to $50? What is the size of the consumer surplus?

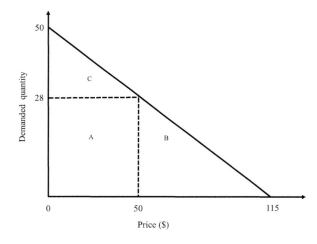

8. A company that sells a homogeneous product is operating in a market with many small producers. Can this company use price to increase profits? Explain.
9. You have the following information about demand (Q), price and costs:

$$Q = 100{,}000 - 10{,}000 \times P$$
$$P = 10 - 0.0001 \times Q$$
$$VC = 5 \,(constant)$$
$$FC = 10{,}000$$

What is the profit-maximizing price and quantity?

10. You have the following information about the relation between price and number of units sold for a service offered by a given firm:

Price	Units sold
100.00	0
90.00	10
80.00	20
70.00	30
60.00	40
50.00	50
40.00	60
30.00	70
20.00	80
10.00	90
0.00	100

The variable costs are $20/unit and the fixed costs are $500. Illustrate in a graph: (a) marginal revenue; (b) marginal costs; and (c) profit across the various levels of units sold. What is the profit-maximizing price/quantity?

11. Do the same as in problem 10, but now assume that the fixed costs jump from $500 to $1,000 if going from 20 to 30 units sold. What is now the profit-maximizing price/quantity?

Notes

1 See for example Pindyck and Rubinfeld (2018).
2 The consumer's income, or more correctly, fraction of total income used for that specific product or service category.
3 This assumption is called *completeness*. It means that consumers can compare and rank all possible market baskets (coffee sold at various coffee shops in our example). The assumption of *transitivity* (a consumer who prefers A to B, and B to C, also prefers A to C) and that consumers prefer *more of any good or service to less*, are also included to form the basis of consumer utility theory. Consult any textbook on microeconomics for details on the basic underlying assumptions about consumer preferences.
4 Note the similarity between the demand curve for one given product or service faced by one firm and the definition of the price–response function.

Chapter 3

Segmentation and price differentiation

When firms face finite customer responses from price changes, they have market power. This means that they can set prices more freely compared with firms operating in markets recognized by perfect competition. The question the managers of such firms must ask is how they can use their market power to maximize profit. One important answer to this question is that they should look for ways of charging *different* prices for, more or less, the *same* product or service offered to the market. That is, firms should look for ways to *price differentiate* based on *certain criteria*. Identifying the certain criteria that can be used to price differentiate is often referred to as *segmentation*. Price differentiation and segmentation are at the heart of pricing analytics in general, and variable pricing specifically. This chapter is devoted to explaining the theory and practice of these concepts and why firms (always) and customers (sometimes) should both be eager to have more of it. The following topics will be covered:

- Definitions and degrees of price differentiation.
- The economics theory behind price differentiation.
- Ways to segment and price differentiate in practice.
- Challenges of segmentation and price differentiation.

The calculations of optimal differentiated prices and the implementation of this practice in Excel will be presented in later chapters. In this chapter we limit the Excel implementation to simple examples that illustrate the impact from various approaches to price differentiation on profit.

3.1 Price differentiation defined

Price differentiation can be defined as:

> *"The practice of charging different prices for identical or similar goods or services based on certain criteria."*[1]

A given firm can perform price differentiation if it:

1. Can identify at least *some* variation in the maximum price its customers are willing to pay for the product or service of interest. This maximum price is called the *reservation price*.

2. Can identify certain criteria that can be used to segment the market into groups with somewhat different reservation prices.

Variation in the customers' *reservation prices* is an important prerequisite for price differentiation to be possible. This simply means that some customers are willing to pay more for a product or service than others. Note here that it could also refer to variation in reservation prices for the same customer buying different quantities of the same good or service, *or* the same customer buying the good or service at *different points in time*. In any case, such variation in the reservation prices induces a non-vertical shape of the aggregate price–response function, which can be utilized by the firm to obtain a higher profit by charging different prices.[2]

To succeed with this, the firm needs to identify those customers who are behind various parts of the aggregate price–response function. Only then can the firm charge higher prices to those prepared to pay a lot and come up with discounts to customers who are more price-sensitive or have lower reservation prices. The extreme case is when the firm can identify exactly what each customer's reservation price is and then make the customer pay this price. This is called *first-degree price differentiation* or *perfect price differentiation*. We shall define this and the two other broad forms of price differentiation next.

Degrees of price differentiation

Price differentiation can be classified into three broad categories:

- **First degree:** This is also called *perfect price differentiation*. In this case each buyer is charged the maximum price he or she is willing to pay.
- **Second degree:** The firm charges different prices for different quantities of the same good or service.
- **Third degree:** The firm segments the market based on certain criteria and sells the product or service of interest at different prices in each segment.

First-degree price differentiation is almost impossible to achieve in practice. The costs associated with figuring out how much every customer would be willing to pay are simply too high compared to the benefits. While the era of *big data* enables firms to obtain better and better estimations of their customers' reservation prices, there is still a way to go before they can charge all their customers their exact reservation price in most practical situations. There are also legal and other constraints that make such extreme price differentiation difficult to implement. One exception is the Dutch auction used by Royal Flora Holland. In this type of auction, wholesale dealers meet in an auction room where the price for a given lot of flowers or plants starts at a fixed, high amount. Then an auction clock starts running down and the price is reduced until a buyer hits a button. The lot is then sold to the buyer hitting the button at the price indicated by the auction clock. This is the reservation price of the buyer. Why? Because the buyer is competing against other buyers, and he or she does not know when they may hit the button to buy the same lot. The only way to make sure the lot is acquired at an accepted price level is to stop the clock once it hits the buyer's reservation price.

Second degree price differentiation is based on the principle that consumers' have *diminishing marginal utility* from consuming more and more of a given product or service. This does not contradict the principle that *more is better than less*, but it means that increasing consumption of the same good or service yields smaller and smaller additions to the consumer's total utility. The principle of diminishing marginal utility is reflected in each customer's individual price–response function for a given product or service. In Table 2.1 this concept was illustrated for two potential consumers. As the price level increased, the quantity demanded of black coffee decreased. This can also be expressed as consumers are willing to pay a lot for the first few cups, but once these are consumed the price must be reduced for the customers to increase consumption.

Firms can use this insight to *charge different prices to the same buyer* in various ways. The most common approach is to offer quantity discounts. Examples you may have seen in stores are "buy two, get one free," "get 50% of the third unit," or something similar. Another approach is to offer *loyalty cards* where buying the same product at different times will induce discounts (for example, a lower price for every fifth unit purchased).

Third degree price differentiation is probably the most used form by companies in practice. A common example of a criterion used to segment the market is students with valid student IDs. The same product or service is then sold to two distinct consumer groups (or segments: students and non-students) at different prices. In general, high prices should be set in the segments where demand is less price-sensitive and vice versa. The criteria used to segment the market do not have to be related to the customers themselves (such as age, gender, students, senior citizens, etc.), but could also be based on the product, the sales channel, time of consumption/purchase, or other things. Approaches to selecting the criteria and various ways of charging different prices in practice will be examined further in section 3.3 of this chapter, but first we shall briefly look at the theory of why both firms (always) and consumers (sometimes) will gain from price differentiation.

3.2 The economics theory behind price differentiation

In Chapter 2 we defined the total *consumer surplus* of the customers purchasing black coffee at Shop Y as the aggregated difference between the price charged per cup and the customers' willingness to pay. One way the coffee shop can earn a higher profit is to capture some of the consumer surplus. We shall look at a simple example to see how this can be done.

Consider Figure 3.1, which depicts a new version of Shop Y's price–response function together with shaded areas denoted with the letters A–F. If Shop Y charged a single price of $1.00 in this case, the total consumer surplus would be the area below the price–response function and above the price. That is, the area A+B+C+D+E+F. This is similar to the illustration of the aggregate consumer surplus presented in Figure 2.8.

Now consider a situation where the variable unit cost (marginal cost) of one cup of coffee is $1.00 and the price charged to all customers is $1.50. What is the consumer surplus in this situation? The answer is the area of the price–response function where the reservation prices are higher than the price charged. That is, the sum of the areas D+E+F. The customers in this area of the price–response function all have a maximum

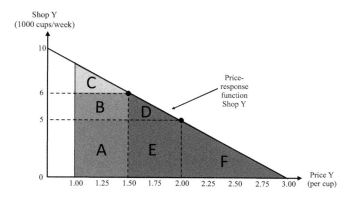

Figure 3.1 Illustration of Shop Y's price–response function and contribution opportunities if implementing price differentiation.

willingness to pay higher than the price level and gain the difference between the two. In this situation, the firm would earn a contribution equal to area A+B of Figure 3.1. This area can be easily calculated as:

$$(\$1.50 - \$1.00) \times 6,000 = \$3,000$$

Assume now that the coffee shop has identified who the customers behind various parts of the price–response function are. A market survey reveals that all the customers with a reservation price below $2.00 are *all* students, and *all* the customers with a reservation price higher than this are non-students.[3] The coffee shop uses this information to set two prices: a student price of $1.50, and a price for all other customers of $2.00. How will this affect the coffee shop's contribution? The answer is that they will increase their contribution with area E of Figure 3.1, earning a total contribution of A+B+E. The new contribution can be calculated as:

$$(\$2.00 - \$1.00) \times 5,000 + (\$1.50 - \$1.00) \times (6,000 - 5,000) = \$5,500$$

an increase of $2,500, or more than 83%. This change in profit can also be calculated directly by taking the price difference and multiplying it with the number of customers paying the highest price:

$$(\$2.00 - \$1.50) \times 5,000 = \$2,500.$$

The consumer surplus is reduced by the same amount, that is, area E, and now only consists of area D – the students with a willingness to pay of more than $1.50 and less than $2.00 (which holds for all students) – and area F – all other customers with a willingness to pay of more than $2.00.

The conclusion here is clear; if the coffee shop can capture more of the consumer surplus, it can increase profit substantially. It turns out that it can do even better, though. If the coffee shop can find ways of charging students and other customers their exact reservation price it can also capture area C (students with lower reservation prices than $1.50), D (students with reservation prices of between $1.50 and $2.00), and F (all other customers with reservation prices of $2.00 or more). This would be a situation where the coffee shop charged a price exactly equal to all customers' reservation prices and is what we described as *perfect* or *first-degree price differentiation* in the previous section. In practice, this is rarely possible because it would mean that we (1) knew all the customers' reservation prices and (2) were able to find acceptable ways of charging these.

The illustration given in Figure 3.1 is nevertheless important to show the potential impact on operating profit even from a simple two-price approach. Note here that the impact on profit, and whether the customers are better off or not, depends on the level of the base price and whether the firm increases or decreases this price to capture more of the area under the price–response function. This point is illustrated in Tables 3.1 and 3.2. Table 3.1 shows the impact as described in this section with a base price of $1.50. Under this scenario the average price increases by 16.67% and the total contribution goes up by 83.33%. Additionally, the consumer surplus is reduced with area E and *no* customers are better off compared to a situation where a single price was charged.

Table 3.2, on the other hand, shows that if the firm is charging a single price of $2.00 to all customers and then decides to go for a two-price policy where students pay only $1.50, the corresponding impact on profit is reduced to an increase of 10% (compared with 83.33% in Table 3.1). Additionally, in this case the consumer surplus will *increase* from area F of Figure 3.1 to area D+F. The reason is because the students with reservation prices of above $1.50 and below $2.00 will now buy coffee. This leads us to a general rule when it comes to price differentiation:

> *"If a price differentiation scheme increases profits for a seller but does not result in additional production, it must reduce total consumer surplus."* (Phillips, 2005: 95)

In the above example, we assume that the coffee shop can perfectly identify customers with high and low reservation prices (students versus non-students). In practice, though, some students may have higher reservation prices than $2.00, and some regular customers are likely to have lower reservation prices than this. It is also important that the coffee shop chooses a price differentiation scheme that (most) customers perceive as fair and

Table 3.1 Example of impact from price differentiation when going from a single low price of $1.50 to two prices of $1.50 and $2.00

Going from low to high price

	Single price	Students	Non-students	Total	Change
Price	$1.50	$1.50	$2.00	$1.75	16.67%
Demand	6,000	1,000	5,000	6,000	0.00%
Variable cost	$1.00	$1.00	$1.00	$1.00	0.00%
Contribution	$3,000.00	$500.00	$5,000.00	$5,500.00	83.33%

Table 3.2 Example of impact from price differentiation when going from a single high price of $2.00 to two prices of $1.50 and $2.00

Going from high to low price

	Single price	Students	Non-students	Total	Change
Price	$2.00	$1.50	$2.00	$1.75	−12.50%
Demand	5,000	1,000	5,000	6,000	20.00%
Variable cost	$1.00	$1.00	$1.00	$1.00	0.00%
Contribution	$5,000.00	$500.00	$5,000.00	$5,500.00	10.00%

that is not in conflict with the law. Therefore, we shall look at various ways firms can segment the market and perform price differentiation next.

3.3 Ways to segment and price differentiate in practice

To be able to charge different prices for identical or very similar products, the firm must segment the market based on certain criteria. A starting point for selecting such criteria could be the PRO cube introduced in Chapter 1. The three dimensions in this PRO cube are (1) customer type, (2) product and (3) channel.

Segmentation and price differentiation based on customer types

Firms can segment the market based on specific criteria or attributes among its customers. Examples include gender, age, members/non-members, or other groups of customers that can be easily identified based on certain characteristics. A much-used customer-based criterion to segment and price differentiate is the use of student discounts. This criterion is also easy to accept by most customers as students often have less spending power than other customers, although there may be big variations within both these segments.

The use of memberships is also a possible approach to segment and price differentiate. This can be done in many ways, where one alternative is to offer special discounts for the same product or service if the customer is a member. Another approach is to have one price for members and another price for non-members. Such a price differentiation scheme could, for example, be used at gyms and various events (sporting events, concerts, festivals, etc.). This approach is similar to a two-part tariff, which we shall discuss soon.

Price differentiation based on customer types will be successful if the various segments have sufficiently different price–response functions and if it is hard (or impossible) for customers in the segment with higher willingness to pay to buy the product or service at the lower price. We shall return to the concepts of *demand shifting* and *cannibalization* when we discuss the calculation of optimal differentiated prices in Chapters 7 and 9.

Segmentation and price differentiation based on product versions

The second element of the PRO cube is *product*. Firms can offer products or services with only minor differences compared with the original product or service and then charge different prices for the various versions. This could be both *superior* and *inferior* variants. In some cases, the only difference between the two could be the name, label or general packaging. For example, a restaurant may use the same ingredients to create two dishes with different names. One of the versions could be named *scrambled eggs* aimed for customers with low willingness to pay. The other version could be named *oeufs brouillés* and aimed at customers with a higher willingness to pay (and who do not speak French). Producing various versions of the same base product or service is an important way for firms to increase profit and this approach is heavily used in practice. Examples include various versions of software, liquor, food, plane tickets, seating at concerts and sporting events, etc. This approach to segmentation and price differentiation also allows the customer themselves to select what version to buy and induce a higher chance of them accepting the pricing scheme.

Segmentation and price differentiation based on sales channel

The last element in the PRO cube is the sales channel. Firms can use this as a criterion to price differentiate. Examples include:

- A ski resort could charge one (lower) price for online purchases of ski lift tickets and another (higher) price for purchases at the cash desk.
- A coffee shop with multiple outlets could charge one (lower) price for a cup of black coffee sold at a downtown shop and another (higher) price for the same product sold at the home games of the local basket ball team.
- A clothing store could charge one set of (higher) prices at their regular stores and another set of (lower) prices at factory outlets.
- A given widget could be sold at one (lower) price if it is sold by a member of a sales team (direct sales) and at another (higher) price if it sold via a dealer or retailer of some sort.

There are many channels a firm can use to distribute its products or services. The cost structure is likely to be different in the various channels. This legitimizes the use of different prices across channels. If the firm wants to move demand from one channel to another (for example, from the cash desk to online sales to make operations more efficient), price can be used to give customers strong incentives to choose the *right* channel.

Segmentation and price differentiation using the two-part tariff

There are also other criteria firms can use to segment and price differentiate. A pricing scheme that is based on a combination of a fixed and a variable element is called *the two-part tariff*. This approach involves differentiating between heavy and light users using fixed and variable cost structures. This is illustrated in Figure 3.2, which relates to subscriptions to a mobile telephone service. Subscribers can choose between different plans depending on their expectations of what plan will result in the lowest total costs. Subscription A has no fixed costs, only variable costs per gigabyte of data traffic used. Subscription B has a low fixed fee that includes a predetermined amount of free gigabytes of data traffic (gigabytes B) combined with a lower variable fee once the

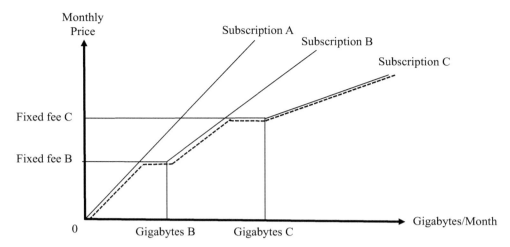

Figure 3.2 Illustration of two-part tariff for three potential mobile phone subscriptions. The dashed line indicates the lowest possible price for the consumer based on various levels of data traffic used per month.

free gigabytes are used. Subscription C has a higher fixed fee, but a lower variable fee for each gigabyte, relative to B, once the free amount is used up. By offering different tariff structures, the mobile telephone company can differentiate customers according to their usage and willingness to pay. Customers usually have no problems with accepting such tariffs as they are dependent on usage. In most EU countries today, mobile phone subscriptions include a fixed fee with a predetermined number of minutes, texts, MMS and data bundles. However, if one should use more than the included amount for any of these, a variable fee is charged for the extra usage. This variable fee varies across the bundled services; for example, an extra minute may cost €0.50 whereas an extra megabyte of data may cost €0.1. In recent years the included amounts in data bundles are what is restrictive for most users, rather than the other attributes of the subscription (such as minutes of calling, texts and MMS).

Another example of two-part tariffs is credit cards that charge a fixed annual fee for using the card and a variable per-transaction fee. Amusement parks also often take advantage of this pricing scheme as they charge one general admission fee and then a certain amount for the various attractions.

The question managers of companies where a two-part tariff is relevant must ask themselves is what fixed and variable fees to set in order to maximize total profit. This is an optimization problem where we aim at maximizing the total profit (the sum of the fixed and variable fees) by changing the fixed and variable fees, simultaneously. In the case of the amusement park, the fixed fee would be an entrance fee (E) and the variable fee would be the price per ride (p). The problem of finding the optimal entrance fee and price per ride problem can be formulated as follows:

$$\max_{E,p} Z = Ed(E) + (p - c_v)d(p) - c_f \tag{3.1}$$

44   Segmentation and price differentiation

where Z is the profit, E is the entrance fee, $d(E)$ is the price–response function (demand function) for the entrance as a function of the entrance fee, $(p-c_v)$ is the contribution margin ($price - variable\,unit\,costs$), $d(p)$ is the price–response (demand) function for the usage of the various attractions in the park as a function of the price level per ride. c_f is the fixed costs (this will not affect the solution, why?). Hence, the optimal level of the entrance fee can be found by setting this function to maximum by changing E and p.

Other approaches to segmentation and price differentiation

The specific tactics firms use for price differentiation can, in most cases, be categorized into the general forms of segmentation mentioned above. There are examples of other approaches that may be effective, though. Examples are the so-called *self-selection* approach, *time-based price differentiation,* and *regional pricing.* We briefly explain these approaches next before we round off this chapter by mentioning some important challenges and limitations to segmentation and price differentiation.

Self-selection price differentiation is based on the idea that all customers have access to various prices or discounts for the same product or service. However, to redeem a given discount, or get access to a lower price, the customer must put in some effort, or have the necessary flexibility to do so. Examples include the use of discount coupons distributed in newspapers and magazines, and discount codes used by web retailers. The service industry can make customers with more flexibility self-select by offering lower prices when there is a lot of available capacity. The airline and hotel industries have used this approach for decades by offering lower prices during low seasons and vice versa. This type of self-selection is related to **time-based price differentiation**. The idea behind this approach is to use time as a criterion to differentiate the price in various ways. In addition to using time of consumption as a criterion (such as low prices in periods with low demand), companies can also differentiate if the customer is willing to commit to the purchase in advance, such as early-bird discounts. These forms of time-based price differentiation are at the heart of variable pricing and revenue management, and we shall return to them in detail in later chapters. Time can also be used as a factor to improve a service by shortening delivery time (if buying items online, for example) or increasing the number of days (time) of the return policy. Such time-based changes will also justify differentiated prices. Finally, **regional pricing** is based on the idea that location of customers, or of the store/outlet itself, can be used as a criterion to price differentiate. An example is new cars where the list price differs depending on the region/country.

3.4 Challenges of segmentation and price differentiation

There are some challenges of segmentation and price differentiation that firms should be aware of when implementing it in practice. Some constraints include:

- *Regulation:* Segmentation and price differentiation based on specific criteria can be prohibited by law. Examples include segmentation based on race or other sensitive characteristics. Even if such segments were related to cost differentials in offering the product or service to the various segments, the firm could face legal action if it violates the regulations of the market the firm competes in.

- *Competition:* Strong competition in a market makes price discrimination difficult. In such cases customers would choose a competitor's products instead of the firm's if the price difference is sufficiently big. This is related to the degree of market power the firm has in the market it competes in.
- *Imperfect segmentation:* It is not possible to segment the market perfectly. In some cases, the average willingness to pay across segments may be very similar and the costs associated with charging different prices to different segments can eliminate the gains.
- *Arbitrage:* Third-party arbitrageurs will have strong incentives to find ways to buy the firm's products at a lower price and resell to high willingness-to-pay customers below market price, pocketing the difference.
- *Cannibalization:* Customers in high-price segments are motivated to find ways to pay the lower price. In this case, the producer surplus is reduced accordingly.
- *Commitment and reputation:* If the firm follows a given pricing scheme (e.g., high prices at introduction and lower prices subsequently) and customers learn this over time and are sufficiently patient, price differentiation breaks down. The firm may claim that this will not happen, but then it must keep its promise to be credible. This is sometimes referred to as the *curse of dynamic pricing* as the optimal price at the introduction of the product or service (i.e., at $t = 0$) tends towards the firm's marginal cost.

Some of these challenges have been addressed in the various subsections of this chapter. Other challenges, such as cannibalization, will be addressed when we discuss the actual implementation and calculation of optimal differentiated prices in later chapters.

3.5 Summary

- Price differentiation is about charging different prices for identical or similar goods or services based on certain criteria.
- For price differentiation to be possible, there must be at least some variation in what customers are willing to pay for the product or service.
- The criteria used to segment the market and differentiate prices can be based on the dimensions of the PRO cube. Other approaches include, (but are not limited to), two-part tariff, self-selection and time-based price differentiation.
- Price differentiation is usually classified as first, second, or third degree, and can be used to increase profit substantially.
- There are several challenges when it comes to implementing price differentiation in practice. Legal constraints, competition, and cannibalization are examples of this.

3.6 Problems

1. What is price differentiation?
2. What conditions must be satisfied for a firm to perform price differentiation?
3. How can you recognize first, second and third degree price differentiation?

46 Segmentation and price differentiation

4. Consider the figure below and answer the following questions:

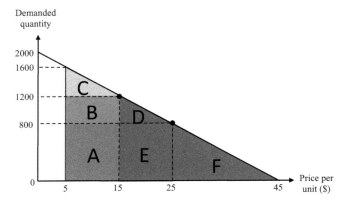

a) If this firm charges a single price of $15, what is the total consumer surplus?
b) If the firm charges a single price of $25, what is the consumer surplus?
c) Assume now that the firm can exactly identify the customers behind various parts of the price–response. All customers with a reservation price below $25 are students, and all customers with a reservation price higher than this are in the general public. Assume further that the variable unit costs are $5. Calculate the total contribution if the firm (1) charges a single price of $25, and (2) charges a price of $15 for students and $25 for the general public. What is (3) the impact on the contribution by going from the single to the two-price approach?
d) How will the relative impact on the contribution (% change) be affected by whether we go from a single high ($25) or low ($15) price to a two-price approach?

5. A professional soccer club plays home games once a week, but on different weekdays. How can this club segment and price differentiate tickets for their home games using the PRO cube as a starting point?

6. What is the optimal subscription for a customer who on average uses 107 MB of data, 261 minutes, 95 texts, and 86 MMS per month, given the information in the tables below.

Included in plan			
	Plan A	Plan B	Plan C
MB	250	500	2000
Minutes	100	500	1000
Texts	250	500	1000
MMS	50	50	500

Fixed and variable rate per month

Fixed	99	199	299
VC-MB	5	3	1
VC-Minutes	0.8	0.5	0.1
VC-Texts	1	0.5	0.1
VC-MMS	1	0.5	0.2

7. Focus on the fixed and variable rates of data only (measured in MB) and depict the cost structure of plans A, B, and C as a function of data usage, as done in Figure 3.2. That is, assume that the customer only uses data and depict how the costs would look like for various usage levels.
8. Focus on the fixed and variable rates of minutes only and depict the cost structure of plans A, B, and C as a function of minute usage, as done in Figure 3.2. That is, assume that the customer only uses minutes and depict how the costs would look like for various usage levels.
9. Focus on the fixed and variable rates of texts only and depict the cost structure of plans A, B, and C as a function of text usage, as done in Figure 3.2. That is, assume that the customer only uses texts and depict how the costs would look like for various usage levels.
10. Focus on the fixed and variable rates of MMS only and depict the cost structure of plans A, B, and C as a function of MMS usage, as done in Figure 3.2. That is, assume that the customer only uses MMS and depict how the costs would look like for various usage levels.
11. What plan should the customers go for in problems 7 to 10? Explain.
12. (NB: Consult the examples in Chapter 7 if needed). An amusement park will introduce a new pricing scheme before the next season. It wants to set an entrance fee and a fee for each ride in the park. A market survey shows that the price–response function for the entrance part can be described by the following function:

$$d(E) = 5,000 - 100E$$

where E is the entrance fee. The price–response function for each ride can be described by:

$$d(p) = 5,000 - 500p$$

where p is the price per ride. The variable unit costs are estimated at \$2.00 per entrance and \$1.50 per ride. What is the optimal (profit-maximizing) two-part tariff in this case? You can solve the problem any way you want, but the objective function that shall be maximized is:

$$\max_{E,p} Z = Ed(E) + (p - c_v)d(p) - c_f$$

13. List at least three examples of (1) self-selection, (2) time-based, and (3) regional pricing.
14. Discuss the possible challenges associated with performing price differentiation in practice.

Notes

1 Note that *price differentiation* and *price discrimination* are both used in the literature to refer to the same thing. Phillips (2005) prefers the former because it avoids the negative connotations associated with the word discrimination. Additionally, many authors stress that price discrimination/differentiation is about charging different prices for similar goods/services to *different consumers*. In the definition used here, we have deliberately omitted this part. The reason is that price differentiation can also be carried out for the same consumer. This is especially linked to what is called second degree price differentiation and is discussed later in this section.
2 A non-vertical shape of the price–response function means that the firm faces finite customer responses and, hence, operates in a market without perfect competition. This in turn means that the firm has at least some market power and that it has active pricing decisions to make. In theory, a firm could operate in a market without perfect competition and still face infinite customer responses (vertical price–response function). In this case, the price elasticity of the demand of the product or service of interest is perfectly elastic. We shall return to the concept of price elasticity of demand in Chapter 5.
3 This is an unlikely situation in the real world of course, but we shall use the assumption to illustrate an important point.

Chapter 4
Break-even analysis

Without perfect price differentiation (i.e., the ability to charge each customer their maximum willingness to pay), the firm must make trade-offs between charging higher prices with lower sales and charging lower prices with higher sales. Having a good understanding of what sales volume changes the firm can afford for given price changes is a very useful starting point before doing more sophisticated analysis on price optimization. For example, if the firm considers a price reduction, it is useful to know how much the sales volume would have to increase to profit from it. Alternatively, if the firm considers a price increase, it is useful to know how big a sales reduction the firm can afford before such a price increase becomes unprofitable. The analyses in these cases focus on providing the firm with information about what sales volume accompanying a price change is required to break even exactly. In other words, what sales volume changes will induce the profit to be exactly at the level as before the price change was implemented? As the focus is on the *break-even* point and not profitability, we often refer to the analysis as *break-even analysis*. The following topics will be covered in this chapter:

- Break-even analysis defined.
- Break-even analysis of price changes.
- Break-even analysis with cost changes.
- Brea-even sales curves.

The various break-even analyses are also implemented in the Excel example file accompanying this chapter.

4.1 Break-even analysis defined

In the traditional sense, the break-even point is given as that point at which total revenue equals total cost and profit is zero. If we use the same model to compute the total profit from the number of items sold, as introduced in Chapter 1, we have the following relation:

$$pv - c_v v - c_f = 0 \qquad (4.1)$$

In this model p is the price, c_v is the variable unit costs, v is the volume, that is, the number of items sold, and c_f is the fixed costs. The first term (pv) in (1.1) constitutes the

50 Break-even analysis

revenues, while the two latter terms reflect the total costs. The expression shows that the revenues and costs are of the same magnitude, i.e., the profit is exactly zero.

The relation in Equation (4.1) can be expressed as:

$$v(p-c_v) = c_f \tag{4.2}$$

and the break-even point can then be written as:

$$v = \frac{c_f}{(p-c_v)} \tag{4.3}$$

that is, fixed costs divided by the contribution margin. This definition helps us in answering the following question:

- What is the required sales volume for the firm to break even exactly, given a certain level of variable- and fixed costs and the price?

However, in many cases firms would be more interested in what sales increment is required to profit from a price reduction, or what level of sales decline would make a price increase unprofitable. By making some adjustments to Equation (4.3), we can calculate the required change in sales volume to break even for a given price change. In the section that follows, we go through the steps involved in calculating the break-even volume change stemming from a price change.[1]

4.2 Break-even analysis of price changes

Our prime interest is to find the change in sales that ensures the contribution gained or lost due to a price change is exactly equal to the contribution gained or lost due to a volume change. The concept is illustrated visually in Figure 4.1. Before any price change takes place, this company sells v_1 units, has variable costs equal to area A, and total contribution margin (CM) equal to area $B+C$. The company then decides to reduce the price from p_1 to p_2. This price decrease reduces the total contribution with area C in the figure, which is equal to the change in price times the old sales volume, i.e., the quantity the company would have sold without the price change. This is usually called the price effect on the contribution margin. However, because of a lower price, the company can expect to sell more. In Figure 4.1, the sales volume increases from v_1 to v_2 and the gain in the contribution margin is reflected by area E. This effect is usually called the volume effect, that is, the increased quantity sold (from v_1 to v_2) times the contribution per unit. Area D is due to additional variable costs from selling more units. We can now easily see that a price reduction is profitable if, and only if, area E (gain) is at least as big as area C (loss) in Figure 4.1. Note that the symbol Δ indicates "change in" (stemming from the Greek letter Delta).

To better understand this, consider again the coffee shop introduced in Chapter 1. Table 4.1 summarizes the status of price, units sold (cups), and variable and fixed costs.

Break-even analysis 51

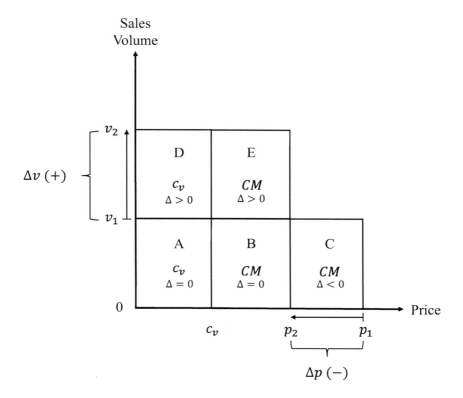

Figure 4.1 Effects of a price reduction on sales volume and contribution margin.

This information is also visualized in Figure 4.2. In this figure, the total contribution margin and the total variable costs are also calculated.

The coffee shop wants to cut its price from $2.00 to $1.50 in order to be more competitive (a 25% reduction in the price). The question is then: how much must the sales volume increase if the price reduction shall be profitable? The effects of this price change are illustrated in Figure 4.3. The contribution lost resulting from the lower price is equal to area C. This area is known: It is the price difference times the number of cups sold before

Table 4.1 Information about current price, sales volume, variable and fixed costs for the coffee shop introduced in Chapter 1

Price/cup	$2.00
Daily sales (cups)	84
Variable costs (per unit)	$0.50
Fixed costs	$20.00

52 Break-even analysis

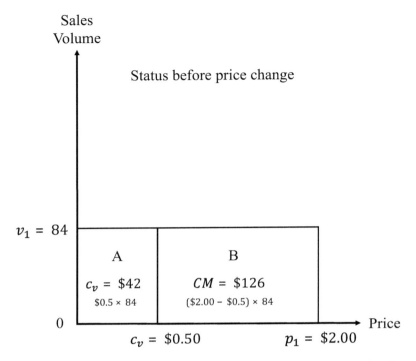

Figure 4.2 Illustration of the status of the coffee shop before the price change is introduced.

the price change occurred: $(\$2.00-\$1.50)\times 84 = \$42$. We now know that for this price change to break even, we need to increase the sales volume such that the total contribution from increased sales (area E of Figure 4.3) is exactly equal to $42. As variable costs (per unit) are $0.50 the contribution per unit is $\$1.00\,(\$1.50-\$0.50)$ after the price change. Since we know that the new contribution times the increased sales volume (that is, area E) must be equal to the lost contribution from the reduced price (the price effect) times the number of units we sold at that price (area C), we can formulate an expression where the aim is to find the change in sales volume required to break even exactly. If we denote the required sales volume change as x, the following equation will solve the problem:

$$\$1.00 \times x = \$42 \Rightarrow x = \frac{\$42}{\$1.00} = 42$$

That is, the coffee shop must sell 42 *more* cups of coffee for a price reduction from $2.00 to $1.50 to break even. If the company sells more than 42 extra cups, the price change is profitable and vice versa. The new sales volume can then be easily found by adding 42 cups to the sales volume before the price change took place:

$$v_2 = v_1 + \Delta v = 84 + 42 = 126$$

Break-even analysis 53

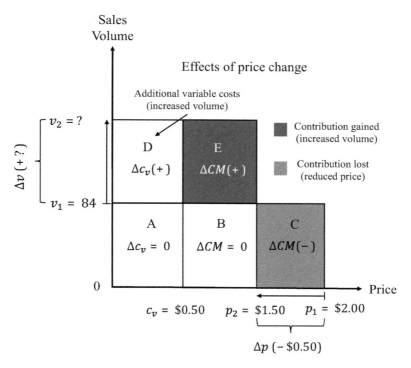

Figure 4.3 Illustration of the effects of a price reduction for one cup of coffee costing $0.50.

In Table 4.2, all the effects of the price change in the coffee shop example are calculated (the areas of Figure 4.3). You can then easily confirm that area C equals area E and that the total contribution before the price change $(B+|C|)$ is exactly equal to the total contribution after the price change $(B+E)$.

Table 4.2 Calculations of the various areas of Figure 4.3. These calculations are also implemented in Example 4.1 of the Excel file following Chapter 4

Area of Figure 4.3	Calculations
A: Total variable costs before price change/part of variable costs after price change	$c_v v_1 = \$0.5 \times 84 = \$42$
B: Part of contribution margin before/after price change	$(p_2 - c_v) v_1 = (\$1.50 - \$0.50) \times 84 = \$84$
C: Contribution lost due to price reduction	$(p_2 - p_1) v_1 = (\$2.00 - \$1.50) \times 84 = -\$42$
D: Additional variable costs due to increased sales volume	$c_v (v_2 - v_1) = \$0.50 \times (126 - 84) = \$21$
E: Contribution gained due to increased sales volume	$(p_2 - c_v)(v_2 - v_1) = (\$1.50 - \$0.50) \times (126 - 84) = \$42$

54 Break-even analysis

We can also use the information from Figure 4.3 to derive a general expression to calculate the relative sales volume change needed to break even from a given absolute price change. We know that area C must be equal to area E for this to be the case. If we use the notation in the figure, we can express the total contribution margin before the price change as $(p_1 - c_v)v_1$ (area $B+C$). After the price change, the margin is $(p_2 - c_v)v_2$ (area $B+E$). Note that $p_2 = p_1 + \Delta p$ and that $v_2 = v_1 + \Delta v$, and remember that both Δp and Δv can be negative. As our objective is to find Δv for which the profit is the same before and after the price change, we can formulate the problem as follows:

$$(p_1 - c_v)v_1 = (p_1 + \Delta p - c_v)(v_1 + \Delta v)$$

If we multiply this equation through, we get:

$$p_1 v_1 - c_v v_1 = p_1 v_1 + \Delta p v_1 - c_v v_1 + p_1 \Delta v + \Delta p \Delta v - c_v \Delta v$$

Collecting terms and setting the expression equal to zero yields:

$$\Delta p v_1 + p_1 \Delta v + \Delta p \Delta v - c_v \Delta v = 0$$

Reorganize and solve for Δv:

$$p_1 \Delta v + \Delta p \Delta v - c_v \Delta v = -\Delta p v_1$$
$$(p_1 + \Delta p - c_v)\Delta v = -\Delta p v_1$$
$$\Delta v = \frac{-\Delta p v_1}{(p_1 + \Delta p - c_v)}$$

which can be written as:

$$\frac{\Delta v}{v_1} = \frac{-\Delta p}{(p_1 + \Delta p - c_v)} \qquad (4.4)$$

In words:

$$Relative\ BE\ sales\ volume\ change = \frac{-Price\ change}{CM + price\ change}$$

Where *BE* stands for "break-even." Using numbers from the example we get:

$$\frac{-(-\$0.50)}{\$1.50 + (-\$0.50)} = \frac{\$0.50}{\$1.00} = 0.50 = 50.0\%$$

Hence, an increase in sales of 50.0%, or 42 units $(0.50 \times 84 = 42)$, is needed to break even for a price reduction of $0.50.

Once we know the break-even sales change, we can also easily calculate the profit or loss associated with any change in volume. In both cases, the profit/loss associated with

Break-even analysis 55

a price change is simply the difference between the break-even volume change and the actual (observed) volume change times the new contribution margin. In the example above, if the observed volume change from a price reduction of $0.50 was 50 (and not 42), the profit from the price reduction would be $8 ($1.00×(50−42)). Similarly, if the volume change from the price reduction was only 40, the net effect would be a loss of $2 ($1.00×(40−42)).

4.3 Break-even with cost changes

What happens if there is a change in either fixed or variable costs when a price change is introduced? Fortunately, this can be easily handled. Let us first consider a situation where a price change will induce a change in variable costs. In this case, the only thing needed is a slight modification of Equation (4.4) to incorporate change in variable costs:

$$\frac{\Delta v}{v_1} = \frac{-(\Delta p - \Delta C_v)}{(p_1 + \Delta p - c_v - \Delta C_v)} \tag{4.5}$$

Where, as before, Δ indicates "change in" (stemming from the Greek letter "Delta"). Hence, by simply including any change in variable costs associated with the price change we get the break-even sales change accounted for new variable costs. We can now express a more general break-even sales change formula as:

$$BESC = \frac{-\Delta CM}{New\,CM} \tag{4.6}$$

where *BESC* stands for *break-even sales change*. Figure 4.4 illustrates a situation where there is both a price reduction (from p_1 to p_2) and a simultaneous reduction in variable costs (from c_{v_1} to c_{v_2}). It is clear from this figure that there is an additional gain in contribution due to reduced variable costs (area F). Hence, the required gain from increased volume (area E) does not have to be as big as if there were no reduction in the variable costs. This makes perfect sense as a reduction in the variable costs affects the contribution margin positively. The relation that will induce no change in overall profit in the general case presented in Figure 4.4 can now be expressed as:

$C = E + F.$

That is, the lost contribution caused by a lower price is equal to the gained contribution resulting from higher sales volume plus the gained contribution caused by lower variable costs. Consider again the coffee shop example from the previous section, but now assume that a price reduction of $0.50 (from $2.00 to $1.00) is associated with a reduction in variable costs (per unit) of $0.10 (from $0.50 to $0.40). What is now the required sales volume change to break even?

To solve this problem, we can apply Equation (4.6) directly:

$$BESC = \frac{-\Delta CM}{New\,CM} = \frac{-(-\$0.40)}{\$1.10} = \frac{0.4}{1.1} = 0.3636 = 36.4\%$$

56 Break-even analysis

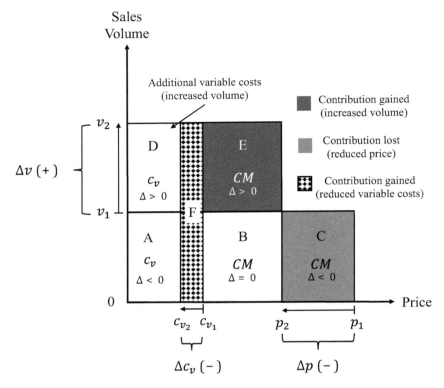

Figure 4.4 Break-even sales change, given change in price and variable costs.

That is, an increase in sales volume of 36.4% is required to break even in the given example. This corresponds to $84 \times 0.364 \sim 31$ extra units and the new required total sales volume would be $84 + 31 = 115$. The detailed calculations of the break-even sales change and the sizes of the various areas of Figure 4.4 are provided in Example 4.2 in the Excel file following Chapter 4.

In some cases there is a need to undertake an investment in order to later implement a price change. For example, a new machine may be needed in order to reduce the variable costs associated with producing an item, which in turn is needed in order to reduce the price. These were defined as *incremental fixed costs* in Chapter 2. Such costs remain fixed within certain ranges of production/sales volumes. For a price change to be justified, the decision-makers must account for these additional costs associated with implementing a price change.

Calculating the break-even sales volume to cover incremental fixed costs is straightforward. It is simply to apply the regular formula for finding the break-even point as given in Equation (4.3). The only difference is that the numerator is "change in fixed costs" associated with the pricing decision and not the overall fixed costs of the production process. Hence, the right question to ask is: "How many units must be sold in order to cover an incremental investment of x dollars?" The answer to this question is the number of items that must be added to the original unit break-even sales change number as obtained from Equation (4.6). Hence, the general formula for calculating unit break-even sales change is:

$$UBESC = \frac{-\Delta CM}{New\,CM} \times initial\ unit\ sales + \frac{\Delta C_f}{New\,CM} \quad (4.7)$$

where $UBESC$ stands for "unit break-even sales change." The corresponding relative (per cent) break-even sales change can be calculated like this:

$$\%BESC = \frac{-\Delta CM}{New\,CM} + \frac{\Delta C_f}{New\,CM \times initial\ unit\ sale} \quad (4.8)$$

You can now verify that these formulas can be used in any scenario. If there is no change in fixed costs, then the last term of Equations (4.7) and (4.8) is zero. In the following example, these formulas are applied to calculate both unit and percentage break-even sales change for changes in the price, variable costs and fixed costs for the coffee shop. The implementation of these calculations in Excel can be found in Example 4.3 in the Excel file following Chapter 4.

Example 4.1: Break-even sales change with change in price, variable costs and fixed costs.

p_1: $2.00, p_1: $1.50, c_{v_1}: $0.50, c_{v_2}: $0.40, Change in fixed costs to handle increased sales volume: $20. Initial sales are 84 cups. What is the minimum required sales increase to justify the given price reduction?

$$\frac{-(-0.40)}{(1.50-0.40)} \times 84 + \frac{20}{(1.50-0.40)} = 0.3636 \times 84 + 18 = 49$$

$$0.3636 + \frac{20}{1.1 \times 84} = 0.5801$$

4.4 Break-even sales curves

When managers make pricing decisions, it is very useful to illustrate the break-even sales volume for a range of price changes. Using a spreadsheet, such as Microsoft Excel, it is very simple to automatically calculate the numbers necessary to draw a so-called *break-even sales curve*. An illustration of these calculations is provided in Figure 4.5 and the corresponding break-even sales curves in Figure 4.6. The upper panel shows a break-even sales curve where price changes induce no change in the costs. The lower panel

58 Break-even analysis

	A	B
1	**BEFORE PRICE CHANGE**	
2	Price/cup	$2.00
3	Daily sales (cups)	84
4	Revenues	$168.00
5	Variable costs (per unit)	$0.50
6	Variable costs	$42.00
7	Contribution (per unit)	$1.50
8	Contribution	$126.00
9	Fixed costs	$20.00
10	Profit	$106.00

	D	E	F	G	H
1	Price Change	Price	Break-Even Sales Change	Unit Break-Even Sales Change	Unit Break-Even Sales Volume
2	0.5	=$E$7*(1+D2)	=-(E2-$E$7)/((E2-$E$7)+$B$7)	=F2*$B$3	=$B$3+G2
3	0.4	=$E$7*(1+D3)	=-(E3-$E$7)/((E3-$E$7)+$B$7)	=F3*$B$3	=$B$3+G3
4	0.3	=$E$7*(1+D4)	=-(E4-$E$7)/((E4-$E$7)+$B$7)	=F4*$B$3	=$B$3+G4
5	0.2	=$E$7*(1+D5)	=-(E5-$E$7)/((E5-$E$7)+$B$7)	=F5*$B$3	=$B$3+G5
6	0.1	=$E$7*(1+D6)	=-(E6-$E$7)/((E6-$E$7)+$B$7)	=F6*$B$3	=$B$3+G6
7	0	2	=-(E7-$E$7)/((E7-$E$7)+$B$7)	=F7*$B$3	=$B$3+G7
8	-0.1	=$E$7*(1+D8)	=-(E8-$E$7)/((E8-$E$7)+$B$7)	=F8*$B$3	=$B$3+G8
9	-0.2	=$E$7*(1+D9)	=-(E9-$E$7)/((E9-$E$7)+$B$7)	=F9*$B$3	=$B$3+G9
10	-0.3	=$E$7*(1+D10)	=-(E10-$E$7)/((E10-$E$7)+$B$7)	=F10*$B$3	=$B$3+G10
11	-0.4	=$E$7*(1+D11)	=-(E11-$E$7)/((E11-$E$7)+$B$7)	=F11*$B$3	=$B$3+G11
12	-0.5	=$E$7*(1+D12)	=-(E12-$E$7)/((E12-$E$7)+$B$7)	=F12*$B$3	=$B$3+G12

	D	E	F	G	H
1	Price Change	Price	Break-Even Sales Change	Unit Break-Even Sales Change	Unit Break-Even Sales Volume
2	50%	3.00	-40.0%	-34	50
3	40%	2.80	-34.8%	-29	55
4	30%	2.60	-28.6%	-24	60
5	20%	2.40	-21.1%	-18	66
6	10%	2.20	-11.8%	-10	74
7	0%	2.00	0.0%	0	84
8	-10%	1.80	15.4%	13	97
9	-20%	1.60	36.4%	31	115
10	-30%	1.40	66.7%	56	140
11	-40%	1.20	114.3%	96	180
12	-50%	1.00	200.0%	168	252

Figure 4.5 Illustration of a spreadsheet with calculations needed to build a break-even sales curve.

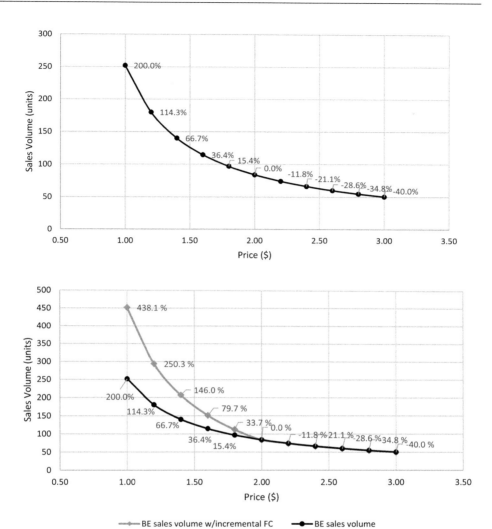

Figure 4.6 Break-even sales curves. Upper panel: Break-even sales curve with no changes in costs. All the combinations on the curve induce the same profit level as the base case (that is, a profit of $106). The base case is given by the information in the upper panel of Figure 4.5 (that is, a price of $2.00, a sales volume of 84 yielding a total profit of $106). The various price changes used to calculate the required sales changes needed to break even are [−50%, −40%, −30%, −20%, −10%, 10%, 20%, 30%, 40%, 50%]. The data labels indicate the required change in sales volume from the base level (84) for any given (new) price level. For example, a change in the price from $2.00 to $1.00 will require a sales change of 200% from the base level (i.e., $84 \times 2 = 168$). The new required total sales volume will then be $84 + 168 = 252$. Lower panel: Break-even sales curve with incremental fixed costs in addition to the break-even sales curve illustrated in the upper panel. The incremental fixed costs used are given in the example Excel file following Chapter 4 (Example 4.4). The figure is adapted from Nagle et al. (2011, p.221), but the axes are switched and the numbers used are different.

shows the corresponding curve with changes in some of the costs for some price changes. The details are provided in the figure caption.

By examining such curves as those illustrated in Figure 4.6, management gets a very quick overview of the sales required for any given price change to break even. You may also notice that this break-even sales curve looks similar to the price–response function introduced in previous chapters. All points on the break-even sales curve show the association between price and demanded quantity. In fact, there is a relationship between the price–response function and the break-even sales curve, where the sensitivity of demand, which can be illustrated with the steepness of the price–response function, decides whether a price change is profitable or not. Put simply; for very elastic demand (i.e., a very big change in demanded quantity for small price changes) a price decrease is generally profitable (and vice versa), while for very inelastic demand (i.e., only small changes in demanded quantity for a given price change) a price increase is profitable. We shall return to the important aspects of price elasticity of demand, price sensitivity and willingness to pay, and the relations between these and price–response functions in the next chapter.

4.5 Summary

- The break-even point is where total revenue equals total cost and profit is zero.
- The break-even sales volume can be found by:

$$v = \frac{c_f}{(p - c_v)}$$

- To analyze effects on profits from price changes we have to compare the lost (gained) revenue from a reduced (increased) price with the gained (lost) revenue from increased (decreased) sales volume.
- The percentage change in sales volume needed for a price change to break even can be found by:

$$\%BESC = \frac{-Price\ change}{CM + price\ change}$$

- In the case of price changes and cost changes occurring simultaneously we modify the formula slightly:

$$\%BESC = \frac{-\Delta CM}{NewCM} + \frac{\Delta C_f}{NewCM \times initial\ unit\ sale}$$

- To obtain the unit sales change needed we multiply the percentage change by the initial unit sales.
- Break-even sales curves illustrate the trade-off between price and sales volume required for constant profitability.

4.6 Problems

1. Calculate the break-even sales volume for a company where the market price is $25, the variable unit costs are $10 and the fixed costs are $25,000. Verify your calculations by calculating the profit for this sales volume.
2. A coffee shop is considering investing in a new machine that produces a brand new type of coffee. The manager believes the new type of coffee can be sold for $5/unit. The variable cost is $3/unit. The machine costs $1,000. Determine how many cups of coffee must be sold to break even?
3. If the coffee shop in the previous problem sells ten cups of the new coffee per day on average, how many days will it take to break even?
4. The manager of the coffee shop in problems 2 and 3 says that the input used in the break-even analysis may be a bit too optimistic. The variable unit costs will be 25% higher than previously stated. How will this affect the break-even sales volume if the price remains the same?
5. Calculate the percentage break-even sales volume change needed to justify a price decrease of 10% in the scenarios given in the table below. Do the same calculations for a price decrease of 15%. Finally, how much sales can the company afford to lose if it increases the price by 20%?

		Change in price		
Price	Current CM	10% decrease	15% decrease	20% increase
10	5			
15	10			
25	20			
90	40			
150	50			

6. Use the information in the table below to calculate the percentage break-even sales change:

	Time 1	Time 2
Price	90	85
VUC	40	38
CM	50	47

62 Break-even analysis

7. A firm produces and sells a widget. Information about the current price, yearly sales, and costs are given in the table below:

Price/unit	$10.00
Yearly sales	20,000
Revenues	$200,000.00
Variable costs (per unit)	$7.00
Variable costs	$140,000.00
Contribution	$60,000.00
Fixed costs	$10,000.00
Profit	$50,000.00

The firm considers a price reduction from $10 to $8.90. Use this information to calculate (1) the break-even sales change both in absolute and relative terms, and (2) the reduced contribution due to the price reduction, the increased contribution due to the sales volume increase and the increase in total variable costs.

8. Use the information from the table in problem 7, but now assume that that the variable costs are also reduced from $7 to $6. How will this affect the results?

9. Use the information from the table in problem 7 and the updated information given in problem 8, but now assume that the fixed costs also change because of the price change (and hence increased sales volume) from $10,000 to $20,000. How will this new information affect the results?

10. Provide a graphical illustration of (1) contribution lost due to price, (2) contribution gained due to volume, and (3) total contribution and total variable costs for the new break-even sales volume, given the numbers presented below. The illustration should be similar to that presented in Figure 4.4, but also include the actual amounts of (1), (2), and (3).

	Time 1	Time 2
Price	20	15
VC	13	12
CM	7	3
Sales volume	1,200	?
Tot VC	?	?
Tot CM	?	?

11. A company is considering investing in a new machine that makes the production process more efficient. The machine costs $15,000 and will lower the variable costs by $2. The goal of the investment is to increase production by selling the product $3 cheaper than the current price of $38. What is the percentage break-even sales volume change when we know that the company currently is producing and selling 10,000 units of the product and has a (current) contribution of $10 per unit sold?

12. Calculate the required sales change (%) for various price changes (%) given in the table below. Assume a current contribution margin of $75 and a sales volume of 20,000. Present your results in a break-even sales curve.

Price change	Price $
25%	187.50
20%	180.00
15%	172.50
10%	165.00
5%	157.50
0%	150.00
-5%	142.50
-10%	135.00
-15%	127.50
-20%	120.00
-25%	112.50

13. Use the information from the table above, but now include incremental fixed costs as given in the table below. Present the results in a break-even sales curve.

Sales volume	Incremental fixed costs
20,000,25,000	$15,000
[25,000,28,000	$30,000
[28,000,33,000	$50,000
[25,000,30,000	$100,000
[33,000,50,000	$200,000

Note

1 For example, one could first just add the profit level in the numerator: $v_f + profit$. Then a new break-even volume with a new price (for example, by multiplying the price by 1.1 for a 10% increase or 0.9 for a 10% decrease) can be calculated.

Chapter 5

Price sensitivity and willingness to pay

5.1 Price sensitivity

In the last part of Chapter 4 we depicted a break-even sales curve for the coffee shop. This figure depicted the sales volume required (measured by number of cups), for a range of prices per cup, to produce a constant profit. However, the figure did not say anything about how the actual demand for coffee varies with the various price levels, only that if we move along the curve, the profit will remain the same.

We can include such information about demanded quantity in this break-even plot, though. By doing so, we know more about whether a specific price change is profitable or not. Why? Because if demanded quantity changes very little from a given price change, a price increase would be profitable (we lose few customers by increasing the price) and vice versa.

In Figure 5.1 the break-even sales curve from Chapter 4 is depicted together with an *inelastic* and *elastic* price–response function (upper and lower panel, respectively). The price range is narrower in Figure 5.1 compared with Figure 4.6, for expository purposes. Demand is inelastic when the sales volume changes little for a given price change. This is clearly the situation in the upper panel. A reduction in the price from $2.00 to $1.60 per cup of coffee hardly affects demanded quantity at all (from 84 units to 92 units – see the dashed line in the upper panel). In this case the coffee shop would gain a lot if it were to *increase the price* per cup. This is because the price–response function is above the break-even sales curve for all prices above the current baseline price ($2.00). The actual profit obtained from increasing the price will then be higher than the no-change (in profit) scenario, which is represented by the break-even sales curve (solid line).

How much will the profit rise from a given price increase? The answer is the difference in the actual demanded quantity (dashed line) for a given new price and the required sales volume to break even at the new price, multiplied by the contribution margin. If using the information from the upper panel of Figure 5.1 the coffee shop would increase profit by ~ $10 if changing the price from $2.00 to $2.20 (($2.20 − $0.50) × (80 − 74)). That is, the new contribution margin ($2.20–$0.50) times the difference between the actual sales (80) and the required sales volume to break even (74).

In the lower panel of Figure 5.1 the same break-even sales curve is depicted, but now with an elastic price–response function. In this scenario, the sales volume will change a lot for a given price change. In such cases, the coffee shop (or any firm) would generally profit from reducing the price. The reason is that the actual increase in demanded quantity from a price reduction will be far higher than the required (minimum) sales increase

Price sensitivity and willingness to pay 65

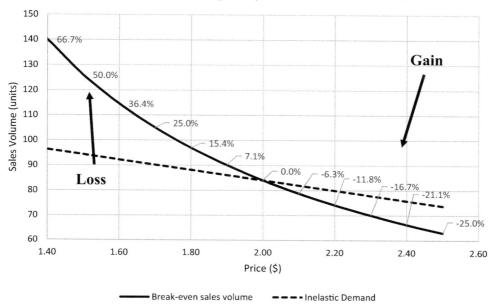

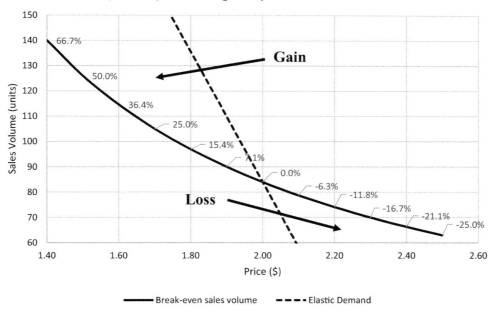

Figure 5.1 Break-even sales curves (solid lines) with inelastic (upper panel) and elastic (lower panel) demand (dashed lines).

to break even. This is clearly illustrated in the figure. If reducing the price from $2.00 to $1.80, the number of cups demanded increases from 84 to 136. This corresponds to an increase of 61.4%. The break-even sales curve, on the other hand, shows that the required increase in sales from this price reduction is only 15.4% to remain at the same profit level as before the change (i.e., to break even from a price reduction from $2.00 to $1.80).

As we understand it, how sensitive customers are to price changes can be measured by how steep the price–response function is. In general, when facing a steep price–response function, the volume (quantity) will change much more than if we were facing a more moderately sloping price–response function. The slope of a price–response function can be calculated by dividing the change in demanded quantity by the price change:

$$\varepsilon = \frac{(d(p_2) - d(p_1))}{(p_2 - p_1)} \quad (5.1)$$

Applying this formula on the price–response functions given in Figure 5.1 and for a price increase of $0.10 from the base price of $2.00, we find a slope of approximately −20 for the PRF in the upper panel $((82-84)/(2.1-2.0))$, and -260 for the PRF in the lower panel $((58-84)/(2.1-2.0))$. This means that for a $1 increase in the price for one cup of coffee, demanded quantity will go down by 20 cups in the upper panel and by 260 cups for the same price increase ($1.00) in the lower panel. The implementation of these approximate calculations of the slopes are given in Example 5.1 in the Excel file following this chapter. An illustration of how the slope is affected by units of measurements (such as cents per unit, instead of dollars per unit) is also included in the example Excel file.

Formally, we say that a steep price–response function reflects an *elastic demand* and that a slowly declining price–response function tells us that demand is *inelastic*. Compared to how the relation between price and demand is usually presented in microeconomic texts, the axes in a price–response function are switched. The reason is that the price–response function is usually estimated using econometric techniques (regression analysis). In this case it is common practice to express the demand as a function of price. Hence, demand is the dependent variable and price is the independent variable. In econometric terminology this is the same as saying that demand is the *y-variable* and that price is the *x-variable*. Consequently, demand is represented on the Y-axis and price on the X-axis. The switch of axes may confuse some readers. Therefore, Figure 5.2 illustrates the inelastic (left panel) and elastic (right panel) demand for both approaches. The upper panel shows *inelastic* (left panel) and *elastic* (right panel) price–response functions where the demanded quantity is a function of price. The lower panel shows traditional *inelastic* (left panel) and *elastic* (right panel) demand curves, as usually presented in microeconomic texts. In this case, price is a function of demanded quantity. Both ways of illustrating the price elasticity of demand induce the same conclusion, though. For a price change of a given magnitude, the change in demand will be (relatively) high if demand is elastic and (relatively) low if demand is inelastic.

We now understand that the price elasticity of demand is determined by the steepness of the price–response function. This statement is a little too general, though. The reason

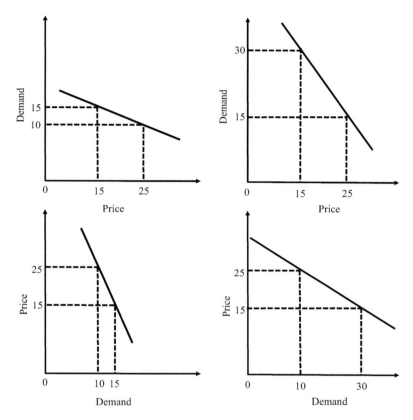

Figure 5.2 Illustration of inelastic (left panel) and elastic (right panel) demand. In the upper panel demand is used on the Y-axis (as commonly done in price–response functions). The lower panel illustrates inelastic and elastic demand with price on the Y-axis (as commonly done in the economics literature).

is that for most functional forms of price–response functions, the estimate of the price elasticity will depend on what part of the curve we choose to use to calculate an elasticity estimate. To see this, consider the following expression that can be used to estimate the price elasticity of demand:

$$\varepsilon = \frac{(d(p_2) - d(p_1))/d(p_1)}{(p_2 - p_1)/p_1} \qquad (5.2)$$

This measure is known as the *point elasticity of demand*, although it requires two combinations of prices and quantities. This estimate will depend on both the old price (p_1) and the new price (p_2), and where we are on the price–response function (the general level of demand at the two prices). An example is given below.

> **Example 5.1: Calculation of price elasticity of demand for a specific product.**
>
> A company increased the price of one of its products from $59 to $64. As a result, the sales went down from 12,000 units to 11,300 units. What is the point elasticity in this case?
>
> $$\varepsilon = \frac{(D_{p_2} - D_{p_1})/D_{p_1}}{(p_2 - p_1)/p_2} = \frac{(11300 - 12000)/12000}{(64 - 59)/59} = -0.69 \quad (5.4)$$

So, what does an elasticity of −0.69 mean? It means that a 10% increase in price will result in a 6.9% decrease in demanded quantity. Alternatively, with a 10% decrease in price, demanded quantity will increase by 6.9%. A price elasticity of less than −1 (for example, −1.5) indicates that demanded quantity changes more than the given price change (in relative terms) and demand is then described as *elastic*. If price elasticity is estimated to more than −1 (for example, −0.69 as in the above example), demanded quantity changes less than the given price change (in relative terms) and demand is referred to as *inelastic*. However, it is important to note *again* here that the estimated elasticity of −0.69 depends on the price levels, and the corresponding demanded quantity, applied in the estimation. Using other price levels will in most cases induce different estimates of the price elasticity. The estimated elasticity does not depend on units of measurements directly – such as demand measured in kilograms or tonnes, or prices measured in dollars or pounds because we calculate percentage changes in both demand and price. However, the general level of the units used can lead to calculations of other percentage changes for either demanded quantity or price. An example could be that we calculate the percentage change in the price for a $1 change versus a €1 change. This would lead us to use slightly different parts of the price–response function in the calculations and the estimate would be affected.

To resolve some of these issues, or if we are more interested in calculating price elasticity over some portion of the demand curve, and not only at one specific point or for a very narrow range, we can calculate what is referred to as the *arc elasticity of demand*:

$$\varepsilon = \frac{(d(p_2) - d(p_1))/\bar{d}(p_1, p_2)}{(p_2 - p_1)/\bar{p}_{1,2}} \quad (5.3)$$

Instead of using the old (original) demanded quantity and price level when calculating the percentage changes, we use the average of the old and new values of both demanded quantity and price. By making these adjustments the arc elasticity becomes less influenced by the levels of both the demanded quantity and price.

If we, on the other hand, are most interested in the elasticity at a certain price level, the *point elasticity* can be more precisely calculated using the following formula:

$$\varepsilon = \frac{p \times d'(p)}{d(p)} \tag{5.4}$$

That is, the price times the slope of the price–response function $(d'(p))$ at *a given price level*, divided by the demand at *that same price level*. In practice, this is the same as calculating the point elasticity using (5.2) when the new price (p_2) approaches (p_1), i.e., for a very small increment in price. We shall return to this when we discuss price–response functions in more detail in the next section.

A final note about price elasticity of demand is that the estimates for most goods and services depend on the time horizon involved. This means that demanded quantity will have one short-run effect and one long-run effect from a given price change. This makes sense as it takes time for consumers to adapt to price changes. For example, if gasoline prices increased by 20% from one day to another, many consumers would probably continue to drive almost as much because they would not have any readily available alternatives. However, in the long term, many consumers would have to look for other alternatives as it would have a big impact on the household budget. In this case, we would therefore expect the long-term demand to be more price elastic than the short-term demand. This is also empirically confirmed by Havranek et al. (2012), who estimate the average short-run demand for gasoline to be −0.09 while the average long-run estimate is −0.31.

In Table 5.1, examples of estimated elasticities for various products are presented. The various goods or services are sorted from most inelastic (top) to most elastic (bottom). As seen from this table, most products have an elasticity of less than 1 (in absolute terms), meaning that demand is inelastic. This is the same as saying that the consumers of these products will not reduce their consumption much if the price goes up. For eggs, for example, the demand will be reduced by only 1.0% if the price goes

Table 5.1 Estimated price elasticities of demand for various products

Product	Mean elasticity
Eggs	−0.10
Airline travel (1st class)	−0.35
Broadband	−0.43
Commuter parking	−0.52
Wine	−1.00
Cinema visits	−0.87
Airline travel (discount)	−0.90
Spirits	−1.50
Coca-Cola	−3.80

Source: Wikipedia article: "Price elasticity of demand," available at: https://en.wikipedia.org/wiki/Price_elasticity_of_demand.

up by 10%. These estimates are based on the U.S. market. In other countries demand for eggs is more elastic. However, in the U.S. eggs are an example of a product that is relatively cheap compared with the consumption level for most consumers. One may argue the same way about Coca-Cola, though, so, why is the elasticity for Coke so high (in absolute terms)? First, for many consumers, the soft drink budget is probably somewhat larger than the eggs budget. A price change will then automatically have a bigger impact on the overall household budget. Second, Coca-Cola is a brand operating in a market where the competition is tough. If the price of Coca-Cola increases, customers will probably quickly look for alternative soft drinks that they perceive to be almost equally good. This is one important reason why Coca-Cola and other brands worldwide spend billions of dollars on marketing every year: to make their customers more loyal (or, in more technical terms, to make demand for their products or services less elastic). Third, the estimated price elasticity for eggs was for the whole product category. If we do the same calculations for the whole *soft drink category*, the price elasticity estimate is much lower (in absolute terms). This is confirmed in a review article by Andreyeva et al. (2010), who found the average elasticity of soft drinks to be −0.79 (based on 160 studies reviewed).

This highlights the important difference between the market demand curve and the price–response functions. What matters to all firms is how demand for the products or services *the specific firm* offers is affected by the price the *same firm charges for those specific products or services*. In other words, what matters are the shapes of the price–response functions. These shapes are based on the consumers' willingness to pay (WTP) for the given products or services of interest. We shall therefore introduce the concept of willingness to pay next and see how this is related to the shape of price–response functions.

5.2 Willingness to pay

Uniform willingness-to-pay distribution

The term maximum willingness to pay refers to the maximum price at which a given potential customer will buy the product or service of interest. This is also referred to as the *reservation price* of the customer. If the price charged is higher than this (reservation) price, the customer will not buy the product or service. If the price charged is lower, the customer will buy the product or service. To see this, consider the example presented in Figure 5.3, which could be for any product or service offered by a given company. For simplicity, we assume in this example that all the customers are interested in buying only one unit of the product or service within the time period considered, even though their reservation price is higher than the listed price. Column A lists five price levels and column B provides information about how many customers have a reservation price equal to the price listed on the same row in column A. That is, two customers have a reservation price of $1, two customers have a reservation price of $2, and so forth. Column C computes the number of customers with a reservation price less than or equal to the price listed in column A. Two customers have a reservation price of $1.00 or less, four customers have a reservation price of $2.00 or less (two customers at $RP = \$1.00$ and two customers at $RP = \$2.00$), and so forth. Column D calculates the total demanded quantity if the price charged was that listed on the same row in column A. This is simply the sum of customers with a reservation price greater than or equal to the listed price. Note that this is the demanded quantity at the various prices, which is the basis of the

Price sensitivity and willingness to pay 71

	A	B	C	D	E
1					
2	RESERVATION PRICES (MAX WTP) AND SHAPE OF PRICE-RESPONSE FUNCTIONS				
3					
4	Price (p)	# of customers with this RP (RP=p)	# of customers with RP ≤ p	# of customers with RP ≥ p (d(p))	Fraction with RP=p
5	$1.00	2	2	8	0.25
6	$2.00	2	4	6	0.25
7	$3.00	2	6	4	0.25
8	$4.00	2	8	2	0.25

Figure 5.3 Excel spreadsheet used to illustrate the relation between reservation prices (maximum willingness to pay), the price–response function and the corresponding WTP distribution.

price–response function. Column E calculates the fraction of customers with reservation prices equal to the corresponding listed price in column A. This is simply the number of customers with a given reservation price (for example, two customers with $RP = \$1.00$) divided by the total potential number of units sold of this product or service by this firm.

Figure 5.4 illustrates the results of the calculations in columns D and E for the various prices listed in column A of Figure 5.3. This figure clearly shows that when the WTP distribution (lower panel) is uniform, i.e., the fraction of customers is constant across all reservation price levels, we end up with a linear relation between demanded quantity and price (upper panel). There is no doubt that a straight line would make the best fit to the data points in this case. We could simply use a ruler and draw a straight line through the points to estimate a continuous price–response function. In doing so, we can see with the naked eye that this line will cross the Y-axis at ten units and the X-axis at $5.00. We also quickly see that for every dollar increase in the price, the demanded quantity goes down by two units.

The general formula to estimate a linear price–response function can be expressed as:

$$d(p) = D + m \cdot p \tag{5.5}$$

This is simply the function for the simple linear regression model. D is the intercept and can be interpreted as the estimated total potential number of units sold, that is, the demand if the price drops to zero. m is the slope and indicates how demanded quantity is affected by a one-unit increase in the independent variable – the price (p).

When plugging in the numbers we can extract with our bare eyes from the upper panel of Figure 5.4 to get the following price–response function:

$$d(p) = 10 - 2 \cdot \$1$$

Figure 5.5 depicts this continuous linear price–response function (upper panel) and the corresponding WTP distribution (lower panel). As the linear (continuous) price–response function is essentially an extrapolation of the discrete price–response function, we indirectly assume that there are two additional customers who would buy the product if the price drops to zero ($D = 10$). This affects the WTP distribution (right panel) as we now divide by a higher number of total (potential) customers (ten instead of eight).

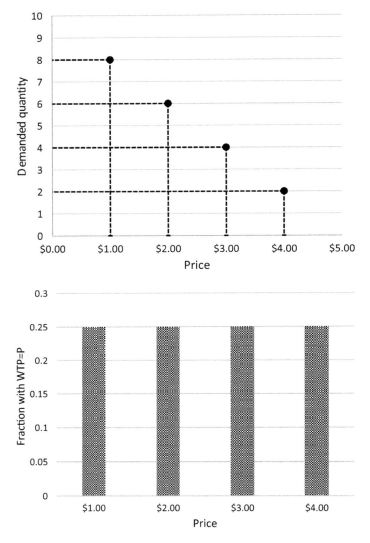

Figure 5.4 Discrete price–response based on the information in Figure 5.3 (upper panel) and the corresponding distribution for willingness to pay (lower panel).

Therefore, we now have a uniform distribution at 20% across prices between $0 and $4. Additionally, we can extrapolate from the other tail to estimate the price for which no customers are willing to buy the product, i.e., the satiating price. In the given example, it is easy to see that this price is $5, but it can also easily be calculated by setting Equation (5.5) equal to zero and solve for p ($-2p = -10 \Rightarrow p = 5$). It is important to note the difference between the discrete and continuous results. From our discrete data, we know that no customers have a willingness to pay of more than $4, while the estimate of the satiating price based on the linear price–response function is $5.

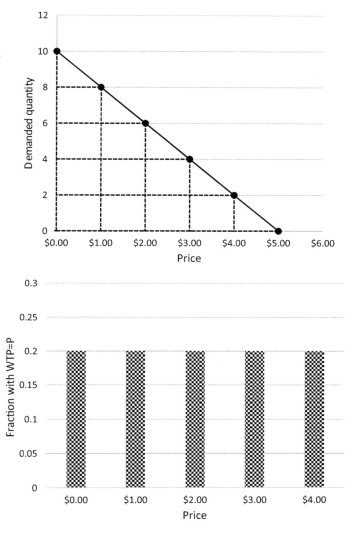

Figure 5.5 Linear price–response function for the same product or service as that presented in Figure 5.4 (upper panel) and the corresponding WTP distribution (lower panel).

The general relationship between a uniform WTP distribution and a linear price–response function is illustrated in Figure 5.6. As seen in this figure, a linear price–response function implies that an equal fraction of the total consumer population is willing to purchase the product or service at every possible price point between 0 and the satiating price P. This constant fraction is equal to $1/P$, where P can be calculated as D/m. Such a uniform WTP distribution is not common in practice, though. Most consumers would probably have a reservation price around the center of the distribution, and the number of potential consumers with very high or very low reservation prices will make up a smaller fraction. Put differently, it is likely that the impact on demanded quantity from a

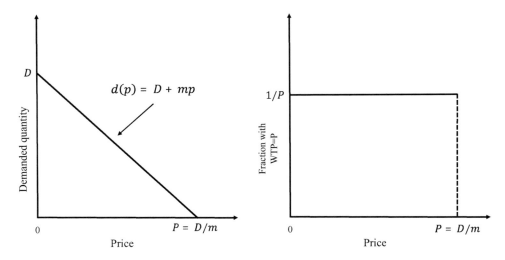

Figure 5.6 General relationship between a linear price–response function (left panel) and corresponding WTP distribution (right panel). The figure is adapted from Figures 3.3 and 3.4 in Phillips (2005).

given price change differs depending on the price level. We shall therefore examine other WTP distributions and the corresponding price–response functions next.

Other willingness to pay distributions

In some cases, the linear price–response function could be used to inform about the general relation between demanded quantity and price. For the most part, though, this price–response function will provide accurate estimates only for *some* price levels. That is, it will not provide a realistic representation of the relation between demanded quantity and price across *all* price levels (that is, globally). For example, for most goods and services sold in a market, it is likely that the fraction of potential consumers with very low and very high reservation prices is lower compared with the fraction of consumers with more moderate reservation prices. An example illustrating this is presented in Figure 5.7 with an illustration of the corresponding WTP distribution and price–response function given in Figure 5.8. In this example, we simply add two customers for each reservation price level from $0 up to $2.50. Then we subtract two customers for each reservation price level from $3.00 to $5.00. This means that $2.50 is the most common reservation price level in this case (16.7% of the customers have $2.50 as their reservation price). The corresponding price–response function (upper panel of Figure 5.8) now has a non-linear form that generally better reflects consumer behavior for most goods and services. For very low and high prices, demanded quantity is barely affected by price changes. For more moderate prices (in relative terms), demand is very sensitive and even small price changes will induce big changes in demanded quantity.

The example just provided can be formalized somewhat by saying that the number of customers with various reservation prices (as given in column B of Figures 5.3 and 5.7) shall be drawn from a known probability distribution. In Examples 5.5 and 5.6 in the

	A	B	C	D	E
1					
2	RESERVATION PRICES (MAX WTP) AND SHAPE OF PRICE-RESPONSE FUNCTIONS				
3					
4	Price (p)	# of customers with this RP (RP=p)	# of customers with RP ≤ p	# of customers with RP ≥ p (d(p))	Fraction with RP=p
5	$0.00	2	2	72	2.8%
6	$0.50	4	6	70	5.6%
7	$1.00	6	12	66	8.3%
8	$1.50	8	20	60	11.1%
9	$2.00	10	30	52	13.9%
10	$2.50	12	42	42	16.7%
11	$3.00	10	52	30	13.9%
12	$3.50	8	60	20	11.1%
13	$4.00	6	66	12	8.3%
14	$4.50	4	70	6	5.6%
15	$5.00	2	72	2	2.8%

Figure 5.7 Excel spreadsheet used to illustrate the relation between reservation prices (maximum willingness to pay), the price–response function, and the corresponding WTP distribution, when fewer customers have very low- and very high reservation prices (in relative terms) compared with more moderate reservation prices.

Excel file following Chapter 5, an implementation of the binomial and normal distribution is illustrated.

Figure 5.9 shows the results for the implementation of normal WTP distribution with mean value equal to $5.00 and with a standard deviation of $2.00 (lower panel). The corresponding price–response function is also depicted in the upper panel.

Using such known probability distributions is particularly useful when building simulation models of how various pricing decisions may influence the general performance of the firm. We shall return to this in Chapter 13 where Monte Carlo simulation for pricing decisions is introduced. However, as the focus in the next chapter will be on fitting price–response functions to empirical price/demand data, we shall briefly examine some *common functional forms* of price–response functions.

5.3 Functional forms of price–response functions

The functional form of the linear PRF was introduced in Equation (5.5). It is given again here together with three other common price–response functions:

Linear: $\quad d(p) = D + m \cdot p$ \hfill (5.6)

Constant ε: $\quad d(p) = C \cdot p^{\varepsilon}$ \hfill (5.7)

Power: $\quad d(p) = \alpha \cdot D/(p^{\beta} + \alpha)$ \hfill (5.8)

Logit: $\quad d(p) = \dfrac{C \cdot e^{a+b \cdot p}}{1 + e^{a+b \cdot p}}$ \hfill (5.9)

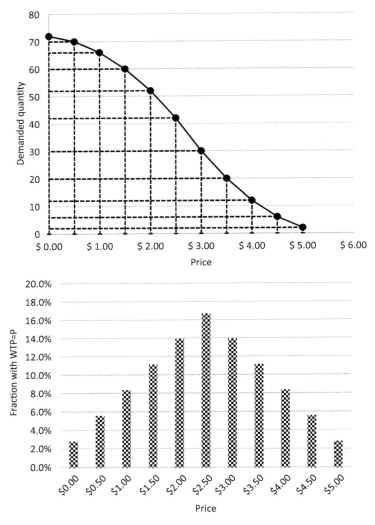

Figure 5.8 Illustration of WTP distribution (lower panel) and corresponding price–response function (upper panel) using data from Figure 5.7.

The general shape of these four price–response functions are illustrated in Figure 5.10. As the properties of the linear price–response function have been introduced and discussed earlier, we focus on the other three price–response functions now.

The constant elasticity price–response function has a point elasticity fixed across all price levels. For almost all goods and services, this is very unlikely. The reason is that this price–response function induces a demand that is neither finite nor satiating. This means that demand never goes to zero as price increases towards infinity, and that demand is unbounded (approaches infinity) as price moves towards zero: there is no limit. These properties infer that the constant elasticity PRF is generally not a good

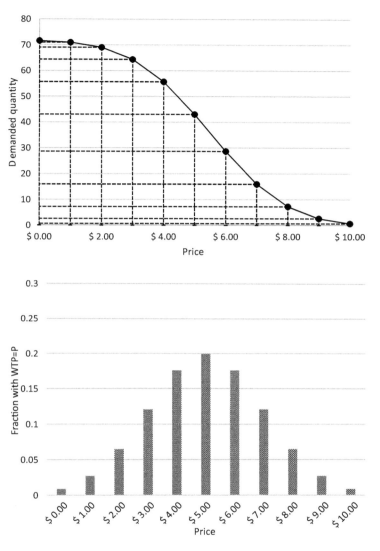

Figure 5.9 Implementation of a normal WTP distribution with a mean equal to $5.00 and a standard deviation of $2.00. See the details in the Excel file following Chapter 5.

global representation of price–response. For some *local* parts of the price/demand relationship, for example around the current market price, it could fit the data well, though. We shall look at some examples when we estimate various price–response functions in the next chapter.

Phillips (2005) also shows that the direction of the slope of the revenue function for a constant elasticity price–response function is determined by $(1-\varepsilon)$. That is, if demand is inelastic (below 1 in absolute terms), then the slope of the revenue is positive, meaning that the seller can continuously increase revenue by increasing price (forever). In the

78 Price sensitivity and willingness to pay

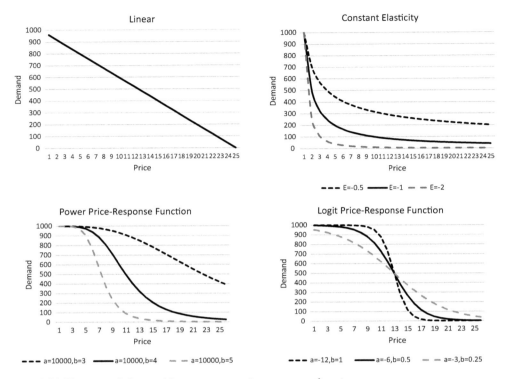

Figure 5.10 The general shape of four common price–response functions.

opposite case, if elasticity is above one the seller can increase revenue by decreasing price. In fact, the maximum revenue in this case is when the price is as close to zero as possible because demand will then move rapidly towards infinity.

For all the reasons mentioned above, we understand that the constant elasticity price–response function is not realistic when moving to the regions of the curve with very low/high prices. In such cases the lower panel of Figure 5.10 provides better approximations of the price/demand relationship. The left panel illustrates a *power price–response function* and the right panel a *logit price–response function*. Both have a similar reverse S-shape. This shape is generally a good description of how demanded quantity is related to price across all price levels for most products or services. For very low prices, consumers will not demand less of the product if price increases, and for very high prices demand is practically zero already, so increasing the price more will not induce a (much) lower demanded quantity. Of the two price–response functions (power and logit), the logit is usually preferred because it is easier to estimate empirically.

Information about the parameters going into the various price–response functions is given in Table 5.2. This information is useful when implementing, or estimating, the various functions. In the Excel example file following Chapter 5 the various price–response functions are implemented. It is a good idea to experiment a little with the

Table 5.2 Functional form of four common price–response functions (left column) and corresponding properties of the parameters going into the PRF

Price–response function	Parameters
Linear: $d(p) = D + m \cdot p$	$D > 0,\ m < 0$
Constant ε: $d(p) = C \cdot p^{\varepsilon}$	$C > 0,\ \varepsilon < 0$
Power: $d(p) = \alpha \cdot D / (p^{\beta} + \alpha)$	$D > 0,\ \alpha > 0,\ \beta > 0$
Logit: $d(p) = \dfrac{C \cdot e^{a+b \cdot p}}{1 + e^{a+b \cdot p}}$	$C > 0,\ a \in \mathbb{R},\ b < 0$

various parameters in Example 5.7 before we move on to estimate them in next chapter. By doing so, you may, for example, notice that the C parameter in the logit model indicates the size of the overall market (when price is zero) and that b specifies the price sensitivity. The larger the value of b, the more price sensitive the customers of this product or service are.

5.4 Summary

- Price elasticity of demand can be either elastic or inelastic.
- Elastic demand means that the sales volume changes a lot for a given price change and can be illustrated through a steep price–response function.
- Inelastic demand means that sales volume changes little for a given price change and can be illustrated with a moderately sloping price–response function.
- Point elasticity of demand and arc elasticity of demand are measures that can be used to quantify the price sensitivity.
- Products/services with inelastic demand are typically those that make up a small fraction of the total household budget and are considered essential in day-to-day life.
- Products/services with elastic demand are typically those that make up a bigger fraction of the total household budget and are considered somewhat extravagant.
- The maximum willingness to pay is also called the reservation price and it is defined as the maximum price at which a customer will buy the product or service of interest.
- Willingness to pay distributions can take many forms and they are directly linked to the shape of the price–response function.
- The uniform WTP distribution corresponds to a linear price–response function.
- Common functional forms of price–response functions are (1) linear, (2) constant elasticity, (3) power and (4) logit.

5.5 Problems

1. What is the difference between elastic and inelastic demand? Illustrate with figures and explain.

2. Calculate the *point* and *arc* elasticities in the following cases:

	a)	b)	c)	d)	e)	f)	g)	h)	i)	j)
D_p2	5,955	6,595	6,078	5,168	5,133	1,3260	1,031	10,881	13,043	14,725
D_p1	12,924	10,897	14,845	11,948	10,760	6,509	7,521	5,112	6,009	5,698
p2	59	69	54	54	56	33	34	31	45	43
p1	47	38	45	46	46	54	60	51	56	58

3. What insights do you get from the calculations done in problem 2?
4. The slope of a PRF is −750. What is the point elasticity at a price of $50 if the corresponding demand at that price is 20,000?
5. Assume that the information given in the previous question still holds, but that the price is $20 rather than $50. What is the point elasticity?
6. What if the slope still is −750, the price is $50 and the demand is only 10,000?
7. Give an interpretation of the point elasticities you calculated in problems 3-6. What do the numbers mean?
8. Calculate $d(p)$ using the price–response functions presented below. Do the calculations in Excel and present the result in graphs. What price–response function is given in each case (linear, logit, etc.). Explain.

$$(a): d(p) = 10,0000 - 500 \cdot p$$
$$(b): d(p) = 50,000 \cdot p^{-0.75}$$
$$(c): d(p) = 15,000 \cdot 50,000 / \left(p^2 + 15,000\right)$$
$$(d): d(p) = \frac{50,000 \cdot e^{(10-0.1 \cdot p)}}{1 + e^{(10-0.1 \cdot p)}}$$

9. Try new values in the price–response functions according to this information:
   (a) Slope equal to −1,500.
   (b) Elasticity −0.5 and −0.1.
   (c) Change b to 2.5 and 3.
   (d) Change a to 5 and b to −0.05.
   Comment on all the changes associated with implementing the new values. How do these affect the various price–response functions? Interpret the results using your knowledge within this field.
10. A linear price–response function is given by $d(p) = 450 - 18p$.
    What does the corresponding WTP distribution look like? Estimate the numbers and illustrate with a figure in Excel. How would you interpret the results?
11. Use the example 5.4 in the Excel file following Chapter 5 and play around with the number of customers that have RP=p. What insights do you get from this?
12. Use the example 5.5 in the Excel file following Chapter 5 and play around with the number of customers that have RP=p. What insights do you get from this?

13. Use the example 5.6 in the Excel file following Chapter 5 and play around with the number of customers that have RP=p. What insights do you get from this?
14. The demand for milk in a specific region is 22,000 gallons at a price of $2.50. When the price increases to $3.00 demand goes down to 15,000 gallons. Calculate the slope in both gallons per $ and liters per $ (1 gallon is 3.785 liters). Calculate also the arc price elasticity using both units of measurement (that is, both gallons and liters). What is your conclusion?

Chapter 6

Empirical estimations of price–response functions

In this chapter, the focus will be on what sources you can use to get access to price and demand data and how to empirically estimate price–response functions once such data points are available. The empirical estimation of price–response functions will also be implemented in a step-by-step manner in Excel. The following topics will be covered in this chapter:

- Sources for price and demand data.
- Measuring price/demand relation in a direct survey.
- Empirical estimation of price–response functions.
- Implementation in Excel.

6.1 Sources for price and demand data

If we want to empirically estimate price–response functions and corresponding price elasticities, we essentially only need information about (1) prices and (2) the corresponding expected demanded quantity at those price levels. There are several sources of such data and there are pros and cons associated with all of them. Breidert et al. (2006) divide the various methods into the following categories:

- Historical market data.
- Experiments.
- Direct surveys.
- Indirect surveys.
- Expert judgements.

Historical market data

Historical *market data* on price/demand is often readily available and reflects actual purchase behavior. A drawback could be that there is little variation in the historical pricing levels, which makes estimations of price–response functions very hard. Additionally, these data are backward-looking. That is, if the market conditions are changing rapidly, the history may not represent the future relationship between price/demand well. In some cases, for example when introducing a new product/service, historical price/demand data are not available.

Price experiments

This approach involves testing various price levels on real customers. Such experiments could either be carried out in a physical store or online. There are several benefits to carrying out price experiments, the most prominent one being that we get information about actual purchase behavior and not *intended* purchase behavior. The drawback is that experiments in many cases are inefficient both from a cost and time perspective. However, if using a flexible online platform, running price experiments can be very efficient. Before conducting price experiments on real customers, it is important to carefully consider potential issues related to legal constraints or customer acceptance more generally. We shall return to this in Chapter 15.

Direct surveys

This method involves asking customers and potential customers about their willingness to pay (WTP) for specific products or services. It is also known as contingent valuation. Broadly, the approach can be considered as a hypothetical experiment because respondents are provided with hypothetical information such as a description of the good or service being offered and a method for eliciting preferences for the good. Such surveys have several advantages. First, they are usually cost-efficient. The questionnaires can be developed in-house and employees in the company can go out in the field and gather the data. Alternatively, the data collection could be outsourced, but the costs would still probably be lower than setting up full-scale experiments. Second, it is time-efficient. Data can be collected rapidly once the questionnaire has been developed. Third, it enables us to measure likely price responses to new products that have not been on the market, and the potential impacts of prices outside ranges that have previously been offered in the marketplace. However, there are some drawbacks. Some studies claim that direct surveys provide biased estimates, and that this method does not reflect actual purchase or choice behavior. The related literature is summarized in section 6.3.

Indirect surveys

Conjoint analysis and discrete choice modeling (DCM) are techniques that fall into this category. Conjoint analysis is mainly about asking respondents to rank various competing products with some differing attributes (where price is one of the attributes). The price sensitivity is then backed out (indirectly) from this ranking. The DCM technique is similar to conjoint analysis, but the underlying estimation method is somewhat different. We have devoted Chapter 14 to the use of rating-based conjoint analysis for pricing decision.

Expert judgement

Another approach to obtaining price and demand estimates for various products or services is simply to ask the experts in the field. This approach is perceived to provide reliable, accurate and cost-efficient estimates (Bodea and Ferguson, 2014). However, the quality of the estimates using this method can never be better than the experts involved.

As we understand, all methods have both advantages and drawbacks when it comes to obtaining accurate, reliable and cost and time-efficient data on price and demand. The pros and cons associated with each approach must be evaluated carefully before committing to a specific one. However, as direct surveys are the most cost-efficient approach for most companies that do not have the relevant historical data available, we shall provide an introduction to how one can use this technique to gather price/demand data. Before the actual survey takes place, there are several important factors to consider. Some of these will be addressed before we describe how one can go about measuring the price/demand relation in a direct survey.

6.2 Preliminaries to data collection

When collecting the data in a direct survey ourselves, the first thing we should be aware is that it is enough to create a sample that is representative of the population of interest. For example, let us suppose that we wanted to find how the demand for hamburgers varies with price at the university cafeteria. Our population is users of the cafeteria on campus and includes students, faculty, staff and outsiders (nearby residents, alumni, visiting families and friends, etc.). From the overall student-to-staff and student-to-faculty ratios, we can approximate the proportions of these groups to include in our sample. This is necessary because it is not unreasonable to believe that, for example, students and faculty are heterogeneous groups. For one, faculty members will on average have higher disposable incomes and therefore their demand for hamburgers may be relatively price inelastic compared with that of students who rely on student loans, part-time work, or handouts from family members for their upkeep. Secondly, the age profile of faculty members would differ from that of students, with the average age of the latter being lower. We could identify a handful of other attributes that would suggest that these two groups are different. If we therefore oversample faculty members relative to students, the resulting price–demand data will not reflect how demand responds to price changes in the population, potentially leading to biased inference.

We should also note that within the groups there may be heterogeneous subgroups, and this needs to be considered when creating the sample. In many countries, there is a wide pay gap between skilled and unskilled employees. If we are in such countries, the ratio of skilled staff members to unskilled should be considered and our sample should be adjusted accordingly. Several experiments in economics have shown that, depending on the topic of study, students are not a homogeneous group (refer to Camerer (2003) for a survey of experiments). Information such as program of study, year of study and level (undergraduate or graduate) may thus be required to discriminate between the different kinds of students. Some other key attributes that need to be accounted for when creating our sample include gender and age.

In summary, we need to first identify the population that we want to study and attributes of this population. Thereafter, we create a representative random sample of the population and then proceed to collecting data either through survey-based methods or experiments. In recent times, open-source software programs have emerged that facilitate the recruitment and sample selection process, for example ORSEE (Greiner 2004). Such software programs allow one to maintain a pool of potential respondents who are recruited over time and based on attributes specified by the researcher.

6.3 Measuring price–demand relationships in a direct survey

Once we have a representative sample of the population we are interested in measuring the price–demand relationship for, we can start to focus on what method to use for collecting the data points we are interested in. Directly asking customers about their willingness to pay for specific products or services has some important limitations. In order to obtain as reliable estimates of the price–response functions as possible using this approach, we should be aware of these and, if possible, adjust the way we carry out the survey to minimize the impact from the flaws.

The most important drawback of the direct approach is that it can generate hypothetical bias, which can be defined as the bias induced by the hypothetical nature of the task. This bias can also be present in indirect approaches (such as the choice-based conjoint analysis) because in both cases we ask respondents about their intended (hypothetical) behavior. Some reasons for why the stated purchase behavior differs from actual purchase behavior are mentioned by Breidert et al. (2006, p. 14):

- Unnatural focus on price (and too little on other attributes of the product).
- Customers may not have an incentive to reveal their true willingness to pay.
- A right statement of maximum willingness to pay cannot necessarily be translated into buying intention.
- Directly asking for willingness to pay for complex and unfamiliar products is a challenging task for respondents. It is unclear whether it leads to over- or understating, but it is likely that it will induce biased estimates.
- Misjudgment of price/value if the product or service is not frequently bought.

These flaws lead some scholars to the conclusion that the direct method of asking customers' willingness to pay for different products may not be reliable. But is it really that bad? And can we do anything about the various drawbacks in the list above to increase the reliability of the estimates obtained from direct surveys?

First thing first. A more recent study carried out by Miller et al. (2011) evaluate four different methods for measuring consumers' willingness to pay. They estimate price–response functions based on the WTP data obtained from various methods using a logit model. The performance of each method is then assessed by comparing the results to real (actual) purchase data. Some of the main conclusions from this study are:

- Mean WTP analysis shows statistically unbiased results for all evaluated methods (including direct approach).
- Hypothetical methods (of which the direct approach is an example) can capture real WTP distributions well.
- Hypothetical methods largely biased in intercept of price–response function, but not much in terms of slope.
- Direct approach can do a good job in forecasting optimal price, quantity and profit.

The findings in this study are important as they to a large extent acquit the direct approach for use in pricing decisions, especially when forecasting optimal price and quantity. Hence, even though some researchers within the academic field are negative to one approach, it does not mean that all agree on this or that the method is not useful. The above conclusions from a thorough empirical analysis confirm this.

86   Empirical estimations

However, the drawbacks with the direct approach could still be present and could potentially influence the results significantly. To reduce some of the potential impact from the flaws associated with this method the following comments can be useful.

First, the concern about an exaggerated focus on price, and the potential difference between actual and stated willingness to pay, can be addressed by *not* asking directly about the price, but instead about how much customers would consume at various price levels. The researchers can then list a range of price alternatives and ask what consumption level is likely at specific listed prices. When the consumption level reaches zero, one can assume that the maximum willingness to pay is reached. By asking about likely consumption at various price levels, the customer is not forced to reveal any hypothetical maximum willingness to pay but is rather asked to state how many (if any) the customer would purchase if the price was at certain levels. This approach is likely to reduce the impact of over- or understating how much the respondent is willing to pay as the consumer is never asked directly about prices or willingness to pay, but rather about consumption quantity. However, in cases where it is hard to estimate exactly how much the consumption is on a given basis, the revealed quantity could potentially be biased. To reduce the aspect of impressing the researcher the responses should be given anonymously.

The relationship between hypothetical and actual purchase decisions may still be present, though. That is, if the respondent states that he or she would consume five apples per week if the price was $1 per apple, the actual purchase behavior may differ from this amount. If not using an approach where customers are obligated to buy the specific amount over a specified time period, one cannot easily control for this.

To meet the criticism regarding potential bias in willingness to pay estimates using this method on complex or unfamiliar products/services there is one good answer: avoid using this approach on such products or services.

The same solution goes for potential biased estimates for products or services that are infrequently purchased: avoid using the direct method in such cases.

Example of a direct survey to obtain price/demand data

In the following section, we present one example of how questions for a direct survey can be formulated to obtain price/demand data points. Before any questions about price/demand are asked, it is important that the respondent is introduced properly to the product/service under consideration. This could be a thorough written description, a picture, a video that illustrates the product/service, a model, and so forth. The important part is that the respondent knows exactly what he or she is about to evaluate.

Moreover, in most cases it is preferable if the respondent can hand in the evaluation anonymously. In the case of online surveys this can usually be arranged easily. If carrying out surveys on site, one can use a box where the filled-in forms can be deposited.

Example of key questions

One example of how to we can obtain the data we need to estimate price–response function is given below. The question reads like this:

> *Q: How many units of ...[the given product] would you be likely to consume on average per [frequency, e.g., day, week, month, season], for the various prices listed below:*

Price	Units per [frequency]
$ 0.20	_____
$ 0.40	_____
$ 0.60	_____
$ 0.80	_____
$ 1.00	_____
$ 1.20	_____
$ 1.40	_____
$ 1.60	_____
$ 1.80	_____
$ 2.00	_____
$ 2.20	_____
$ 2.40	_____
$ 2.60	_____
$ 2.80	_____
$ 3.00	_____

Q: If you would still consume this product for a price of $3.00 per unit, what is your maximum willingness to pay for one unit?

This approach is very similar to the open-ended contingent valuation method where common practice is to first have two closed alternatives to which the respondent should answer *yes* or *no* before revealing the exact amount he or she is willing to pay for the product or service. However, with the approach above "yes" and "no" are changed to the actual quantity that the respondent would consume at the various price levels. As we can see, only at the end is the consumer asked to indicate a *price* that may reflect the maximum willingness to pay and *only* if the quantity has not dropped to zero before the highest closed price is reached.

Variables relevant for segmentation purposes should, of course, be included in the form in order to estimate separate price–response functions for each segment. We shall look at examples of how data collected with this method look like shortly, but first we shall briefly look at how we can address potential hypothetical bias using experiments instead of a direct survey.

6.4 Addressing hypothetical bias using experiments

As noted in the previous section, some empirical evidence shows that eliciting willingness-to-pay information using direct surveys can result in hypothetical bias where respondents tend to over- or underestimate the price that they are willing to pay for a product or service. While there may be several reasons explaining this problem, price experiments focus on incentivizing choices to induce participants to reveal their true willingness to pay. The typical experimental design entails participants making real purchase decisions in the field. For example, Blumenschein et al. (2008) allow participants to purchase a diabetes management program at a pharmacy after receiving a description of it. The participants use actual dollars to make the purchase and the decision tasks correspond to the real purchase experience. Paying more than the willingness to pay results in a real dollar loss to the participant and not buying the product if the price is less than the willingness to pay has a negative effect on the participant's utility since she misses out on the associated consumption benefits.

A limitation of implementing experiments that involve real purchase decisions is that this may not always be feasible, for example, in the case of high-value assets such as real estate, or for non-tradable goods and services, or those where a market does not exist. However, it turns out that a well-designed laboratory experiment is just as effective at eliciting a participant's true willingness to pay in such cases. While the setting is hypothetical, similar to direct surveys, choices are incentivized so that the participant incurs a loss if she does not exert the necessary effort in completing the decision tasks set out. If the firm has an online platform where the products or services are offered, the hypothetical setting can also be avoided. In this case, a price experiment can be set up to extract real purchase data for various price levels. When designing such a web-based price experiment it is very important to be aware of the potential drawbacks associated with implementing it on real customers. The most important of these is related to customer acceptance and the potential of having very upset customers who purchased the product or service at a (random) high price and who later figure this out. To avoid any potential pitfalls, it is a good idea to think carefully about the experimental design and relate it to customer acceptance and potential ethical and legal issues.

One example of an online price experiment that has the potential of being accepted by most customers is to send an offer via e-mail to all customers in the firm's database. The offer should be for the same product or service, but the price level could be randomized at some predetermined levels, preferably all at a lower level than the current list price. The share of customers receiving the offer should be approximately equal across price levels. The firm can then easily extract datapoints containing the total demanded quantity at each price level and use these to estimate price–response functions.

The use of real-life experiments is increasing rapidly in many fields, including pricing analytics. A full overview of how to run such experiments in practice is beyond the scope of this book. Interested readers can consult Glennerster and Takavarasha (2013) for a practical guide.

6.5 Empirical estimation of price–response functions

Once we have data on the price/demand relationship we can start to estimate the various price–response functions presented in the previous chapter. We shall focus on (1) the linear price–response function, (2) the constant elasticity price–response function, and (3) the logit specification in this chapter, as those are the most applied techniques in practice.

Estimating a linear price–response function in Excel

The linear price–response function was presented Chapter 5 like this:

$$d(p) = D + m \cdot p \tag{6.1}$$

where $d(p)$ is the demanded quantity for a specific product at various price levels, D is the intercept, i.e., the demand at a price of zero, m is the slope, and p is the price. The parameters to be estimated in this function are D and m. For those familiar with linear regression these parameters are better known as the intercept (D) and the slope (m) of the simple linear regression model. This model can easily be estimated with ordinary least squares (OLS) in Excel.

The data used in the empirical estimations are taken from a customer survey as presented in Bodea and Ferguson (2014, p. 162). These data are used such that we can compare the estimates we obtain using Excel with those obtained using statistical software (Bodea and Ferguson (2014) use R to estimate the various price–response functions).

To estimate the intercept and the slope in the linear function given in Equation (6.1) we can either use the INTERCEPT and SLOPE functions in Excel, or we can install the Analysis ToolPak (which is an add-in included in Excel) and run a linear regression using this approach.[1] If including more than one independent variable (in addition to the price) we have to use the latter approach as the two formulas, INTERCEPT and SLOPE, only provide estimates for the simple linear regression model (i.e., only one independent variable).[2] The data is illustrated in Figure 6.1. Our objective is to explain variation in demanded quantity (on the Y-axis) as a function of the price (on the X-axis). Simply by visually inspecting the data, we clearly see that there is a negative relationship between these two variables. That is, when price increases demanded quantity goes down and vice versa. Our objective is now to figure out what exactly the price response is.

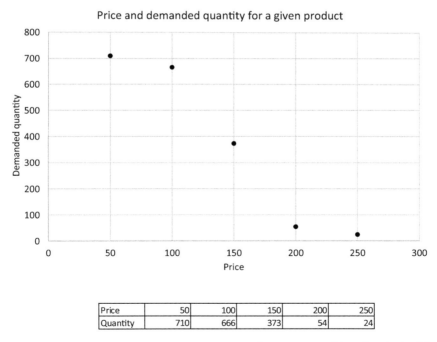

Figure 6.1 Results from a customer survey on the relationship between price (X-axis) and sales (Y-axis).
Source: Bodea and Ferguson (2014, p. 162).

90 Empirical estimations

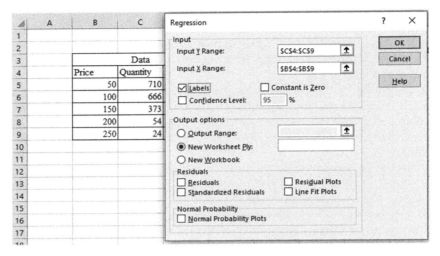

Figure 6.2 Screenshot of the interface for carrying out regression analysis in Excel.

In Figure 6.2 a screenshot of the regression input window in Excel is provided. To get to this window you need to go to the *Data tab → Data analysis* (only available if the Analysis ToolPak is installed. See the appendix of this chapter) and then choose *Regression* in the dialogue box. The Y variable is the dependent variable (always the demanded quantity in our case) and the X variables are always the independent variables, i.e., the variables we want to use to explain variation in the Y variable. When estimating price–response functions the aim is always to explain variation in the demanded quantity from various price levels. Hence, demanded quantity is the Y variable (dependent variable) and price is the X variable (independent variable) in these analyses.

The range of the Y and X variables is simply the range of the cells with the numbers we need to run the regression model. The headings of the variables can be included in this range, but then you must check the *Labels* tab in the input window. The Output options area can be used to set the location of where the results should appear after the analysis is carried out. The default option here is that it will appear in a new worksheet, but this may be changed to any location within your workbook (just refer to any cell within your workbook). That's it. The only thing remaining at this stage is to hit the OK button and Excel will perform the simple linear regression model we have just specified.

Right after you hit the OK button in the user form, the output presented in Figure 6.3 will appear in your specified output range. There is quite a lot of information in such a summary output. However, if you are familiar with the standard linear regression model, there is nothing new here. In our case, the important parts to focus on are (1) adjusted R square, (2) intercept, and (3) price. Additionally, we should have an idea of what the *standard error, t Stat*, and *P-value* mean.[3]

Adjusted R square essentially tells us how much of the variation in the dependent variable (demanded quantity) can be explained by variation in the independent variable (price). This will always be a number between zero and one (a fraction) as it is impossible to explain either less than 0% or more than 100% of the variation in a variable.[4] In our

SUMMARY OUTPUT

Regression Statistics	
Multiple R	0.965006113
R Square	0.931236799
Adjusted R Square	0.908315732
Standard Error	98.43034762
Observations	5

ANOVA

	df	SS	MS	F	Significance F
Regression	1	393625.6	393625.6	40.62798635	0.007816805
Residual	3	29065.6	9688.533333		
Total	4	422691.2			

	Coefficients	Standard Error	t Stat	P-value	Lower 95%	Upper 95%	Lower 95.0%	Upper 95.0%
Intercept	960.6	103.2346195	9.30501807	0.002627546	632.0613665	1289.138633	632.0613665	1289.138633
Price	-3.968	0.622528179	-6.374008656	0.007816805	-5.949162502	-1.986837498	-5.949162502	-1.986837498

Figure 6.3 Screenshot of summary output from a regression analysis performed in MS Excel.

case we can explain almost 91% of the variation in demanded quantity just by including the price.

The coefficient next to *intercept* is the constant term (the D in Equation (6.1)) and the value of the price–response function when price is zero. In this case, the value is 960.6 and it can be viewed as the total potential size of the market for specific product or service of interest. However, as we know that the relationship between price and demanded quantity generally is not linear, and especially not so in the tails, it is a little bit dangerous to draw this conclusion. We shall return to this shortly when we compare the predicted values with the actual values.

The coefficient for the *price* variable tells us the following: by how much does demanded quantity change with a one-unit increase in price? The answer in our case is −3.97. That is, for a one-unit increase in price, demand goes down by almost four units, on average. This is the *slope* of the price–response function and can be used to calculate price elasticity as shown in Chapter 5.

The concept of statistical significance loses some of its meaning when working on price/demand data. Why? Because we have already made the assumption that price and demand always go in the opposite direction. Hence, we have already stated that the slope of the price–response function is negative. If we are uncertain about this, e.g., if we have a hypothesis that there could be a positive relation between the two, the test of statistical significance becomes more interesting.[5] Even if the slope is very close to zero, we still do not care too much about whether it is significantly different from zero or not. The reason is that the predicted slope is still our best estimate and it will be used in the subsequent optimization model. In the case of a non-linear price–response function, the slope will even be different at each specific point of the curve.

Once we have the estimated coefficients of the linear price–response function we can calculate the predicted values. This is done by plugging the estimated coefficients into Equation (6.1):

$$d(p) = 960.6 - 3.968 \times p$$

If using the same values for the price as those used in the survey data, we obtain the following predicted values for $d(p)$:

Price	Quantity	Prediction
50	710	762.2
100	666	563.8
150	373	365.4
200	54	167
250	24	−31.4

The actual and predicted values are also depicted in Figure 6.4. This figure shows that the linear price–response function fits the data fairly well, at least for "normal" prices in the middle region of the price–response function. However, we also see that the linear function has at least two problems: (1) it declines below zero as prices go beyond approximately 240, and (2) it continues to grow linearly for lower prices. The former is simply not possible in any market. We will never sell a quantity of fewer than zero units. The latter tells us that it is very dangerous to make predictions outside the range for which we have actual observations. In our case we do not have any observations for prices between zero and 50. Hence, to continue to draw the straight line until it crosses the Y-axis may give a wrong impression of the market size as we know that the curve flattens out substantially in this area.

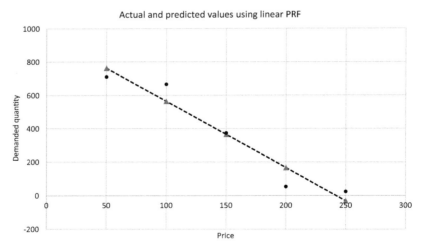

Figure 6.4 Actual and predicted values using the linear price–response function.

Estimating the constant elasticity price–response function

To estimate a constant elasticity price–response function, we need to do a transformation of the two variables used in the linear regression model. That is, instead of using the original values of these variables, we take the log of both. The functional form then looks like this:

$$\ln(d(p)) = D + m \cdot \ln(p) \qquad (6.2)$$

This transformation has the following impact on the interpretation of the slope (the m parameter in Equation (6.2)). For a 1% increase in price, demand changes with m percent. In Excel, the log transformation is straightforward using the =LN() formula. An illustration of this is provided in Figure 6.5.

When this is done, a standard linear regression model can be performed on the log-transformed values using the specification in Equation (6.2). The estimated coefficients along with the standard errors, t-statistic and p-value are given in the screenshot of the Excel output below.

The interpretation of these results is: For a 1% increase in price, demand goes down by 2.1%, on average.[6] The estimated elasticity is constant across all price levels in this model. To estimate predicted values, we first must calculate the log predictions by using the estimated coefficients and plug them into Equation (6.2):

$$\ln(d(p)) = 15.44 - 2.0965 \times \ln(price)$$

	A	B	C	D
1	CUSTOMER SURVEY DATA OF PRICE AND DEMANDED QUANTITY - LOG			
2	TRANSFORMATION			
3				
4	Price	Quantity	lnPrice	lnQuantity
5	50	710	=LN(A5)	=LN(B5)
6	100	666	=LN(A6)	=LN(B6)
7	150	373	=LN(A7)	=LN(B7)
8	200	54	=LN(A8)	=LN(B8)
9	250	24	=LN(A9)	=LN(B9)

Figure 6.5 Screenshot of how to perform a log transformation of the two variables.

	Coefficients	Standard Error	t Stat	P-value
Intercept	15.4400	3.5404	4.3611	0.0223
lnPrice	-2.0965	0.7221	-2.9032	0.0623

Figure 6.6 Screenshot of regression output of the constant elasticity price–response function.

94 Empirical estimations

This induce the following predicted log values in our case:

lnPrice	lnQuantity	lnPrediction
3.91	6.57	7.24
4.61	6.50	5.79
5.01	5.92	4.94
5.30	3.99	4.33
5.52	3.18	3.86

To obtain actual predicted values, the log predictions must be transformed back using the exponential function (antilog). In Excel, this is done by writing EXP(Cell-reference) as seen in column F in Figure 6.7. The predicted values can then be depicted together with the various price levels in a graph. This is done in Figure 6.8.

The overall fit of the constant elasticity price–response function is clearly not as good as the linear price–response function. For low price levels, the estimates are too high. For the middle region, this price–response function undershoots the real demanded quantity, but for high prices the fit is acceptable. One of the benefits with this specification is that we will never end up with negative predicted values for demanded quantity (as the antilog of any negative value is positive). Even though this price–response function does not provide a good fit in this case, it is useful to know how to estimate it for later use and comparison with other models.

Estimating the logit price–response function

To overcome some of the problems with the linear and the constant elasticity price–response function, we now turn to one of the most popular non-linear, and much more flexible, price–response functions: the logit specification. Even though Excel does not have a formal add-in for running logit models, the next few pages will walk you through how to estimate parameters for this model using the solver add-in. It is important to note that the procedure presented here may not work on all sorts of data, and it also relies somewhat on your ability to set good starting values of the parameters in the model.

	A	B	C	D	E	F
1						
2		CUSTOMER SURVEY DATA OF PRICE AND DEMANDED QUANTITY - LOG TRANSFORMATION					
3						
4	Price	Quantity	lnPrice	lnQuantity	lnPrediction	Prediction
5	50	710	=LN(A5)	=LN(B5)	=$B$27+$B$28*C5	=EXP(E5)
6	100	666	=LN(A6)	=LN(B6)	=$B$27+$B$28*C6	=EXP(E6)
7	150	373	=LN(A7)	=LN(B7)	=$B$27+$B$28*C7	=EXP(E7)
8	200	54	=LN(A8)	=LN(B8)	=$B$27+$B$28*C8	=EXP(E8)
9	250	24	=LN(A9)	=LN(B9)	=$B$27+$B$28*C9	=EXP(E9)

Figure 6.7 Screenshot of how to calculate predictions from log predictions using the exponential function.

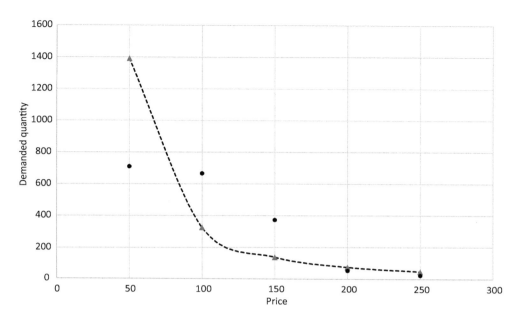

Figure 6.8 Estimated values using the constant price–response function (gray triangles and dotted line) and corresponding real observed values (black dots).

Before starting to estimate the parameters of the logit model, it is a good idea to depict the data in a scatter plot and define cells for the various parameters of the model. The functional form of the logit model was given in Chapter 5 like this:

$$d(p) = \frac{C \cdot e^{a+b \cdot p}}{1 + e^{a+b \cdot p}} \tag{6.3}$$

Hence, there are three parameters to be estimated in this model: (1) C, a, and b. These must be estimated based on an objective function of some sort. In this example the sum of the squared deviations is used as the objective function to be minimized. The deviations are calculated as the actual demanded quantity minus the predicted (based on the model) demanded quantity at each price level. An example of how the model can be set up in Excel is given in Figure 6.9. The steps involved in creating the setup can be summarized as follows:

1. Provide starting values of the parameters C, a, and b, given in cells B4, C4 and D4.
2. Calculate predictions (predicted demanded quantity) using Equation (6.3) in column C.
3. Calculate squared deviations at each price level in column D.
4. Calculate the sum of the squared residuals in cell D14.

96 Empirical estimations

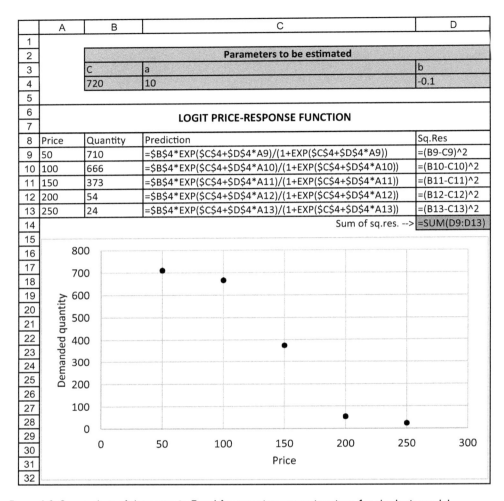

Figure 6.9 Screenshot of the setup in Excel for carrying out estimations for the logit model.

The starting values should be as good as possible based on common sense and, if needed, some trial and error. The C parameter is the constant, which can be understood as the total number of units sold of the product or service the firm offers when the price is zero. It is very important that we provide a value here that is higher than the number of units sold at the lowest price level we have in our data set (that is, a value higher than the quantity sold for a price of 50, i.e., 710 in the example given). To find the starting values of the parameters a and b, some trial and error may be needed. However, before doing that, it is important to note the general restrictions on these parameters as given in the previous chapter. Table 5.2 showed that a could take both positive and negative values and that b is restricted to be negative (when price increase, demanded quantity goes down). Another tip in this initial phase is that the fraction $-(a/b)$ is where the price response is steepest, and that it also can be understood as an approximate market price.

In the example given in Figure 6.9, *a* is set to 10 and *b* to −0.1, yielding an approximate market price of 100, which seem like reasonable starting values.

However, to further examine this, some trial and error can be carried out. To do this efficiently, it is a good idea to include in the graph the predicted values. This is done by simply adding the series of predictions in the existing scatter plot showing the actual price/demand data (right-click in the graph area and then choose *select data* and then *add series*). Additionally, you can draw a line between the predictions to get a better feel for the fit, as done for both the linear and constant elasticity price–response function earlier in this chapter. Figure 6.10 illustrates the effect of some trial and error on the values of the parameters C, a and b. In the upper left panel C is set to 800, a to 50 and b to −0.2. Clearly, in this case the price–response function is overshooting the actual demanded quantity for all price levels. By reducing the a parameter from 50 to 30, the fit is improved substantially (upper right panel), but the constant (C) is still clearly too high.

In the lower left panel, all three parameters are adjusted down. However, the predictions now generally undershoot the actual demand at all price levels. In the lower right panel, all parameters are therefore adjusted up again somewhat and the shape of the price–response function now better follows the actual values at all price levels. We

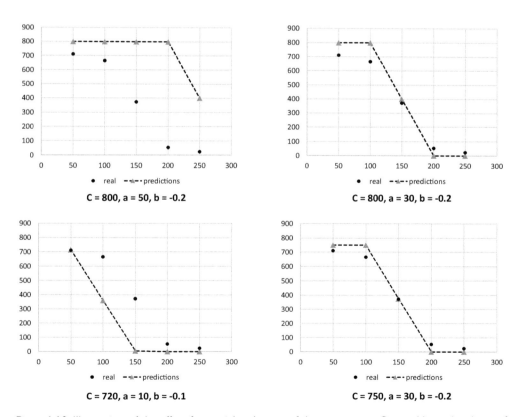

Figure 6.10 Illustration of the effect from trial and error of the parameters C, a, and b on the shape of the logit price–response function.

98 Empirical estimations

could continue this trial and error for a long time, but if we have a reasonable fit to the data, we can ask Excel's solver to do the rest of the job.

To do this, we need to open solver and define the optimization problem. The solver add-in can be found under the *Data* tab on the ribbon (note again, the solver needs to be installed before it is available. See the appendix of this chapter). Figure 6.11 shows the solver interface together with the worksheet where the model is formulated. The objective is to minimize the sum of squared residuals by changing the various parameters in the model. In the solver interface this is defined by setting the objective cell to the cell where the sum of the squared residuals is calculated (D14) and the variable cells should refer to the cells where the parameters to be estimated are located (B4:D4). Additionally, we add a few constraints for reasons mentioned before. In the current example the constant (C) is restricted to be above 710 and below 800, and the b parameter should be less than or equal to zero. Again, to get an idea of the restrictions for the C parameter we can look at the figure of the actual price/demand data and also the fit of the various trial and error curves in Figure 6.10. We then clearly see that the total potential demanded

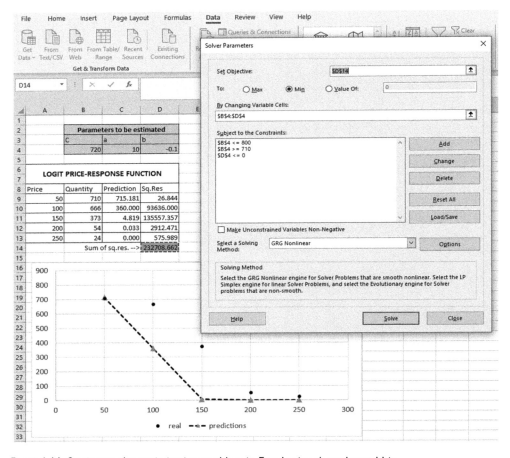

Figure 6.11 Setting up the optimization problem in Excel using the solver add-in.

volume must be above the demanded quantity for the lowest price we have in our data (that is, 710). Additionally, from the upper left panel of Figure 6.10 we see that it is unlikely that the constant will be above 800. Providing good starting values with some restrictions is important for the success of the optimization. Once the problem is defined properly using the solver interface, the only thing left is to choose a solving method (here we choose GRG non-linear, because it is a non-linear optimization problem) and to hit *Solve*. The solver will then change the parameters (the variable cells) such that the objective cell (the sum of the squared residuals) is minimized.

The result of the optimization in our example is provided in Figure 6.12. The final value of the parameters C, a, and b are 714.55, 7.66, and −0.05, respectively. The graph

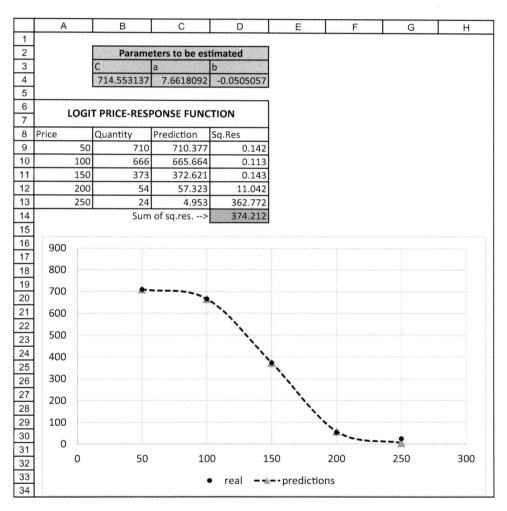

Figure 6.12 The result of the optimization. The parameters are estimated such that the sum of the squared residuals is minimized. In the figure the fitted values (dashed line) are depicted together with the actual values.

in the lower part of the figure shows the fit of the model against the actual values. Clearly, the model does a good job of predicting the actual values. Interestingly, we get the exact same estimated values of the three parameters as those obtained using a more sophisticated statistical software (R, as used by Bodea and Ferguson (2014)). However, you should note that for more complicated data sets, you may encounter problems related to non-convergence or estimates that are far off. In such cases, you would need either to use more specialized software, or spend more time on figuring out what the starting values should be.

Estimating other non-linear price–response functions

Once we know how to perform non-linear optimization in Excel, most other functional forms of price–response functions can also be implemented, such as the power price–response function. One important thing to remember is that you must feed Excel's solver with good starting values. If you do this, the chances are good that you will get similar results as those obtained with more sophisticated statistical software. We will show more examples of how various price–response functions can be estimated using data from a movie theater case in Chapter 8.

6.6 Summary

- Price-demand data can be obtained from several sources including (1) historical market data, (2) experiments, (3) direct surveys, (4) indirect surveys, and (5) expert judgements.
- There are pros and cons associated with the various methods. Costs and reliability of the data are important aspects that must be considered.
- Direct surveys have been criticized in the literature for, among other things, (1) having too much focus on price, (2) failing to capture true willingness to pay, and (3) lacking a direct link between willingness to pay and buying intention. Still, this method has been found to perform well in an empirical evaluation when compared to other methods.
- A way of reducing the focus on price in a direct survey could be to ask for demanded quantity for various price levels instead of what price the (potential) customer is willing to pay.
- Price experiments can also be used to potentially address the hypothetical bias from surveys. The drawback is that such experiments can be very expensive to carry out.
- Estimation of various price–response functions in Excel can be done by using the built-in functions for the INTERCEPT and SLOPE (simple linear regression) or by using the solver add-in.
- When estimating the logit price–response function the starting values of the parameters should be as good as possible. Trial and error in combination with a visualization of the price–response function can be used to set good starting values.

6.7 Problems

1. What are the main methods one can use to obtain data on the price–demand relationship? Briefly explain potential pros and cons associated with each method.
2. What factors should you be aware of *before* collecting data in a direct survey?
3. Provide some reasons for why stated purchase behavior is not the same as actual purchase behavior.
4. Give an example of how you can obtain price–demand data in a direct survey. Assume that the product/service of interest is visits to the hairdresser per year.
5. In what ways can the hypothetical bias in willingness to pay from direct surveys be addressed?
6. Consider the following price–demand data for a given product:

Price	Quantity
5	25,291
10	22,265
15	18,273
20	8,874
25	2,513

    a) Depict the price–demand relationship in a scatter plot.
    b) Estimate a linear price–response function using the INTERCEPT and SLOPE functions in Excel.
    c) Illustrate the estimated price–response function together with the scatter plot.
    d) How would you assess the fit of the linear price–response function to these data?

7. Use the same data as those given in problem 6 and perform the following tasks:
    a) Depict the price–demand relationship in a scatter plot.
    b) Estimate a constant elasticity price–response function using the INTERCEPT and SLOPE functions in Excel based on log-transformed data.
    c) Illustrate the estimated price–response function together with the scatterplot.
    d) How would you assess the fit of the constant elasticity price–response function to these data?

8. Use the same data as those given in problem 6 and perform the following tasks:
    a) Depict the price–demand relationship in a scatter plot.
    b) Estimate a logit price–response function using Excel's solver add-in.
    c) Illustrate the estimated price–response function together with the scatter plot.
    d) How would you assess the fit of the logit price–response function to these data?

9. Use the same data as those given in problem 6 and perform the following tasks:
    a) Depict the price–demand relationship in a scatter plot.
    b) Estimate a power price–response function using Excel's solver.
    c) Illustrate the estimated price–response function together with the scatterplot.
    d) How would you assess the fit of the power price–response function to these data?

10. Do an overall assessment of the various price–response functions. Which function would you choose for further analyses? Discuss briefly.

6.8 Appendix

Follow the steps below to install the Analysis ToolPak in MS Excel:

1. Go to *File* and then *Options:*

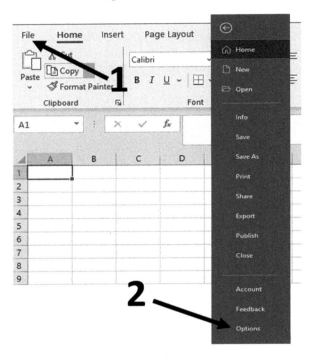

2. Go to the *Add-ins* options and mark the *Analysis ToolPak*. Then hit the *Go* button.

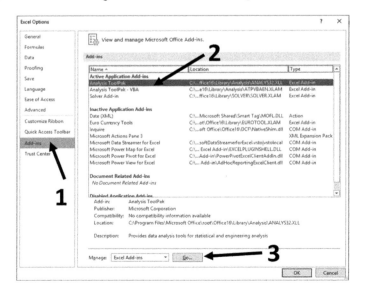

3. Make sure that the *Analysis ToolPak* is checked and hit the *OK* button.

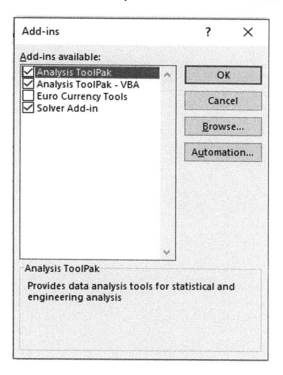

4. The *Data Analysis* tools should now be available to the far right of the ribbon under the Data tab.

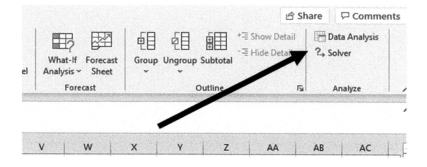

Notes

1 See the appendix of this chapter for a guideline on how to install the Analysis ToolPak in MS Excel.
2 Another option is to apply a so-called user-defined function to estimate a multiple regression model. We show how this can be done in Chapter 14.

3 We will not go through these concepts in detail here, but refer you to text books on introductory econometrics in general.
4 Since we are looking at the adjusted R square measure it is not entirely true that the value of this cannot be less than 0%. It can go below this because we are adjusting (penalizing) for the number of independent variables in the model. Hence, if we have many independent variables in the model and if these are not able to explain much of the variation in the dependent variable, the adjusted R square measure could come out as a negative number.
5 This could be due to so-called *Giffen goods* where demand rises as their price rises because of the substitution effects. An example is when the consumer is on a strict budget and the price of a good that is frequently purchased increases. In order to stay within the budget the consumer then has to stop buying another, more expensive good, which enables him or her to buy one additional unit of the frequently purchased product.
6 Formally, the change in the dependent variable for any p percentage change in the independent variable (price in our case) can be calculated as follows: percentage change in demand = $\left(1.p^{\beta} - 1\right)$. For example, for a 1% increase in price, the change in demand using the estimates in the example above would yield: $\left(1.01^{-2.0965} - 1\right) = 0.9794 - 1 = -0.02064 = -2.06\%$.

Chapter 7

Price optimization

Once we have estimated the price–response function, and we have information about the cost structure of the product or service of interest, we can start the process of optimizing the price. This chapter will focus on the theory of price optimization and how we can calculate optimal prices in practice using Excel. To do so, we will analyze real-life data from various industries in a step-by-step manner. The chapter will cover the following topics:

- Basic price optimization.
- Price optimization with capacity constraints.
- Optimal price differentiation with capacity constraints.
- Optimal time-based price differentiation.
- Elasticity and optimization.
- Pricing with competition.

7.1 Basic price optimization

To calculate the optimal price, we first must formulate the optimization model. This involves three steps:

1. Define the decision variable.
2. Define the objective function.
3. Define the constraints.

In our case, the decision variable is always the price. The objective function is usually defined as either *total contribution* or *total profit*, but in some cases it could also be *total revenues*. The constraints are often related to the total available capacity, but for now, we shall assume that capacity constraints are not an issue. Remember that the contribution margin, or just the margin, is the difference between price and variable unit cost. The total contribution is then the sum of all the unit margins, and the total profit is the total contribution minus the fixed costs. Given this, the objective function can be defined as follows:

$$\max_{p} Z = (p - c_v)d(p) - c_f \qquad (7.1)$$

106 Price optimization

Note that we use the letter Z to define the objective function. In the formula above, p is the price, c_v is the variable cost, $d(p)$ is the demanded quantity at price p (the price–response function), and c_f is the fixed costs. The $d(p)$ part could follow any price–response function, for example one of those estimated in the previous chapter. Standard optimization theory suggests that the price can be found by taking the derivative of Z with respect to p and setting it equal to zero. The reason is that the profit function will be hill-shaped with one single peak. Hence, when the slope of Z is flat it has reached its maximum level. However, the golden rule that we mentioned in Chapter 2, that the optimal solution is where marginal revenue equals marginal costs, still holds (again, in most cases, consult Chapter 2). Hence, we have that:

$$Z'(p) = 0 \tag{7.2}$$

and that this point is found where:

$$MR = MC \tag{7.3}$$

Fortunately, there is nothing new in terms of finding MR and MC. If we have the price–response function and the cost function, the calculations of the total revenues and total costs are straightforward. We illustrate the calculation of the optimal price (p^*) of a cup of coffee in a student canteen using the two approaches presented in Equations (10.2 and 10.3) in Examples 7.1 and 7.2.[1]

Example 7.1: Finding the optimal price by differentiating the revenue and cost function and setting MR=MC.

A linear price–response function has been estimated for the # of cups of coffee demanded at a student canteen:

price–response function:

$$d(p) = 250 - 10p$$

c_v The variable costs per extra cup of coffee sold $c_v = NOK\, 2.25$. The total revenue is given by:

$$R(p) = (250 - 10p)p = 250p - 10p^2$$

Marginal revenue is the derivative of the revenue function with respect to price:

$$R'(p) = 250 - 2 \times 10p = 250 - 20p$$

The total cost is:

$$(250-10p)2.25 = 562.50 - 22.5p$$

The derivative with respect to p of this expression is -22.5.
Hence, the maximum profit is obtained when $250 - 20p = -22.5$

$$p^* = 13.63$$

is the profit-maximizing price.

Example 7.2: Finding the optimal price by differentiating the objective function and setting it equal to zero.

The previous example can also be solved by taking the derivative of the objective function directly and setting it equal to zero.

Price–response function:

$$d(p) = 250 - 10p$$

The incremental costs per extra cup of coffee sold are equal to the variable unit costs c_v = NOK 2.25. Fixed costs c_f are equal to zero (but will not affect the optimal solution, why?). The total profit, Z, is then given by:

$$Z = p(250-10p) - (250-10p)2.25 - 0 = 250p - 10p^2 - 562.5 + 22.5p$$

Collecting terms yields:

$$Z = -10p^2 + 272.5p - 562.5$$

The derivative of Z with respect to p is then:

$$Z'(p) = -20p + 272.5$$

Setting this equal to zero and solving for p yields:

$$p^* = \frac{272.50}{20} = 13.63$$

is the profit-maximizing price.

It is worth mentioning a note about the cost parameters. In our optimization problems, the relevant costs are those associated with one additional unit of our product or service sold. Phillips (2005) refers to such costs as the *incremental costs of a customer commitment*, and he defines it as the difference between the total costs a company faces with or without that commitment. When c_f is fixed across all levels of demanded quantity (no incremental increase in the fixed costs) and the variable unit costs are constant and equal to c_v, the incremental costs associated with one more unit sold are c_v. However, both c_v and c_f in the optimization problem may vary, at least to some degree, with the level of activity. Solving the optimization problem is still straightforward, but it is important that the function for both c_v and c_f is as correctly specified as possible.

Solving the basic price optimization problem in Excel

It is nice to know how the optimal price can be calculated by setting MR=MC or by solving $Z'(p) = 0$. However, in most practical situations it is far more efficient to let the computer do the job. This is particularly true when the number of products/services we are going to set a price for increases, and/or the frequency of how often the price should be adjusted is high. The problems presented and solved in Examples 7.1 and 7.2 are therefore most efficiently solved using the computer.[2]

Screenshots of how this can be done using Microsoft Excel are presented in Figure 7.1 on the next page. The important steps involve: (1) Write the price–response function in one cell (the demanded quantity as a function of price), as done in cell B9 in the upper panel of the figure; (2) write the function for the variable and fixed costs in separate cells; (3) let the price be represented in its own cell and set an initial value for it (just set a random value of your own choice); and (4) calculate the value of the objective function in a separate cell. It is important that this is a function referring to the other cells that is part of the objective function (such as the cells where price, demand, and the variable and fixed costs are defined). Excel will not understand what you are attempting to do if you forget this. The final step in the optimization process is to ask the solver in Excel to maximize the objective function (total profit) by changing the price (using non-linear optimization). It is also good practice to add the constraints that both the price and demand should be non-negative (B9 >= 0 and B10 >= 0). The procedure is the same for all price–response functions and cost functions. We will return to more advanced examples when we analyze a few case studies in the next chapter.

7.2 Price optimization with capacity constraints

In the previous section, we assumed that capacity constraints were not an issue. In real life, however, most businesses have capacity constraints, and they must take this into account when setting the price. This is true for both manufacturers and service providers. Examples include hotels, sporting events, airlines, and manufacturing companies producing snow shovels or any other good.

In all these cases we need to modify the objective function such that it considers the constraints. In the simple case, when the price–response function is the same across all segments and time periods, the only adjustment needed is the capacity of the business. This can be formally presented as in Equation (7.4):

Price optimization 109

	A	B
1		
2	BASIC OPTIMIZATION: LINEAR PRF	
3		
4	INTERCEPT	250
5	SLOPE	-10
6	cv	2.25
7		
8		
9	d(p)	=B4+B5*B10
10	price	10
11	cv	2.25
12	cf	0
13	Z (total profit)	=(B10*B9)-(B11*B9)-B12

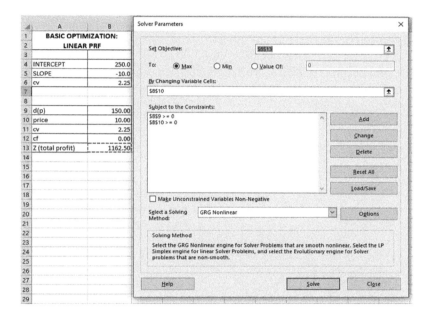

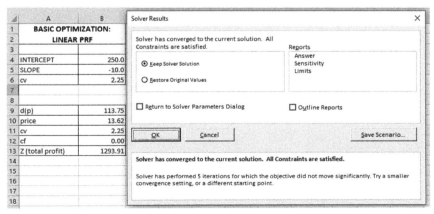

Figure 7.1 Screenshots of how to implement basic price optimization in Excel.

$$\max_{p} Z = (p - c_v)d(p) - c_f$$
s.t. (7.4)
$$d(p) \leq C$$

where *s.t.* means *subject to* and C is the available *capacity*. The other parameters are as before. In this case, the decision rule is simple. If the unconstrained optimal price, p^*, induces a demand $d(p^*)$ lower than the capacity constraint, i.e., $d(p^*) < C$, then this is both the unconstrained and the constrained optimal price. However, if the optimal unconstrained price leads to $d(p^*) > C$, we need to calculate a new, higher price such that we satisfy the capacity constraint.

In Figure 7.2 we illustrate the problem of setting optimal prices with a capacity constraint using the numbers from Examples 7.1 and 7.2. The straight dashed line in the figure show the capacity constraint of 50 cups of coffee per day. The optimal unconstrained price (p^*) is 13.62,[3] but what is the optimal price if the coffee machine in the student canteen can only produce 50 cups of coffee per day? The figure shows that the optimal constrained price is the price that makes the demanded quantity equal to the capacity constraint. That is, $d(p) = 50$ in our case. This is called the *runout price*, i.e.,

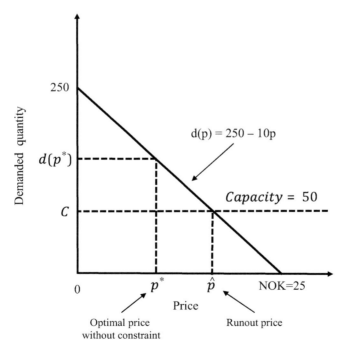

Figure 7.2 Optimal pricing with a capacity constraint. The capacity constraint is $C = 50$ cups of coffee per day. The same price–response function as in Example 7.1 and Example 7.2 is used. Adapted from Figure 5.1 in Phillips (2005, p. 102).

the price that would make demand exactly equal to the capacity constraint. To calculate this *runout price*, we simply solve this equation with respect to p:

$$d(p) = 250 - 10p = 50$$
$$10p = 200$$
$$\hat{p} = \frac{200}{10} = 20.00$$

Hence, the price that exactly induces a demanded quantity equal to the supply constraint (*runout price*) is NOK 20.00 in this case. If we set the price at this level, we will sell exactly 50 cups of coffee per day and maximize the total contribution given the supply constraint. Note that if the capacity constraint (C) is larger than the used capacity at the optimal price (p^*) the *runout price* is no longer the optimal price. To verify this, consider a situation where the capacity of the coffee machine is 150 cups per day. The runout price can be found by setting $d(p) = C$:

$$d(p) = 250 - 10p = 150$$
$$10p = 100$$
$$\hat{p} = \frac{100}{10} = 10.00$$

That is, if we set a price of NOK 10.00 we would sell exactly 150 cups of coffee. But what would the value of the objective function in this case? To find this, we plug the numbers into Equation (7.4):

$$Z_{p=10.00} = (10.00 - 2.25) \times 150 - 0 = 7.75 \times 150 = 1,162.50$$

and compare it to the total profit using the optimal price of 13.62:

$$Z_{p=13.63} = (13.63 - 2.25) \times 113.75 - 0 = 11.37 \times 113.75 = 1,293.91$$

As clearly seen from the above results, when the runout price is lower than the optimal price, we should always choose the optimal price. This leads to the following general principle for calculating the optimal price with a supply constraint (Phillips, 2005, p.102):

> "The profit-maximizing price under a supply constraint is equal to the maximum of the runout price and the unconstrained profit-maximizing price. As a consequence, the profit-maximizing price under a supply constraint is always greater than or equal to the unconstrained profit-maximizing price."

Solving the constrained price optimization problem in Excel

Solving the constrained price optimization problem for one product or service using Excel is almost as simple as solving the unconstrained problem. The only difference is that we must add the capacity constraint before solving the optimization model. The steps involved are illustrated in Figure 7.3. The first step is to write in the actual capacity constraint in one cell in the spreadsheet itself (B15). In our case, we have a constraint of 50 cups of coffee and we therefore plug in the number 50 in this cell. The second step is to define the model using *solver*. The objective function and the decision variable are the same as for the basic example shown in the previous section (the objective is the total profit given in B13, and the decision variable is the price given in cell B10). The new thing that we must now add is the capacity constraint. This is done by hitting Add in the solver interface. The constraint that must be satisfied when Excel solves the model is that the demanded quantity, $d(p)$, is less than or equal to the capacity of the coffee machine. The demanded quantity based on the price–response function (i.e., $d(p)$) is given in cell B9 and this cell reference is therefore inserted. The constraint itself is given in cell B15 and we refer to this cell reference here. One could also simply write the number 50 directly, but it is more efficient to refer to an actual cell if the model is updated with new capacity constraints in the future. The non-negativity constraints of both the prices and demanded quantity can be added in a similar way. Just refer to the relevant cells (B9 and B10) and indicate that they both should be greater than or equal to zero (add one constraint at the time).

The final step is to ask Excel to solve the problem. Make sure that you select the *GRG non-linear as the solving method* before you hit solve. The results are depicted in the lower panel of Figure 7.3. As seen from the results, the optimal price when we have a capacity constraint of 50 cups per day is NOK 20.00. The awake reader can confirm that this is the *runout price* and, hence, the same price we got when calculating this in the previous section. The total profit when setting a price of NOK 20.00 to sell 50 cups is NOK 887.50, a reduction of the total profit of NOK 406.41 (1,293.91 – 887.50) compared with the unconstrained optimization problem.

The reduced profit associated with a capacity constraint is called the *opportunity cost*. It is important for managers to have a good understanding of this concept as it is related to how much he or she should be willing to pay for increasing the capacity. In the next section we discuss the opportunity cost and related terms in more detail.

Opportunity cost, shadow price, and marginal contribution margin

We have just learned that when imposing a capacity constraint in the optimization model the objective function can only (1) stay at the same level, or (2) be reduced. In the first case (i.e., profit stays at same level), the optimal unconstrained price is also the optimal price with the capacity constraint. That is, we have not used all the available capacity in the optimal solution and the capacity constraint is not binding. In this case, it makes no sense to add more capacity. Why? Because we already have more capacity than we use, and you should not be willing to pay anything to add more unused capacity. However, if the constraint is binding, that is, you have used all the available capacity in the optimal solution,[4] what should you be willing to pay to remove the constraint? The answer is that you should be willing to pay the difference in the objective function (e.g., total profit) with and without the constraint. This is called the *opportunity cost* and will always be greater than or equal to zero. For the coffee example, we can calculate this opportunity cost as follows. First, calculate the

Price optimization 113

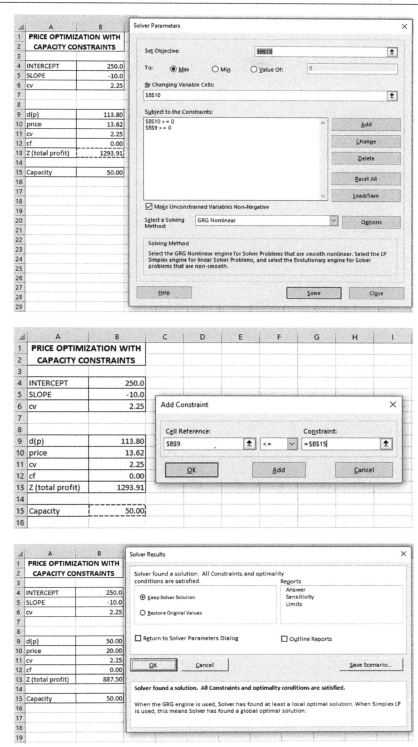

Figure 7.3 Screenshots of how to implement constrained price optimization in Excel.

total profit at the optimal unconstrained price (which we calculated as NOK 13.63 in the previous section):

$$Z_{p=13.63} = (13.63 - 2.25) \times 113.75 - 0 = 11.37 \times 113.75 = 1,293.91$$

Then calculate the total profit using the *runout price* (which we calculated as NOK 20.00 in the previous section) and the corresponding capacity constraint (50):

$$Z_{p=20.00} = (20.00 - 2.25) \times 50 - 0 = 17.75 \times 50 = 887.50$$

Then simply take the difference between the two:

$$Oppurtunity\,cost = 1,293.91 - 887.50 = 406.41$$

Hence, to remove the capacity constraint entirely, the student canteen should be willing to pay NOK 406.41 because the total profit will increase by this amount when removing the constraint at zero cost. If you pay any amount of NOK 406.41 or less for the extra capacity, you will be better off, compared with facing the binding constraint. As the optimization model is defined at the daily frequency, the opportunity cost is also a *per day* number. Hence, from an investment point of view, buying a new coffee machine would probably be highly profitable for the student canteen in this particular case.

The above example shows that the opportunity cost is what the student canteen should be willing to pay to remove the constraint entirely. But what if the capacity of the coffee machine could be gradually increased? What should the manager be willing to pay for one additional cup of capacity? The numeric answer to this question is called the *marginal opportunity cost*. Readers a little familiar with linear and non-linear programming may also see the link between this term and the *shadow price*. The shadow price is defined equivalently: the amount the decision-maker should be willing to pay for one extra unit of capacity.

To calculate the marginal opportunity cost (shadow price), we simply recalculate the objective function for each additional unit of capacity added. The differences in the value of the objective function at each level is the corresponding opportunity cost (shadow price) at that level. To illustrate, consider again the coffee example and the effect on the objective function by moving from 50 units sold to 51 units sold. To do this, we first need to calculate the runout price at this demand level.

To calculate this *runout price*, we simply solve this equation with respect to p:

$$d(p) = 250 - 10p = 51$$
$$10p = 199$$
$$\hat{p} = \frac{199}{10} = 19.90$$

Then calculate the value of the objective function with this price:

$$Z_{p=19.90} = (19.90 - 2.25) \times 51 - 0 = 17.65 \times 51 = 900.15$$

This induce a marginal opportunity cost (shadow price) of $12.65\,(900.15 - 887.50)$. Hence, to increase the capacity of the coffee machine from 50 to 51 cups we should be willing to

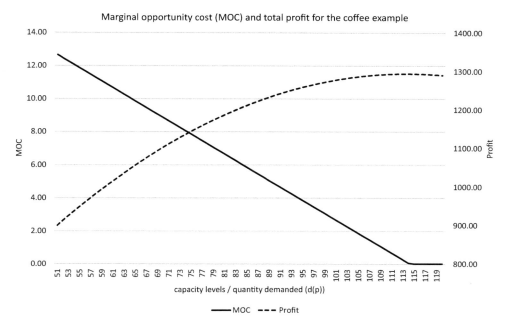

Figure 7.4 Marginal opportunity cost (MOC) and the profit function for the coffee example. The MOC follows the primary vertical axis and the profit function follows the secondary vertical axis.

pay NOK 12.65. If we pay any amount less than this to increase the capacity with one unit, we would be better off. If continuing to do this calculation at every level of capacity, we can depict the marginal opportunity cost across capacity levels. This is done in Figure 7.4.

The results from these calculations are clear: the more binding the constraint, the higher the opportunity cost. The awake reader may also note that the line representing the marginal opportunity cost flattens out at approximately 114 units. The reason is that this is the quantity sold at the profit-maximizing unconstrained price (NOK 13.63). Hence, increasing the capacity beyond this level has no value, and the marginal opportunity cost is zero.

Another interesting finding from the above calculations is the link between the marginal opportunity cost (MOC) and the profit function. Up to the profit-maximizing capacity level (~114) the MOC is equal to the *marginal contribution margin*. Why? Because the MOC is equal to the change in total contribution margin by going from one capacity level to another (which is the same as total change in profit if the fixed costs stay fixed). This in turn may be called the *marginal contribution margin*. In the special case of zero variable costs, the marginal contribution margin/MOC is also equal to *the marginal revenue*, for all capacity levels below the optimal unconstrained demand/price.

Calculating runout prices and opportunity costs in Excel

Calculating runout prices and opportunity costs in Excel is straightforward if we have the price–response function. Let us continue to use the coffee example from the previous sections. We found the runout price for a given capacity level simply by setting the price–response function equal to the capacity level and then solved the equation with respect to the price. Hence, the runout price for a linear price–response function can be found like this:

$$d(p) = C$$
$$D - m \cdot p = C \qquad (7.5)$$
$$\hat{p} = \frac{(D-C)}{m}$$

where C is the capacity, D is the constant term in the linear price–response function, m is the slope, and p is the price. Solving the equation with respect to p yields the runout price, p. The awake reader may notice that this is the inverse of the price–response function.

Once we have this formula, implementing it in Excel is very simple. The upper part of Figure 7.5 illustrate how this is done. In this case, the capacity level is given in column A (from A12 and down) and the parameters of the price–response function are given in C3 (intercept, which is the D in Equation (7.5)) and C4 (the slope, which is the m in Equation (7.5)). The formula to insert in cell B12 is then =($C$3-A12)/ABS($C$4). This can be pulled down for all relevant capacity levels. In columns C and D, the total revenue and profit are calculated, respectively. Once we have these numbers, the calculation of the marginal revenue and MOC is easily done just by taking the first difference of the total revenue and/or the total profit. In Figure 7.5 this is illustrated in columns E and F. To make the calculations of the MOC absolutely correct, we should use the =MAXA() formula in Excel which takes the maximum of the first difference of the profit function and 0 at all capacity levels. Hence, when the capacity is no longer binding, the MOC becomes zero, as it should be according to the theory. If depicting the profit and the MOC, we end up with a similar figure as that presented in Figure 7.4.

7.3 Optimal price differentiation with capacity constraints

In Chapter 2, we argued that one way to increase the total profit would be to offer the same product or service to different buyers at different prices. This can be done if we are able to segment the market and there is no or little risk of arbitrage. Additionally, there must be a difference in the price–response functions (and hence price elasticities) of the various segments. A good example of price differentiation is to offer one price to the general public and then a discounted price to students. This sort of discount is usually also well accepted, as students in general tend to have a lower income level and a tighter budget than the general public.[5] Let us use the same coffee example as in the previous sections, which is based on actual data of students and employees/visitors of a student canteen.[6] Segmenting the total market into students and the general public yields these two linear price–response functions (we shall use more advanced price–response functions in the next chapter):

Students: $d_s(p_s) = 200 - 9p_s$
General public: $d_g(p_g) = 50 - 1p_g$ (7.6)

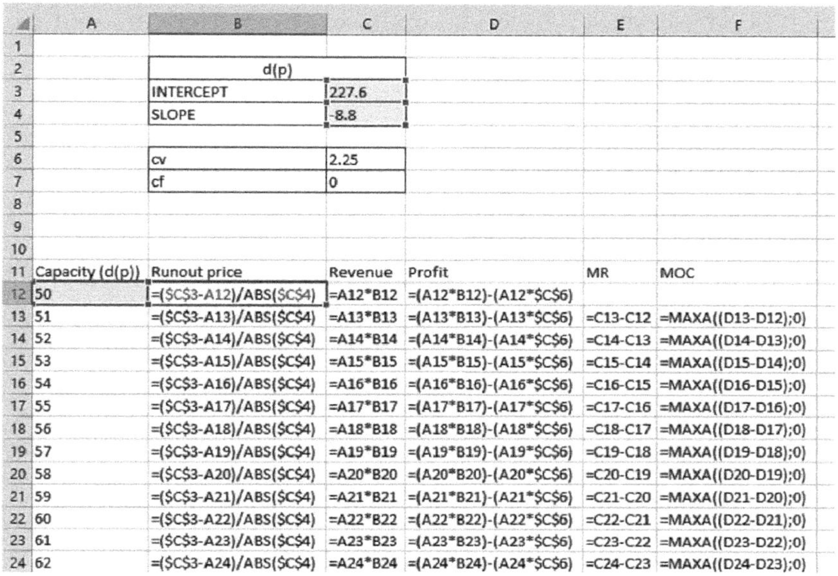

Price optimization 117

Figure 7.5 Screenshots of how to calculate runout prices and marginal opportunity costs in Excel.

Using the general notation, we can formulate the optimization model as follows:

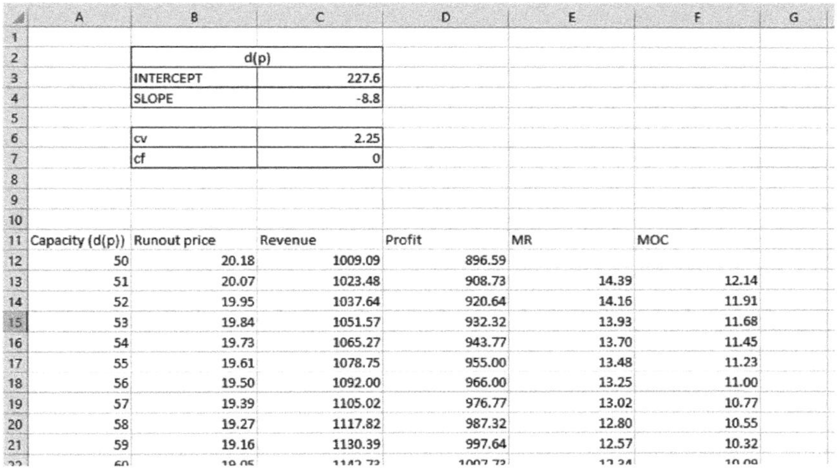

$$\max_{p_{s,g}} Z = (p_s - c_v)d_s(p_s) + (p_g - c_v)d_g(p_g) - c_f$$

s.t.

$$d_s(p_s) + d_g(p_g) \leq C$$

$$p_s, p_g \geq 0$$

(7.7)

118 Price optimization

If we assume that the available capacity is 50, the variable (incremental) cost associated with selling one extra cup of coffee is still NOK 2.25 and the fixed costs are zero, the specific model for us to solve would look like this:

$$\max_{p_{s,g}} Z = (p_s - 2.25)(200 - 9p_s) + (p_g - 2.25)(50 - 1.00 p_g)$$
s.t. \hspace{5cm} (7.8)
$$(200 - 9p_s) + (50 - 1.00 p_g) \leq 50$$

By simplifying and taking the derivative of the two profit functions, we obtain a function for the marginal contribution margin for both the students and the general public:

Students: $\quad MCM_s = -18 p_s + 220.25$
General public: $MCM_g = -2 p_g + 52.25$ \hspace{2cm} (7.9)

We can simplify the two equations for the marginal contribution margins further and equate them:

$$MCM_s = p_s - 12.24$$
$$MCM_g = p_g - 26.13$$
$$p_s - 12.24 = p_g - 26.13 \hspace{3cm} (7.10)$$
$$p_g = p_s + 13.89$$

That is, given the data we have at hand, and by using linear price–response functions, the optimal price for the general public is NOK 13.89 above the optimal price for students. The awake reader may notice at this stage that the optimal price for students and the general public is NOK 12.24, and NOK 26.13 in the case of no capacity constraints. Why? Because these prices make the formula for the marginal contribution margin equal to zero in both cases. But what happens when we include the capacity constraint? If we simplify the equation for the constraint given in Equation (7.8), we get:

$$9 p_s + p_g = 200 \hspace{5cm} (7.11)$$

And then solving both the condition in Equations (7.10) and (7.11) simultaneously, we get:

$$9 p_s + p_s + 13.89 = 200$$
$$10 p_s = 200 - 13.89 = 186.11$$
$$p_s = \frac{186.11}{10} = 18.61 \hspace{4cm} (7.12)$$
$$p_g = 18.61 + 13.89 = 32.50$$

Price optimization 119

If we plug these prices into the respective price–response functions we can calculate the number of cups that will be sold to students and the general public:

Students: $d_s(p_s) = 200 - 9 \times 18.61 = 32.50) : 33$

General public: $d_g(p_g) = 50 - 1 \times 32.50 = 17.50) : 17$

(7.13)

The total contribution margin using these prices is:

$$Z = (18.61 - 2.25) \times 33 + (32.50 - 2.25) \times 17 = 1,054.17 \quad (7.14)$$

This is an increase of almost 19% compared with charging a single price in the case of a capacity constraint of 50 cups of coffee per day (verify it yourself).

7.4 Optimal time-based price differentiation

In many situations, customers have a different willingness to pay depending what time the good or service is consumed. This may induce a unique shape of the price–response functions for the various sub-period. Examples of services where willingness to pay can vary by time of consumption are:

- Alpine skiing.
- Going to the movie theater.
- Going to a restaurant.

In all these cases (and many others) it is likely that the price sensitivity of the customers is affected by the time of consumption. For example, it is likely that alpine skiers and those visiting the movie theater, or a restaurant, are more price-sensitive on midweek days compared with the weekend. Additionally, most consumers would probably value skiing during the daytime more than in the evening, while going to the movies or the restaurant are typically done in the afternoon and evenings. In such cases, and if the businesses have the freedom to adjust prices over different periods – which is often the case in real life – they can exploit these variations in price sensitivity to increase the total profit from the fixed capacity available. This tactic is referred to as *variable pricing* in the literature (see, e.g., Phillips 2005). However, the general concept is identical to that presented in the previous section on price differentiation. The only difference is that we examine the price response for various time periods and not for various segments based on the criteria of the customers themselves (such as age, gender, student, etc.). Hence, the various time periods can now be viewed as segments with their own characteristics. Offering variable prices across time periods is usually also well accepted because the customers can choose themselves if they want to take advantage of a lower price during a less-attractive time period, or not.[7] Consider the following two linear price–response functions for an alpine skiing resort given below:

Midweek: $d_{mw}(p_{mw}) = 700.97 - 1.09 p_{mw}$

Weekend: $d_{we}(p_{we}) = 1,610.01 - 2.09 p_{we}$

(7.15)

120 Price optimization

In Equation (7.15) midweek refers to the time period Monday–Thursday and weekend are defined as the days Friday–Sunday. The objective of the alpine skiing resort is to maximize the total profit over the entire season. If we assume that there is no *demand shifting*[8] resulting from variable intra-weekly prices and that the variable (incremental) costs associated with handling one extra skier is 0, the general formulation of the objective function is:

$$\max_{p_{mw}, p_{we}} Z = p_{mw} d_{mw}(p_{mw}) + p_{we} d_{we}(p_{we}) - c_f$$

s.t.

$$d_i(p_i) \leq C \tag{7.16}$$

where $i = mw, we$

That is, maximize the total profit by changing the midweek and weekend prices and make sure that neither weekend demand nor the midweek demand exceeds the available capacity.[9] If using the price–response functions as given in Equation (7.15), and if we assume that this ski resort can handle 600 skiers per day, the objective function can be expressed like this:

$$\max_{p_{mw}, p_{we}} Z = p_{mw}(700.97 - 1.09 p_{mw}) + p_{we}(1{,}610.01 - 2.09 p_{we}) - c_f$$

s.t. (7.17)

$$700.97 - 1.09 p_{mw} \leq 600$$
$$1{,}610.01 - 2.09 p_{we} \leq 600$$

Hence, the only difference from traditional price differentiation is that the sum of the demanded quantity of the various segments in the optimization model is no longer relevant. Why? Because it cannot be midweek *and* the weekend at the same time. Hence, the important element is that the capacity of the ski resort is not exceeded in any given time period separately.

We can solve this model in the exact same way as we did with the coffee example, as illustrated from (7.6) to (7.12). Table 7.1 below shows the results from the optimization using (1) constant pricing, and (2) variable pricing across midweek/weekend. If the ski resort chooses to offer a single price for all weekdays, the optimal (profit-maximizing) price is NOK 483.26 for a day pass. At this price, the ski resort sells 174 day passes on average during the midweek days and 600 day passes during the weekend days (which is the capacity constraint). The average number of daily visitors using this pricing strategy is 387.[10]

If choosing a variable approach to pricing, the optimal price for the midweek days is reduced from NOK 483.26 to NOK 321.55. This is a reduction of approximately 33%, but it will lead to an increase in demand of more than 101% (from 174 to 350). The change in profit during the midweek days is almost 34%. The average number of daily visitors over the week increases by almost 23% while the average price is reduced by almost 17%. The total profit increases by 7.62%.

This example shows the potential impact a variable approach to pricing can have on the operating profit. By just offering two prices, instead of one, the total profit is

Table 7.1 The results of the price optimization using (1) a single price across all weekdays (upper panel), and (2) a variable pricing approach (lower panel)

Summary of optimization results

Single price

	Midweek	Weekend	Average
Price	483.26	483.26	483.26
d(p)	174.22	600.00	387.11
Profit	84,192	289,955	374,148

Variable price

	Midweek	Weekend	Average
Price	321.55	483.26	402.40
d(p)	350.49	600.00	475.24
Profit	112,697	289,955	402,652

increased notably. Another side-effect is that we also attract more skiers to the slope, which in turn would induce higher ancillary revenues.

However, there is one potential pitfall when implementing variable pricing. Some customers can change their time of consumption among periods with high/low prices. For example, if many alpine skiers choose to go skiing during the lower-priced midweek days instead of the higher-priced weekend days, there is a need to take this *demand shifting* into account when calculating the optimal prices. In the next section, we briefly illustrate how this can be done.

Optimal variable prices with demand shifting

Let us continue with the alpine skiing example, but now assume that for every NOK in price difference between the weekend and midweek days, two customers will shift their skiing activity from the higher-priced weekend to the lower-priced midweek period. The new price–response function can then be presented as:

$$d_i = D_i + m_i p_i + \sum_{j=1}^{2} 2(p_j - p_i) \tag{7.18}$$

where d_i is the daily demand for either the midweek- or the weekend period, D_i is the intercept in the linear price–response function, m_i is the slope, and p_i / p_j is the price in the given period.

Consider again the price–response function for the midweek and weekend as given again below:

Midweek: $d_{mw}(p_{mw}) = 700.97 - 1.09 p_{mw}$

Weekend: $d_{we}(p_{we}) = 1{,}610.01 - 2.09 p_{we}$

(7.19)

122 Price optimization

Combining the information above with that presented in Equation (7.18) and the optimal prices from Table 7.1 gives new demand levels for the two periods:

$$\text{Midweek: } d_{mw}(p_{mw}) = 700.97 - 1.09 \times 321.55 + 2(483.26 - 321.55) = 673.91$$
$$\text{Weekend: } d_{we}(p_{we}) = 1{,}610.01 - 2.09 \times 483.26 + 2(321.55 - 483.26) = 276.57 \quad (7.20)$$

Hence, if two customers shift their demand from the weekend to the midweek for every NOK in price difference between the two periods, the new demand in the two periods would be 674 (midweek) and 277 (weekend). You may notice that the midweek demand has now exceeded the available capacity. Hence, the suggested prices in Table 7.1 and the corresponding demand given in Equation (7.20) are no longer feasible. We therefore need to recalculate the optimal prices where the updated price–response functions satisfy the capacity constraint:

$$\max_{p_{mw}, p_{we}} Z = p_{mw} d_{mw}(p_{mw}) + p_{we} d_{we}(p_{we}) - c_f$$

s.t.

$$d_i(p_i) + \sum_{j=1}^{2} 2(p_j - p_i) \le C \quad \text{where } i, j = mw, we \quad (7.21)$$

The results of the updated optimization are provided in Table 7.2. As seen from this table, new optimal prices are calculated to be NOK 352.33 and NOK 419.24 for the midweek and weekend, respectively. If implementing these prices and there is no demand shifting between periods of high and low prices, the base demand would be 317 during midweek days and 734 during weekend days. However, as two skiers switch their skiing

Table 7.2 The results of the variable price optimization

Summary of optimization results

Without demand shifting

	Midweek	Weekend	Average
Price	321.55	483.26	402.40
d(p)	350.49	600.00	475.24
Profit	112,697	289,955	402,652

With demand shifting

	Midweek	Weekend	Average
Price	352.33	419.24	385.79
d(p)	450.73	600.00	525.37
Profit	158,808	251,542	410,350

Notes: The upper part shows the results for which there is no demand shifting between higher and lower-priced periods and the lower part shows the results when some of the demanded quantity for ski passes shifts according to the information given in Equation (7.18).

consumption from the high-priced weekend to the lower-priced midweek for every NOK in price difference between the two periods (see Equation (7.18)), the real demand at these prices will be NOK 451 and NOK 600 for midweek and the weekend, respectively. This means that a total of 134 skiers will switch from weekend skiing to midweek skiing under the given price regime.

Another interesting finding from the new optimization is that the average number of skiers in the slopes has increased even more compared with the situation where there was no demand shifting. The updated results show that the average demand has increased by 10.5% (from 475 to 525), and that the total profit has increased by 4.1%.

Calculating optimal differentiated prices using Excel

Once we have information about (1) the price–response functions for the various segments/sub-groups/time periods, and (2) the necessary information about the relevant costs, it is straightforward to implement optimization models that provide the profit-maximizing differentiated prices in Excel. The steps involved are similar to those involved when calculating only a single optimal price, as shown in Figure 7.3. The new thing is that we must create an aggregate objective function, which is simply the sum of the profit functions for the various segments/sub-groups/time periods. Additionally, a cell containing a function for the aggregated demanded quantity must be included to make sure we stay within the capacity constraint. An illustration of how the optimization model can be formulated for the coffee example examined earlier in this chapter is provided in Figure 7.6.

The objective function to be maximized now is formulated in cell L3 and the capacity constraint is given in L5. This example, and the example where the optimal time-based differentiated prices for the ski resort are calculated, are both included in the Excel file following Chapter 7. Additionally, an example of optimal time-based variable prices in the case of demand shifting is included.

It is important to note here that demand shifting can also be a problem when we differentiate prices across other criteria than time. As customers rarely can be perfectly segmented, there may be situations where customers who are in a high-price segment find ways of buying the product or service at the lower price. In such cases some of the demand in the higher-priced segment shifts to the lower-priced segment in a similar way as for the variable time-based pricing approach. This is referred to as cannibalization and it will affect the optimal prices in the various segments.

	E	F	G	H	I	J	K	L
1								
2	STUDENTS			GENERAL PUBLIC			Optimization	
3	INTERCEPT	200		INTERCEPT	50		Aggregate Z	=F12+I12
4	SLOPE	-9		SLOPE	-1		Aggregate d(p)	=F8+I8
5	cv	2.25		cv	2.25		Capacity	50
6							Diff	=(L3-C12)/C12
7								
8	d(p)	33		d(p)	17			
9	price	18.6111111335494		price	32.4999997946847			
10	cv	2.25		cv	2.25			
11	cf	0		cf	0			
12	Z (total profit)	=(F9*F8)-(F10*F8)-F11		Z (total profit)	=(I9*I8)-(I10*I8)-I11			

Figure 7.6 Setting up an optimization model for differentiated prices (students and general public).

124 Price optimization

In the next chapter we shall examine several real-life case studies where we analyze the concepts of cannibalization and demand shifting in more detail using Excel.

7.5 Elasticity and optimization

In general, the elasticity tells us something about how revenue will be affected for a small change in price. Around a specific price point, it tells us how much demanded quantity will change for a specific change in price. If the change in sales from a small price change is low, a price increase will increase revenue (price effect outweighs volume effect) and vice versa. In general, we have the following set of rules regarding elasticity and revenue:

$$
\begin{aligned}
&(1): |\varepsilon| < 1 \to p^+ \Rightarrow R^+ \\
&(2): |\varepsilon| = 1 \to p \amalg R \\
&(3): |\varepsilon| > 1 \to p^+ \Rightarrow R^-
\end{aligned}
\qquad(7.22)
$$

where the $\amalg$ sign is used to mean "independent of," that is, price is independent of revenue. In number (1) a price increase induces increased revenue, while in (3) a price increase induces reduced revenue. By combining the equation of point elasticity with the condition that the optimal price is found where the derivative of the profit function is zero, we obtain the following:

$$\frac{(p^* - c)}{p^*} = -\frac{1}{\varepsilon(p^*)} \qquad(7.23)$$

where p^* is the optimal price. The left side of this equation is the contribution margin ratio. This formula is particularly useful as it provides the seller with a set of rules if the variable costs and the point elasticity is known. The rules are as follows (Bodea and Ferguson, 2014):

Current situation	Rule
$(p-c)/p = -1/\varepsilon(p)$	p is optimal (do not change price).
$(p-c)/p < -1/\varepsilon(p)$	p is too low, profit will increase by raising the price.
$(p-c)/p > -1/\varepsilon(p)$	p is too high, profit will increase by lowering the price.

Note that all these rules are local sine $\varepsilon(p)$ changes as the price changes (except in the case of constant elasticity). Hence, for most practical circumstances it is easier to follow the steps as described in the previous sections of this chapter when calculating the optimal price.

7.6 Pricing with competition

Competition is a very important part of all pricing decisions. In fact, most managers identify competition as the number one factor influencing their pricing (Phillips, 2005, p. 55). It is therefore important to know how it affects the price–response function of the firm's product or service and, eventually, how we should account for it in our models.

The good news is that when calculating the price–response function on historical data, competition is already included as the demanded quantity (i.e., historical sales) we observe for various prices are the choices of the consumers, given that we are competing in a market. Hence, the lost sales from a price increase would most likely benefit a competitor (in terms of higher sales volume for the competitor) and vice versa. To some extent the price–response function therefore already includes "typical" competitive pricing. So, assuming that the competitors behave similarly in the future as they have in the past, the price–response function can be used to anticipate market response (including competitor response). If the market changes, in one way or another, new price–response functions must be estimated and the models updated to calculate new optimal prices.

If you have the (dynamic) prices of your main competitors readily available, for example via their webpages, such information can of course be used to potentially improve the predictions of your own price changes. The general methodological framework is called *consumer-choice modeling* and *the multinomial logit model* is the most widely used estimation technique on such data. This model can also be applied on survey data obtained by the so-called *choice-based conjoint method*.

It is beyond the scope of this book to examine the details of consumer-choice modeling and the multinomial logit model, but Chapter 14 is devoted to how rating-based conjoint analysis, which also can be used to include information about competitors' prices and other key attributes, can be used in pricing decisions.

7.7 Summary

- When we have information about the price–response function and the cost structure of the product or service of interest, basic price optimization can be used to find the profit-maximizing price.
- Formulating the optimization model involves three steps: (1) define the decision variable (the price); (2) define the objective function (the total profit); and (3) define the constraints (usually related to capacity).
- The optimal price can be found by setting MR=MC, by differentiation of the objective function and setting it equal to zero, or by using Excel and the solver add-in.
- In the case of capacity constraints, the price that induces a demanded quantity equal to the constraint is called the runout price.
- The profit-maximizing price in the case of capacity constraints is always greater than or equal to the unconstrained profit-maximizing price.
- The opportunity cost can be understood as the amount the firm should be willing to pay to remove a capacity constraint.
- The MOC is the amount the firm should be willing to pay to increase capacity with one unit. Another term used for this is "shadow price."

- If we have information about the price–response functions of separate sub-groups/sub-periods, we can find the optimal differentiated prices using optimization.
- Demand shifting/cannibalization must be considered when calculating optimal differentiated prices.
- Information about price elasticity and costs can be used to decide whether the current price is too low, too high, or optimal.

7.8 Problems

1. A company contacts you to evaluate whether their current price of a widget is optimal or not. The variable costs to produce and sell the widget are $5 per unit and the fixed costs are $10,000. Formulate the optimization problem. Will the fixed costs affect the solution? Why/why not?
2. You just received information about the estimated price–response function for the widget in problem 1. It is estimated to be:

$$d(p) = 50,000 - 58p$$

   Find the optimal price using both calculus and Excel. What is the total profit based on the optimization results?
3. The management is happy with your solution so far, but there is a problem. The current capacity is only 2,000 units. Will this affect your results from problem 2? If so, how?
4. One analyst in the company contacts you to inform about a recent analysis of the price–demand relationship. She has done more estimations and concluded that a logit price–response function should be used instead of a simple linear price–response function. The estimated parameters of the logit model are as follows:

$$(p) = \frac{5{,}285 \cdot e^{3-0.06 \cdot p}}{1 + e^{3-0.06 \cdot p}}$$

   The other information is as given in the previous problems (including a capacity constraint of 2,000 units). What is the optimal price now?
5. Use the linear price–response function provided in problem 2 and the general information from problem 1. Illustrate how the MOC and the total profit varies with various capacity levels.
6. Assume now that the company has identified two segments: (1) students; and (2) the general public. They both have unique price–response functions with the following characteristics:

   Students: $d(p) = 2{,}000 - 40p$
   General public: $d(p) = 3{,}000 - 18p$

   What are the optimal prices for these two segments?

7. A newly established hotel wants to make it simple for its customers by offering only two rates: one weekend rate and a midweek rate. The variable costs associated with making each room ready for new guests are estimated at $10 during midweek days (Monday–Thursday) and $18 for weekend days (Friday–Sunday). The midweek days and weekend days have the following price–response functions:

   Midweek: $d(p) = 1,200 - 8p$
   Weekend: $d(p) = 1,200 - 12p$

   The hotel has a capacity of 500 rooms in both the midweek period and the weekend period. What is the profit-maximizing single price? What are the profit-maximizing variable prices? What is the percentage increase in total profit from introducing variable pricing?

8. It turns out that introducing lower prices for the weekend induces some customers with great flexibility (such as retirees) to move some of their demand from the higher-priced midweek days to the lower-priced weekend days. An analysis shows that ten customers are likely to shift from midweek to weekend for every dollar in price difference between the two periods. What are the optimal variable prices now?

Notes

1 The prices in these examples (and in later examples in this chapter) are given in Norwegian Kroner (NOK). €1 ~ NOK 10.
2 In the Excel file following Chapter 7, the various examples are implemented.
3 As shown in Example 7.1 and Example 7.2.
4 This is the same as saying that the *runout price* is higher than the unconstrained optimal price.
5 We will return to various pricing acceptance/fairness factors in Chapter 15.
6 We round up the parameter estimates in all the examples in this chapter for expository purposes.
7 We will return to the importance of customer acceptance in Chapter 15.
8 Demand shifting refers to the concept of customers moving their consumption from a higher-priced period to a lower-priced period. This is often also referred to as cannibalization. We shall examine the concepts of demand shifting/cannibalization in detail in Chapter 9.
9 If we want to find the single optimal price, we multiply the two price–response functions by one price variable:

$$\max_{p} Z = p \times d_{mw}(p_{mw}) + p \times d_{we}(p_{we}) - c_f$$

s.t.

$$d_i(p_i) \leq C \quad \text{where } i = mw, we$$

10 Note that we have done these calculations by taking the simple average even though there are four midweek days and three weekend days. Strictly speaking, it would be more correct to calculate a weighted average for expository purposes if we treat the two time periods as being of the same length.

Chapter 8

Case study
Optimal prices of movie theater tickets

The most famous examples where dynamic pricing/price optimization is regularly used stem from the service industry and include hotels, airlines and cruise ships. However, the principles of price optimization with capacity constraints are equally relevant for other service businesses. Berman (2005) lists the criteria for which dynamic/variable pricing can be successfully applied in service industries. The most important of these are:

- Predictable seasonality (intra-daily, intra-weekly, intra-yearly) in demand and differences in price sensitivity by market segments.
- Low costs of marginal sales compared to marginal revenues and high fixed costs.
- Fixed capacity that cannot be stored for later use.

You may notice that most service industries are recognized as having these characteristics. A few examples mentioned by Berman (2005) are amusement parks, golf courses, sporting events, restaurants, advertising time and space, and equipment rental.

Another prime example of such a service industry that fulfills all the requirements for the ideal application of dynamic/variable pricing is, you guessed it, *movie theaters*.

In this chapter we shall walk you through a case study where the aim is to find optimal prices for movie theater tickets. The aim is to include all the steps in the process, from data collection to optimization, such that you can use this chapter as a template for your own projects later. The steps covered are:

- Step 1: Develop a questionnaire on price/demand.
- Step 2: Data collection.
- Step 3: Data preparation.
- Step 4: Preliminary analysis:
  - Descriptive statistics and data visualization.
- Step 5: Estimation of price–response functions.
- Step 6: Optimize prices.
- Step 7: Implementation.

8.1 Step 1: Develop a questionnaire

If your firm does not have data on price/demanded quantity readily available, you must either set up a price experiment or collect data via a direct survey. The latter approach is by far the cheapest and easiest way of obtaining the data needed to perform the subsequent analysis, although it has some weaknesses as mentioned in Chapter 6. In the case we examine in this chapter, a direct survey among existing movie theater visitors and the general public was carried out. An illustration of the questionnaire is included in Figure 8.1. The key question in the survey is question 10. Here, the respondent is asked to reveal their annual consumption level for various price levels, both for midweek days (Monday–Thursday) and weekends (Friday–Sunday). These variables alone will enable us to calculate the optimal (profit-maximizing) prices for the midweek and weekend, respectively. However, if we want to carry out price differentiation based on more criteria, such as *time of the day, general public/students, age, distribution channel,* or something else, we must include questions that capture the characteristics we would like to use as the basis for price differentiation later.

Another important aspect that must be considered if the aim is to implement time-based price differentiation is the concept of *demand shifting/cannibalization*. There are various ways this can be captured in a direct survey. One way is to ask respondents directly how various price combinations (for higher-priced periods and low-priced periods) will affect their preferences for when to attend the service of interest (with the risk of bias this direct approach will induce). Another way is to extract this information indirectly from answers given to other questions. We shall examine one such indirect way in this chapter.

The questionnaire in Figure 8.1 is simple and all the questions fit on one page. At a first glance it may be hard to understand why some of the questions are included when the aim is to optimize the ticket prices. An example is the question asking how many times during one year the respondent visits the movie theater (Q6). However, this question can be useful for at least two reasons: (1) it allows us to examine whether there is any bias in the visit frequency the respondent reveals on the key question (Q10); and (2) it can be used to price-differentiate across light and heavy users. We shall examine this further when analyzing the data later. The most important point when developing a direct survey is to make sure that you keep the questionnaire short and to the point,[1] while at the same time ensuring you include the key questions needed to perform the price analyses you desire.

8.2 Step 2: Data collection and punching

Once you have a version of the questionnaire ready, the data collection process can start. It is a good idea to run one, or more, *pretests* before collecting the data that shall be used in the main analyses. A pretest means that you ask a small sample (for example, friends or colleagues) to fill out the questionnaire and provide their feedback. Performing such pretests gives useful information on whether the included questions measure what you aim to measure, if the questions in general are understandable, if the length seems appropriate, and more. Before starting the real data collection process, you should also bear in mind what characteristics your customers have in terms of background variables such as *gender, age, residence, income,* and so forth. The reason is that the sample used for data collection shall be similar to the population of your customers on key characteristics. The more similar the sample is to the population, the better.

SURVEY ON MOVIE THEATER VISITS

This survey is part of a bachelor thesis Inland Norway University of Applied Sciences. I hope you will give your honest responses to all the questions as they will affect the subsequent analyses. Your answers will remain anonymous at it takes about 3-5 minutes to complete the survey. Thank you very much in advance for taking Your time to participate! ☺

Questions:
1. Gender?
   - ☐ Male
   - ☐ Female

2. Age?
   _____ years

3. Are you..? (Multiple answers possible)
   - ☐ Student, _____ (what program?)
   - ☐ Work full time
   - ☐ Work part time
   - ☐ Unemployed
   - ☐ Other, _____

4. Zip code of your residence?
   _____

5. Approximately how much is your total net annual income?
   - ☐ Under 100 000 NOK
   - ☐ 100 000- 200 000 NOK
   - ☐ 200 000- 400 000 NOK
   - ☐ 400 000- 600 000 NOK
   - ☐ More than 600 000NOK
   - ☐ Do not want to answer

6. Approximately how many times during **one year** do you visit the movie theater
   _____ times

7. What days do you visit the movie theater (Multiple answers possible)?
   - ☐ Monday
   - ☐ Tuesday
   - ☐ Wednesday
   - ☐ Thursday
   - ☐ Friday
   - ☐ Saturday
   - ☐ Sunday
   - ☐ No preference

8. At what times to you prefer visiting the movie theater (time the movie starts)?
   - ☐ Before 18:00
   - ☐ 18:00-21:00
   - ☐ After 21:00

9. On a scale from 1 (not interested) to 10 (very interested), how interested in movies are you?
   1 2 3 4 5 6 7 8 9 10

10. How many visits to the movie theater **per year,** would you make during midweek (Mon-Thu) and weekends (Fri-Sun), respectively, if the price per ticket was as follows:
    (Note! The sum of midweek and weekend shall be the total number of visits to the movie theater during one year at that price level)

Price:	MIDWEEK: Visits/year;	WEEKEND: Visits/year;
40 NOK	_____	_____
50 NOK	_____	_____
60 NOK	_____	_____
70 NOK	_____	_____
80 NOK	_____	_____
90 NOK	_____	_____
100 NOK	_____	_____
110 NOK	_____	_____
120 NOK	_____	_____
130 NOK	_____	_____
140 NOK	_____	_____
150 NOK	_____	_____

11. If you still would be willing to visit the movie theater at least one time per year at a price of 150 NOK, either during midweek, or weekend, or both. What is the maximum price you would be willing to pay for a ticket?

    MIDWEEK: _____ NOK

    WEEKEND: _____ NOK

Figure 8.1 Questionnaire used for data collection in the case study.

The data used in the case study examined in this chapter were collected in a direct survey by a bachelor student at the Inland Norway University of Applied Sciences. The data were collected at the movie theater before the various movies started, on the university campus and via online versions of the questionnaire (identical to the paper version).

In total, 241 people completed the form. Not all of these could be used in the main analysis. We shall return to this in the next section.

You may wonder how many observations are needed to perform valid analyses in general. There is no simple answer to this question. The most important criterion is that your sample is as *representative* as possible. That is, it should reflect the total base of your existing and potential customers on key background characteristics (such as gender, age, residence, and so forth). If you do a good job on this, you can get away with a minimum sample size as low as 100 respondents. However, it is generally a good idea to go beyond this minimum as some of the observations may need to be taken out in the data preparation step. This could be because of incompleteness, inconsistency, typos, or other reasons. The longer and more complex the survey, the more responses with missing or inconsistent values. Hence, you should evaluate the quality of the responses as the data collection goes on and potentially adjust the minimum required number of observations accordingly. As a rule of thumb, *the maximum* sample size can be set to the minimum of 10% of your total customer base and 1,000. That is, if you have 500,000 existing or potential customers, you set the maximum sample size to 1,000 (10% of 500,000 is 5,000 and you then choose 1,000). Usually you would end up with a sample size between the minimum and maximum. Whether you end up with a number closer to the maximum or minimum depends on several factors, where your budget and time constraints probably are the most important ones in this matter.

When the data collection is finished, the responses provided by the respondents must be coded into numeric values. Some of the questions, for example Q2, Q4, Q6, Q9, Q10 and Q11, in the questionnaire used in this case study (Figure 8.1) already contain numeric values and these can be directly punched into the data sheet. Other variables, such as gender (Q1), must be coded into numeric values such that they can be efficiently used for filtering, summarizing (sub) results and used directly in the analyses. Figure 8.2 illustrates the explanations and coding of the various categorical variables in the movie theater case. For example, if the respondent is a male, the value 0 is assigned in the column containing the *gender* variable. Even when performing an online survey, the various categories must be coded/recoded into the numeric values you want to use, if it is not possible to set this up when creating the form.

Figure 8.3 illustrates how the data for the first ten respondents on the first six questions in the movie theater case study look like. When the explanations/codes of the various categorical variables are available (Figure 8.2), we can easily interpret the recorded data points for each respondent. For example, the first respondent is a female (Gender = 1), aged 41, working fulltime (Work status = 4), with an income level of between NOK 400,000 and NOK 600,000 (Income = 3), with an annual visit frequency to the movie theater of 10.

The *weekday* variable needs a bit more explanation. The explanation in Figure 8.2 states that this is coded into a *dummy variable*. This means that we create one variable for all seven days of the week (i.e., Monday, Tuesday, Wednesday, Thursday, Friday, Saturday, and Sunday). These variables can only take two values and are therefore called dummy variables. In the current example, we use the value 1 where the respondent has indicated the weekday of interest as a preferred day to go to the movie theater (Q7), and zero otherwise. Additionally, a variable called *all_days* is created if the respondent has indicated the option *No preference*. Figure 8.4 illustrates how these variables should be

	A	B	C
1	**Explanations**		**Code**
2	Gender	Male	0
3		Female	1
4			
5	Work Situation	Student	0
6		Student working part time	1
7		Student working full time	2
8		Working part time	3
9		Working full time	4
10		Unemployed	5
11		Other	6
12		Retiree	7
13			
14			
15	Income	Under 100 000 NOK	0
16		100 000 - 200 000 NOK	1
17		200 000 - 400 000 NOK	2
18		400 000 - 600 000 NOK	3
19		More than 600 000 NOK	4
20		Prefer not to answer	NA
21			
22	Weekday	Dummy variabel	Yes=1/No=0
23			
24	Time of day	Before 18:00	0
25		18:00 - 21:00	1
26		After kl 21:00	2
27		Before 18:00 - 21:00	3
28		After 18:00	4
29		All times	5
30			
31	Version	Paper	0
32		Online	1
33			
34	C/I	Complete	0
35		Incomplete	1

Figure 8.2 Coding of various types of data into numerical data.

recorded in the spreadsheet. In that figure, the recording of the intra-daily time preferences of the respondents is also illustrated (Q8). The interpretation of the weekday dummies and the time of the day variable is straightforward. For example, the first respondent prefers Thursdays and Sundays between 18:00 and 21:00. The second respondent prefers Fridays, Saturdays and Sundays between 18:00 and 21:00, and so forth.

	A	B	C	D	E	F	G
1	Respondent #	Gender	Age	Work Status	Zip Code	Income	Visit Frequency
2	1	1	41	4	1456	3	10
3	2	1	18	0	851	0	4
4	3	0	23	0	873	0	4
5	4	1	20	3	2618	1	12
6	5	0	24	3	2611	1	9
7	6	1	20	3	2838	2	10
8	7	1	20	4	2839	2	10
9	8	0	22	0	2624	NA	5
10	9	0	24	0	2624	0	2
11	10	0	30	2	2670	2	10

Figure 8.3 Example of how the data for the ten first respondents on the first six questions should be recorded in the spreadsheet.

	H	I	J	K	L	M	N	O	P
1	Monday	Tuesday	Wednesday	Thursday	Friday	Saturday	Sunday	All_days	timeOfDay
2	0	0	0	1	0	0	1	0	1
3	0	0	0	0	1	1	1	0	1
4	0	0	0	0	0	0	0	1	1
5	0	0	0	0	0	0	0	1	1
6	0	0	0	0	0	0	0	1	1
7	0	0	0	0	1	1	0	0	2
8	0	0	0	0	1	1	0	0	2
9	0	0	0	1	0	1	0	0	2
10	0	0	0	0	1	1	0	0	2
11	0	0	0	0	0	0	0	1	2

Figure 8.4 Example of how the weekday dummies and the variable on time of day for the ten first respondentsshould be recorded in the spreadsheet.

8.3 Step 3: Data preparation

When the data is collected and punched into a spreadsheet, you can start the process of preparing the data for further analyses. This process involves going carefully through the responses and, if needed, deleting or adjusting observations. Examples of observations that can be completely deleted from the data set are those with unrealistically high consumption levels for some or all price levels, and observations violating the basic downward-sloping property of the price–response function (i.e., observations with higher consumption levels for higher price levels and vice versa). In the Excel file containing the data of the case study, an IF(AND()) function is implemented to check the downward-sloping property. One way of controlling and adjusting for the stated consumption level is to calculate the ratio of the revealed consumption level of the service of interest today (Q6 in Figure 8.1) to the revealed consumption level at today's price level (Q10 of Figure 8.1) as follows:

$$\frac{D_{revealed_{p_t}}}{D_{actual_{p_t}}} \tag{8.1}$$

134 Case study

where D indicates the demanded quantity and p_t indicates today's prices of the service. If the ratio is above 1, it means that the respondent has overstated his or her consumption level at today's price level and vice versa. For example, if the respondent has indicated a total of five annual visits to the movie theater on Q6 in Figure 8.1 and the corresponding number on Q10 at today's price level is 10, the ratio would be 2, meaning that the respondent has overstated the consumption level by 100%. The revealed consumption levels could therefore be adjusted accordingly by dividing them with the calculated ratio as given in Equation (8.1) before using them in the main analyses. In some (rare) cases, the respondent either (1) reveals a demand of zero at today's price level, while the stated actual demand is different from zero, or (2) states an actual demand of zero and reveals a demand different from zero at today's price level. In both these cases the ratio calculated with the formula in Equation (8.1) will not make much sense. In the former case, the expression has no meaning. In the latter case the quantity we obtain will be zero, which also makes little sense to use in an adjustment. Such observations can be deleted from the data set as the respondent has failed to pass this simple "attention check." When going through the ratios of revealed demand to actual demand, we should also pay attention to large deviations from 1 and potentially remove these from the data set. In the data we use in the case study of this chapter, observations with a ratio of less than or equal to 0.3 and more than or equal to 4.0 were removed in the data preparation process (a total of 14 observations removed).

After cleaning the raw data following this and other steps mentioned above, the total number of observations we carry on to the next step of preliminary analysis is equal to 192.

8.4 Step 4: Preliminary analysis

Descriptive statistics

When we have a clean data set, we can start analyzing it. It is usually a good idea to start with some descriptive statistics to check that the sample matches the population on key characteristics. An efficient way of summarizing data is to use a PivotTable. You create this by highlighting the upper left cell of your data sheet (cell A1), then hit "Insert" and choose "PivotTable." In the interface for creating a PivotTable you just check that the data range is correct and hit "OK." These steps are illustrated in Figure 8.5.

When the PivotTable is created, we can drag the variables we are interested in from the list to the fields we are interested in. Let us look at some examples. First, we shall calculate the gender ratio. As females take the value 1 and males 0, we know that the average of the gender variable would represent the fraction of women in the sample. We can find this by checking the box next to the "Gender" variable or drag the variable down to the *Values* field directly. In the *Value field settings*, we choose *Average* and then hit "OK." The steps involved are depicted in Figure 8.6. The result of the calculations performed by the PivotTable appears in the upper left part of the spreadsheet (0.645, meaning that 64.5% of the respondents in the sample are females).

Assume now, that we would be interested in calculating the average movie interest for men and women, respectively. When we have a PivotTable available this is simple. We just drag the "Gender" variable to the *Rows* or *Columns* field and use the "MovieInterest"

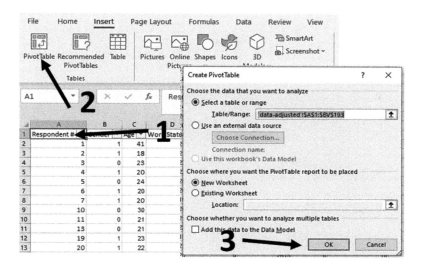

Figure 8.5 Illustration of how a PivotTable is created in Excel.

variable in the *Values* field. The setup and results of the calculations are illustrated in Figure 8.7. In a similar way, we could calculate the fraction of visitors who prefer to visit the movie theater on the various days of the week and at what times during the day. Additionally, the data table we need to estimate price–response functions later can be easily created in the same PivotTable.

We shall look at this soon, but first let us summarize the key characteristics of the sample in a table and compare it to the population of our customer base:

Summary statistics

	Mean	Std dev.
Gender	0.65	0.48
Age	27.45	10.56
Visit frequency	5.83	5.14

The summary statistics show that 65% of the respondents in the sample are female. There is no exact data on the fraction of male/female movie theater visitors in Norway, but the central statistical agency (SSB) collects information on the consumption of cultural events in general. These statistics show that women are generally overrepresented in traditional cultural events, while men to a greater extent go to sports events. The average age of 27.45 also matches the finding of SSB that young people in the age bracket 16–24 go to the movie theater more often compared with people in other age groups. The average visit frequency is also included in the table. We do not have exact numbers on the population's movie theater consumption, but in many cases such information is

136 Case study

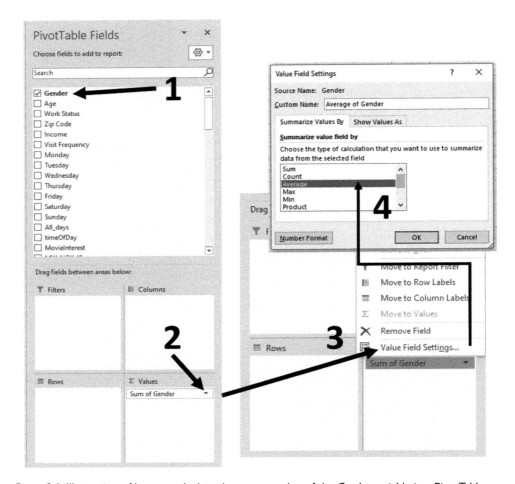

Figure 8.6 Illustration of how to calculate the average value of the *Gender* variable in a PivotTable.

available, and this number should then be compared with the actual consumption level as a general quality check of the data. The summary statistics presented here are not very thorough, but they should give you an idea of what to focus on in your own project. Next, we shall look at how some of the key variables can be visualized for easy interpretation by the decision-makers of your report.

Data visualization

Being able to efficiently visualize the key insights from your data is a skill that is becoming more and more important as the availability of (big) data increases rapidly and managers get busier and busier. The data used in the case study are not very complex or big, but it is still useful to present some of the key variables visually. One example of this is the variable on weekday preferences among movie theater visitors. If there

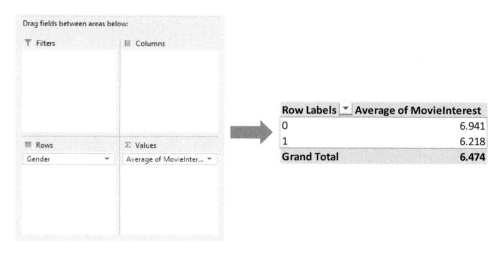

Figure 8.7 Illustration of how to calculate the average *Movie interest* by *Gender* in a PivotTable.

is a systematic (predictable) pattern in preferences across weekdays, this information can be used directly in the segmentation and price differentiation process. Figure 8.8 shows one way of illustrating these preferences by weekday (upper panel) and time of the day (lower panel). We clearly see in this figure that the weekend (Friday–Sunday) is more popular compared with the midweek days (Monday–Thursday). The figure also shows that 37.5% of movie theater visitors have no preference for a particular weekday. Moreover, the by far most preferred time period for going to the movies is between 18:00 and 21:00. Almost eight out of ten visitors prefer this time.

This figure, in combination with historical visitor or ticket purchase data, provides clear indications that variable pricing is applicable. The capacity of the movie theater is fixed and the preferences (and hence most likely, the demanded quantity) seem to vary with a very distinctive (predictable) pattern. In the next step we shall therefore estimate price–response functions for various subsets of the data we have.

8.5 Step 5: Estimation of price–response functions

To estimate price–response functions we need data on demanded quantity at various price levels. Again, the PivotTable is a very useful tool to get the data into the format we want. This time, the *Values* field should contain the demanded quantity at the various price levels. Remember that the values of the number of visits each visitor makes at the various price levels have been adjusted (using Equation (8.1)) to better match the stated actual number of visits (as given in Q6). We therefore use these adjusted revealed annual demanded quantities for the various price levels for both the midweek days and the weekend days. The setup of the PivotTable and the resulting calculations of demanded quantity for both the midweek period and weekend period are illustrated in Figure 8.9.

Next, the demanded quantity at each price level, for the various sub-periods, should be organized in a table and then depicted in a scatter plot. This will help us evaluate

138 Case study

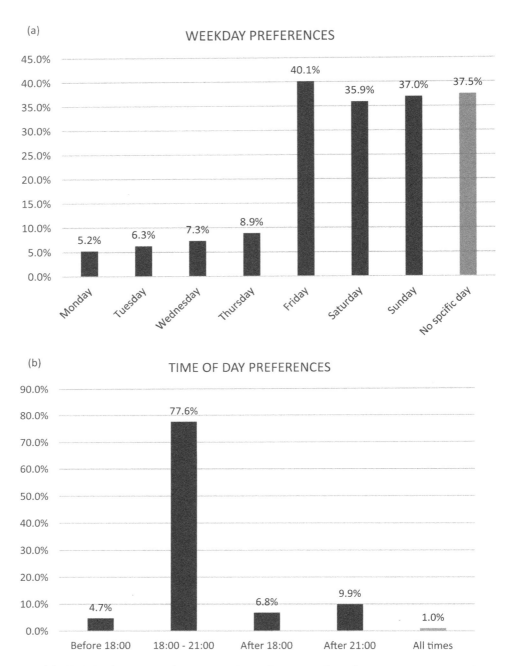

Figure 8.8 Weekday (upper panel) and time of day (lower panel) preferences among movie theater visitors.

Case study 139

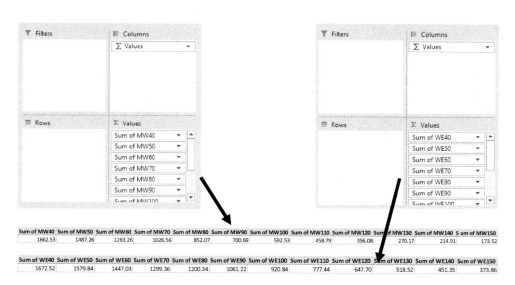

Figure 8.9 Setup of PivotTable to obtain the demanded quantity at the various price levels we need to estimate price–response functions.

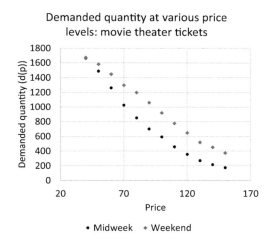

Figure 8.10 Price and corresponding demanded quantity as presented in a table (left panel) and a scatter plot (right panel)

what price–response function that may fit the data well. Figure 8.10 shows how this can be done. By examining the scatter plot, we can right away evaluate what price–response functions would fit the data. The weekend demand data seem to be fairly linear and a linear price–response function may be a good fit, at least in the relevant area of the curve. However, the midweek data exhibit a more non-linear shape, and the logit price–response function or the power price–response function would probably be better choices. To see how the various functional forms of the price–response functions fit the

140 Case study

actual data, we shall depict the various price–response functions together with the actual data when they have been estimated. We start with estimating the linear price–response function, followed by the logit price–response function.

Estimating linear price–response functions

The linear price–response function was introduced in Chapter 5 and an example of how to empirically estimate the parameters was given in Chapter 6. The linear price–response function can be expressed as:

$$d(p) = D + m \cdot p \tag{8.2}$$

The parameters to be estimated are the intercept (D) and the slope (m). To estimate these using Excel we can apply both the data analysis tool or the functions "=INTERCEPT" and "=SLOPE." In Chapter 6 the implementation using the data analysis tool was illustrated and we therefore now use the built-in functions to estimate the intercept and slope of the simple bivariate linear regression model. The "known_Ys" should refer to the cells where the dependent variable is listed. We want to model demanded quantity as a function of price. Hence, the column containing the demanded quantity is the "known_Ys" in our case. The "known_Xs" refers to the independent variable. In our case, this is the price. The setup in Excel with the correct implementation of the various functions and formulas to calculate the predicted values for both the midweek and weekend days, and an illustration of the corresponding predicted values are illustrated in Figure 8.11. The illustration of the predicted values (lower panel) show that the linear price–response function provides an OK fit to the weekend demand data, but for the midweek data it undershoots the actual demand for low price levels, overshoots for moderate prices (70–120) and then undershoots again for high prices. Additionally, the predicted demanded quantities using the linear price–response function become negative for prices above approximately NOK 150. As such, we should consider other price–response functions. We shall now examine the logit price–response function.

Estimating logit price–response functions

The logit price–response function was also introduced in Chapter 5 and examples of how to empirically estimate the parameters was given in Chapter 6. The functional form of this price–response function is given as:

$$d(p) = \frac{C \cdot e^{a+b \cdot p}}{1 + e^{a+b \cdot p}} \tag{8.3}$$

This formula should be implemented directly into the spreadsheet next to the actual, observed, demanded quantity for the periods of interest (midweek and weekend in our case). Then, a prespecified area in the same spreadsheet should contain the parameters to be estimated. In Chapter 6 we also devoted a column to calculate the squared deviations between the predicted and observed values. In the current example this is also done, and

Case study

	A	B	C	D	E
1		PRICE & DEMANDED QUANTITY		PREDICTED VALUES	
2	Price	Midweek	Weekend	Midweek	Weekend
3	40	1662.53018865721	1672.5227481816	=$B$19+$B$20*$A3	=$C$19+$C$20*$A3
4	50	1487.26031020144	1579.83676001331	=$B$19+$B$20*$A4	=$C$19+$C$20*$A4
5	60	1263.26044229771	1447.03087167295	=$B$19+$B$20*$A5	=$C$19+$C$20*$A5
6	70	1026.56459832409	1299.35630031282	=$B$19+$B$20*$A6	=$C$19+$C$20*$A6
7	80	852.071778457931	1200.3410176653	=$B$19+$B$20*$A7	=$C$19+$C$20*$A7
8	90	700.694713887912	1061.2213529637	=$B$19+$B$20*$A8	=$C$19+$C$20*$A8
9	100	592.525818600907	920.839138019999	=$B$19+$B$20*$A9	=$C$19+$C$20*$A9
10	110	458.785666511913	777.43771853111	=$B$19+$B$20*$A10	=$C$19+$C$20*$A10
11	120	356.076751315677	647.699863641299	=$B$19+$B$20*$A11	=$C$19+$C$20*$A11
12	130	270.171704425648	518.51666567863	=$B$19+$B$20*$A12	=$C$19+$C$20*$A12
13	140	214.905776348076	451.345785745425	=$B$19+$B$20*$A13	=$C$19+$C$20*$A13
14	150	173.524166856935	373.863396254447	=$B$19+$B$20*$A14	=$C$19+$C$20*$A14
15					
16					
17		LINEAR PRF - PARAMETERS			
18		Midweek	Weekend		
19	Intercepts	=INTERCEPT(B3:B14;A3:A14)	=INTERCEPT(C3:C14;A3:A14)		
20	Slopes	=SLOPE(B3:B14;A3:A14)	=SLOPE(C3:C14;A3:A14)		

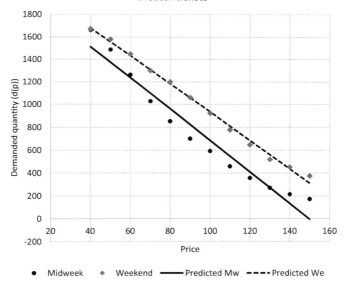

Figure 8.11 Implementation of the linear price–response function in Excel on the movie theater case data (upper panel) and the corresponding predicted values for both the midweek and weekend days (lower panel).

we shall use the sum of these as the objective functions when estimating the parameter values. The setup of the spreadsheet before the estimation starts is illustrated in the upper panel of Figure 8.12. In this spreadsheet the parameters to be estimated are given in the range B19:C21. In cells B22 and C22 the objective functions are defined.

142 Case study

	A	B	C	D	E	F	G
1	PRICE & DEMANDED QUANTITY			PREDICTED VALUES		RESIDUALS	
2	Price	Midweek	Weekend	Midweek	Weekend	Sq.Res MW	Sq.Res WE
3	40	1662.53018865	1672.52274818	=$B$19*EXP($B$20+$B$21*A3)/(1+EXP($B$20+$B$21*A3))	=$C$19*EXP($C$20+$C$21*A3)/(1+EXP($C$20+$C$21*A3))	=(B3-D3)^2	=(C3-E3)^2
4	50	1487.26031020	1579.83676001	=$B$19*EXP($B$20+$B$21*A4)/(1+EXP($B$20+$B$21*A4))	=$C$19*EXP($C$20+$C$21*A4)/(1+EXP($C$20+$C$21*A4))	=(B4-D4)^2	=(C4-E4)^2
5	60	1263.26044229	1447.03087167	=$B$19*EXP($B$20+$B$21*A5)/(1+EXP($B$20+$B$21*A5))	=$C$19*EXP($C$20+$C$21*A5)/(1+EXP($C$20+$C$21*A5))	=(B5-D5)^2	=(C5-E5)^2
6	70	1026.56459832	1299.35630031	=$B$19*EXP($B$20+$B$21*A6)/(1+EXP($B$20+$B$21*A6))	=$C$19*EXP($C$20+$C$21*A6)/(1+EXP($C$20+$C$21*A6))	=(B6-D6)^2	=(C6-E6)^2
7	80	852.071778457	1200.34101766	=$B$19*EXP($B$20+$B$21*A7)/(1+EXP($B$20+$B$21*A7))	=$C$19*EXP($C$20+$C$21*A7)/(1+EXP($C$20+$C$21*A7))	=(B7-D7)^2	=(C7-E7)^2
8	90	700.694713887	1061.22135296	=$B$19*EXP($B$20+$B$21*A8)/(1+EXP($B$20+$B$21*A8))	=$C$19*EXP($C$20+$C$21*A8)/(1+EXP($C$20+$C$21*A8))	=(B8-D8)^2	=(C8-E8)^2
9	100	592.525818600	920.839138019	=$B$19*EXP($B$20+$B$21*A9)/(1+EXP($B$20+$B$21*A9))	=$C$19*EXP($C$20+$C$21*A9)/(1+EXP($C$20+$C$21*A9))	=(B9-D9)^2	=(C9-E9)^2
10	110	458.785666511	777.437718531	=$B$19*EXP($B$20+$B$21*A10)/(1+EXP($B$20+$B$21*A10))	=$C$19*EXP($C$20+$C$21*A10)/(1+EXP($C$20+$C$21*A10))	=(B10-D10)^2	=(C10-E10)^2
11	120	356.076751315	647.699863641	=$B$19*EXP($B$20+$B$21*A11)/(1+EXP($B$20+$B$21*A11))	=$C$19*EXP($C$20+$C$21*A11)/(1+EXP($C$20+$C$21*A11))	=(B11-D11)^2	=(C11-E11)^2
12	130	270.171704425	518.516656786	=$B$19*EXP($B$20+$B$21*A12)/(1+EXP($B$20+$B$21*A12))	=$C$19*EXP($C$20+$C$21*A12)/(1+EXP($C$20+$C$21*A12))	=(B12-D12)^2	=(C12-E12)^2
13	140	214.905763484	451.345785745	=$B$19*EXP($B$20+$B$21*A13)/(1+EXP($B$20+$B$21*A13))	=$C$19*EXP($C$20+$C$21*A13)/(1+EXP($C$20+$C$21*A13))	=(B13-D13)^2	=(C13-E13)^2
14	150	173.524166856	373.863396254	=$B$19*EXP($B$20+$B$21*A14)/(1+EXP($B$20+$B$21*A14))	=$C$19*EXP($C$20+$C$21*A14)/(1+EXP($C$20+$C$21*A14))	=(B14-D14)^2	=(C14-E14)^2
15							
16							
17		LOGIT PRF					
18		Midweek	Weekend				
19	C	2000	2000				
20	a	4	3				
21	b	-0.05	-0.03				
22	SSR	=SUM(F3:F14)	=SUM(G3:G14)				

Figure 8.12 Setup of Excel spreadsheet before estimating the logit price–response function and the predicted values of the price–response functions (next page) given the starting values provided in the range B19:C21.

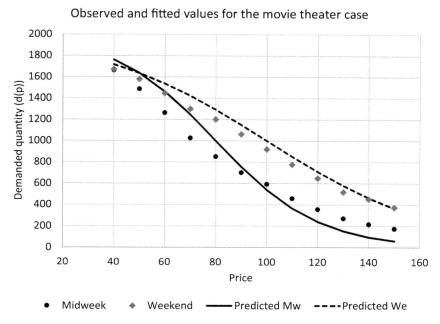

Figure 8.12 Cont.

As mentioned in Chapter 6, it is important that we provide Excel with good starting values before asking Excel's solver to help us optimize the parameter values (such that the sum of the squared deviations is minimized). Hence, we should plot the predicted values together with the observed values in the scatter plot and play around with all the parameters. After some trial and error, we ended up with the starting values as given in in the cell range B19:C21 in Figure 8.12. The corresponding shape of the price–response function using these starting values are illustrated in the lower panel. The next step then is simply to ask the solver to find the parameter values that minimize the sum of the squared deviations as provided in cells B22 and C22. The solver setup to estimate both the midweek and weekend price–response functions using the logit specification is illustrated in Figure 8.13 and the corresponding results are shown in Figure 8.14. Comparing Figure 8.14 with Figure 8.11, it is easy to see that the fit of the logit specification is substantially better than the linear price–response function. When moving to the next step of finding the profit-maximizing prices, we should therefore use the logit price–response function. In the Excel spreadsheet following this chapter, the power price–response function is also included for your benefit. However, the fit of the logit model is more than good enough for the current case and we do not have to test other functional forms. What we should do at this stage though is to consider what other criteria than *weekday* could be used to price-differentiate. We could, for example, separate the students from the general public and estimate price–response functions for both groups to estimate optimal differentiated prices in the next step. All the steps involved in doing this are identical to those involved when estimating separate price–response

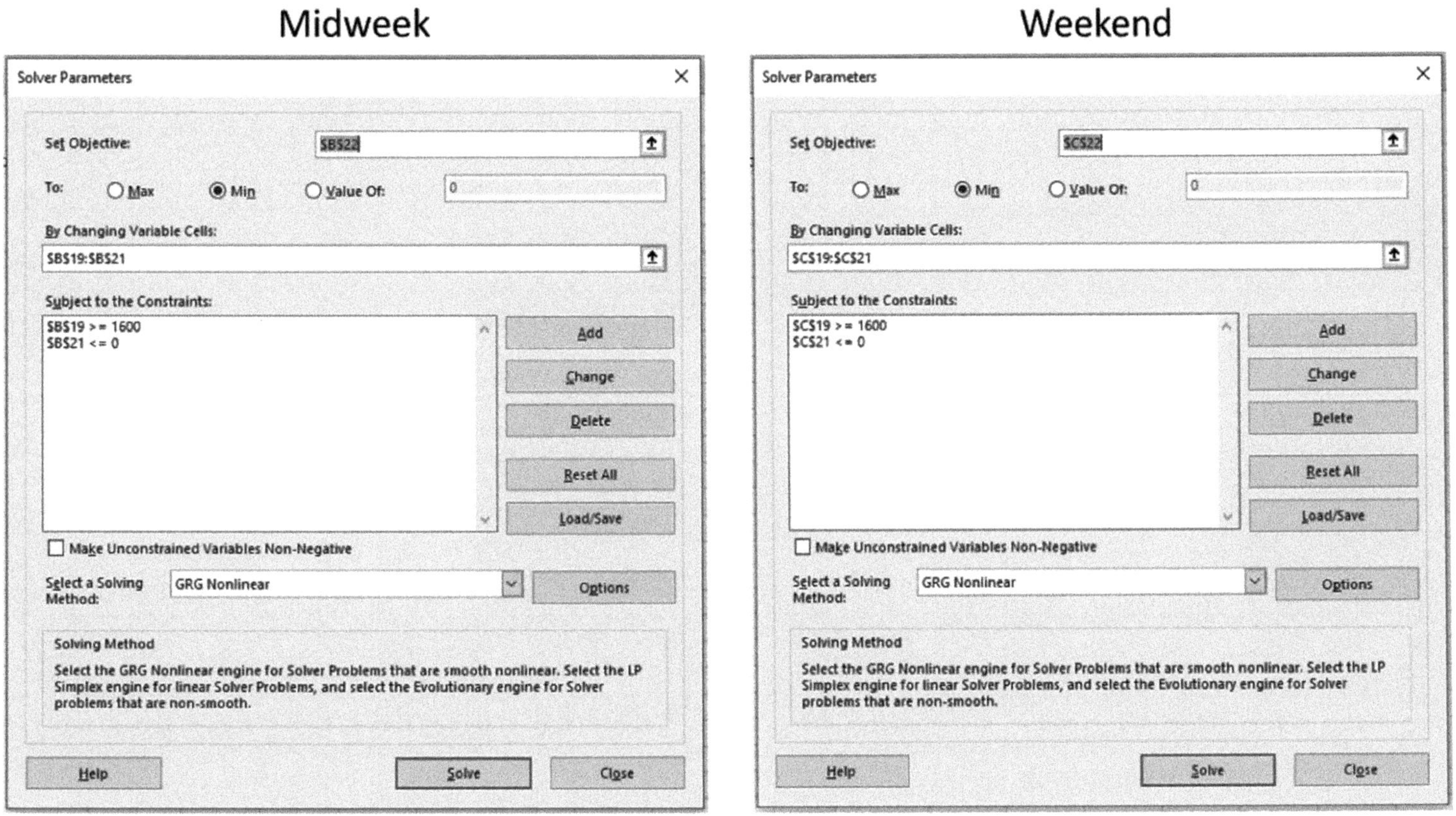

144 Case study

Figure 8.13 Setup of the estimation problem using Excel's solver. The setup to estimate the midweek price–response function is illustrated in the left panel and the weekend price–response function in the right panel.

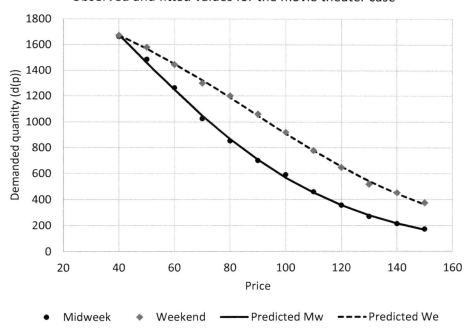

Figure 8.14 The estimated parameters of the logit price–response function for both the midweek and weekend period (upper panel) and the fitted and observed (actual) demanded quantity for movie theater tickets (lower panel).

functions for midweek and weekend days and we will therefore not go through it again here. In the Excel file following this chapter, an example of this is provided for you to follow when you work on your own project. There you will also find an example where the power price–response function is estimated.

	A	B	C	D
1		LOGIT PRF - PARAMETERS		
2		Midweek	Weekend	
3	c	3201.87688225832	2161.57373264241	
4	a	1.18312304418319	2.2657764917832	
5	b	-0.0271581425149206	-0.0258278319368835	
6				
7				
8		OPTIMIZATION MODEL 1: WITHOUT CAPACITY CONSTRAINTS		
9				
10		Midweek	Weekend	
11	d(p)	=$B$3*EXP($B$4+$B$5*B13)/(1+EXP($B$4+$B$5*B13))	=$C$3*EXP($C$4+$C$5*C13)/(1+EXP($C$4+$C$5*C13))	
12	vc	20	20	
13	price	100	100	
14				
15		Midweek	Weekend	Total
16	Total margin	=(B13*B11)-(B12*B11)	=(C13*C11)-(C12*C11)	=SUM(B16:C16)

Figure 8.15 An example of a setup for the optimization model in Excel. The decision variable is the price and is given in the cells B13/C13. The objective function is total profit (total margin) and is given in the cell D16.

8.6 Step 6: Optimize prices

Optimization without capacity constraints and no demand shifting

Once all the price–response functions are estimated, the next step is to calculate the optimal prices that maximize the total profit. To do this we must specify four things: (1) A cell containing the price–response function; (2) a cell containing the cost function; (3) a cell containing the decision variable, that is, the price; and (4) a cell containing the objective function, that is, the total profit. An example of a setup of the optimization model is illustrated in Figure 8.15. In the current case we assume variable unit costs per extra movie theater visitor to be NOK 20. In your own project you may have a very accurate cost function considering incremental fixed costs and potentially non-linear shapes of the variable unit costs. You then simply plug that function into the cells B29/C29 instead of the number 20. Make sure then that if this cost function depends on the demanded quantity, you must refer to the price–response function as defined in the cells B12/C12. The objective function that shall be maximized is defined in the cell D16 and the decision variables in the cells B13 and C13. An initial (random) value can be set here before the optimization just to make sure that the model is working as it should.

When you have set up the optimization model properly (for example, as done in Figure 8.15) we can ask Excel's solver to maximize the objective function (D16) by changing the prices (B13:C13). You do not have to add any constraints, but it is a good idea to check the box indicating that *unconstrained variables should be made non-negative*. The results of the optimization model reveal that the optimal midweek and weekend prices are NOK 73.26 and NOK 92.74, respectively. Compared with today's price level of NOK 115 this is a substantial price reduction. Yet, the modeled results indicate that the total profit could be improved by as much as 18.9% if implementing the calculated optimal prices. However, the present optimization model does not consider capacity constraints, nor demand shifting. We shall therefore update the model in the next step to incorporate this.

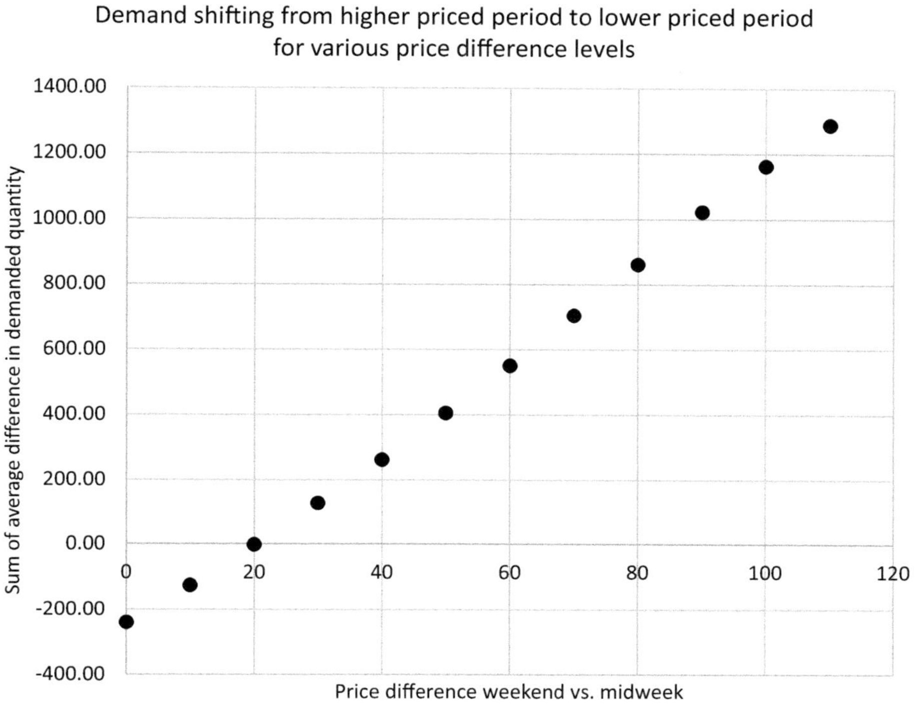

Demand shifting from higher priced period to lower priced period
for various price difference levels

Figure 8.16 Scatter plot of the sum of the average difference in demanded quantity across various price difference levels in the weekend versus the midweek period.

Optimization with capacity constraints and demand shifting

As movie theaters, just as most other service providers, have fixed capacity, we must modify the optimization model to take this into account. Additionally, we should also incorporate any information we may have on how a variable pricing scheme will induce demand shifting from the higher-priced period to the lower-priced period. In this section we incorporate these things and re-optimize the midweek and weekend prices.

As there is limited direct information about how many visitors will switch between weekend and midweek days for various price differences in these two periods, we must estimate it using the data we have. One approach could be to calculate each respondent's average difference in weekend visits versus midweek visits for all possible price differences (including zero). Then we could use this number to estimate the slope of a simple bivariate regression model where the price difference between the midweek and weekend period is the independent variable and the sum of each individual's (average) differences in demanded quantity at each price difference level is the dependent variable.[2]

These calculations, and the estimation of the slope of the bivariate regression model, are included in the Excel file following this chapter. A scatter plot illustrating the relationship between the price difference and demand shifting is provided in Figure 8.16. As seen from this plot, a linear regression line seems to fit these data well. The average

148 Case study

	A	B	C	H	I	J
1				Price Diff	Slope	Customers switching
2				=C28-B28	=SLOPE(F3:F14;E3:E14)	=I2*H2
		LOGIT PRF - PARAMETERS				
		Midweek	Weekend			
3	C	3201.8768225832	2161.5737326424			
4	a	1.18312304418319	2.26577649 17832			
5	b	-0.0271581425149206	-0.0258278319368835			
6						
7						
8						
9						
10						
11		OPTIMIZATION MODEL				
12						
13	DEMAND:	Midweek	Weekend			
14	d(p) - wo/diversion	=$B$3*EXP($B$4+$B$5*B27)/(1+EXP($B$4+$B$5*B27))	=$C$3*EXP($C$4+$C$5*C27)/(1+EXP($C$4+$C$5*C27))			
15	d(p) - base	=$B$3*EXP($B$4+$B$5*B28)/(1+EXP($B$4+$B$5*B28))	=$C$3*EXP($C$4+$C$5*C28)/(1+EXP($C$4+$C$5*C28))			
16	d(p) - real	=$B$3*EXP($B$4+$B$5*B28)/(1+EXP($B$4+$B$5*B28))+J2	=$C$3*EXP($C$4+$C$5*C28)/(1+EXP($C$4+$C$5*C28))-J2			
17	Demand shifting (diversion)	=B16-B15	=C16-C15			
18						
19	COSTS:	Midweek	Weekend			
20	cv	20	20			
21	cf	0	0			
22						
23	CONSTRAINTS:	Midweek	Weekend			
24	Capacity	1000	500			
25						
26	DECISION VARIABLES:	Midweek	Weekend			
27	Prices wo/diversion	73.2595659605839	134.22291143714			
28	Prices w/diversion	89.4651931 63585	109.46916590 0668			
29						
30	OBJECTIVE FUNCTIONS	Midweek	Weekend			Total
31	Profit wo/diversion	=B27*B14/(B14*B20)-B21	=C27*C14-(C20*C14)-C21			=SUM(B31:C31)
32	Profit w/diversion	=B28*B16/(B20*B16)-B21	=C28*C16-(C20*C16)-C21			=SUM(B32:C32)

Figure 8.17 An example of a setup for the constrained optimization model with demand shifting in Excel. The decision variable is the price and is given in the cells B27:C28. The objective function is total profit (total margin) and is given in the cells D31 (without demand shifting) and D32 (with demand shifting).

Case study 149

demand difference at a price difference of NOK 0 is approximately −240. This means that when there is no difference in the midweek and weekend price, the sum of the average demanded quantity is approximately 240 movie theater tickets higher for the weekend, compared with the midweek period. This finding also makes sense when comparing it to the price–response functions for the two sub-periods as provided in Figure 8.14. For the same price levels, the weekend demand is generally higher than the midweek demand. However, when the price difference between the two periods increases, the sum of the average difference in the demanded quantity also increases. For a price difference of NOK 20 the demanded quantity in the two periods is, on average, approximately the same. Beyond this price difference, the demanded quantity is, on average, higher in the midweek period compared with the weekend period. Having the data organized this way makes it easy for us to estimate the average demand shifting per NOK in price difference. This is simply the slope of a simple bivariate linear regression model and can be estimated using the "=SLOPE" function in Excel.

The estimated slope is equal to 14.25. This means that, on average, 14.25 visitors would switch from the weekend to the midweek per NOK increase in price difference between the two periods. If we now also incorporate information about the capacity constraints, the modified optimization model can be set up and solved. This is done in Figure 8.17 and an explanation of the process needed to obtain the solution will be described next.

Sub-step 6.1: Implement the functions for demand and demand shifting

We have already estimated the price–response functions (given in the range B3:C5) and the function yielding the number of customers shifting demand per NOK in price difference between the two sub-periods (given in cell I2). The first step when setting up the optimization model is to use this information to calculate the demanded quantity in the case of: (1) No diversion (given in the range B14:C14); (2) the so-called *base* demand, which is the number of potential visitors using the estimated price–response functions, if there were no capacity constraints or demand shifting (given in the range B15:C15); and (3) the *real* demand, which incorporates the total demand shifting for the price difference of the sub-periods (which is calculated in cell J2) and which is subject to the capacity constraints (given in the range B16:C16. The constraints are given in the range B24:C24).

Sub-step 6.2: Define the objective functions and the constraints

There is no change in the information about variable and fixed costs (given in the range B20:C21) and we can therefore move on to formulate the objective functions and the constraints. The objective functions are still the total profit from selling movie theater tickets and the decision variable is what prices will achieve this objective. We define objective functions both with and without demand shifting (but with capacity constraints in both cases) to show how it affects the profit. The objective function without demand shifting is given in cell D31 and the objective function with demand shifting is given in D32. The capacity constraints are entered in B24 (midweek capacity) and C24 (weekend capacity).

150 Case study

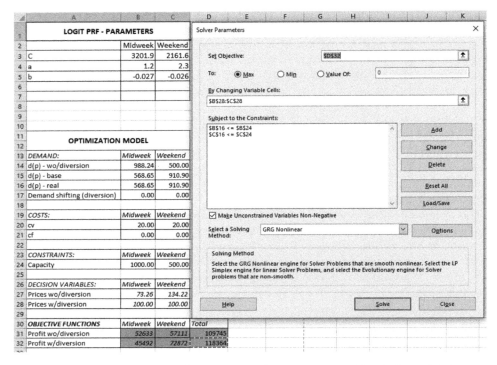

Figure 8.18 Illustration of the setup of the constrained optimization model with demand shifting using Excel's solver.

Sub-step 6.3: Optimize prices

When the previous steps have been implemented the final step is to ask Excel's solver to maximize the objective functions given the capacity constraints. We must focus on one objective function at the time. Figure 8.18 shows how the setup should look when optimizing the prices when also considering demand shifting. To get started we just plug in two random prices for the midweek and weekend periods (in Figure 8.18 a value of NOK 100 is given in cell B28:C28). Then, in the solver interface we define the correct objective function (cell D32) and indicate that it should be set to *Max* by changing the prices of the two sub-periods (that is, the decision variables given in the range B28:C28). The constraints are then entered: The real demanded quantity (given in B16:C16) must be less than or equal to the available capacity (given in B24:C24). Then the problem can be solved using the method *GRG non-linear*.

The results are illustrated in Figure 8.19 and indicate that the profit-maximizing prices for the two periods when considering both capacity constraints and demand shifting are NOK 89.47 for the midweek period and NOK 109.47 for the weekend period. At these prices a total of 285 movie theater tickets will shift from the weekend to the midweek. The optimal variable prices without demand shifting, but with capacity constraints, are NOK 73.26 for midweek and NOK 134.22 for the weekend. Hence, the range of the

	A	B	C	D
1	LOGIT PRF - PARAMETERS			
2		Midweek	Weekend	
3	C	3201.9	2161.6	
4	a	1.2	2.3	
5	b	-0.027	-0.026	
6				
7				
8				
9				
10				
11				
12	OPTIMIZATION MODEL			
13	DEMAND:	Midweek	Weekend	
14	d(p) - wo/diversion	988.24	500.00	
15	d(p) - base	714.95	785.05	
16	d(p) - real	1000.00	500.00	
17	Demand shifting (diversion)	285.05	-285.05	
18				
19	COSTS:	Midweek	Weekend	
20	cv	20.00	20.00	
21	cf	0.00	0.00	
22				
23	CONSTRAINTS:	Midweek	Weekend	
24	Capacity	1000.00	500.00	
25				
26	DECISION VARIABLES:	Midweek	Weekend	
27	Prices wo/diversion	73.26	134.22	
28	Prices w/diversion	89.47	109.47	
29				
30	OBJECTIVE FUNCTIONS	Midweek	Weekend	Total
31	Profit wo/diversion	52633	57111	109745
32	Profit w/diversion	69465	44735	114200

Figure 8.19 Illustration of the results of the constrained optimization model with demand shifting.

optimal sub-period prices becomes much narrower in the case of demand shifting. This is in accordance with our expectations. The more customers that choose to switch from the higher-priced period to the lower-priced period, the closer these two prices need to be for profit to be maximized.

8.7 Step 7: Implementation

When all the previous steps have been implemented, the only thing remaining is to set prices in accordance with the results of the optimization. The managers of the movie theater do not have to set the prices exactly as those provided by the model. The midweek price could for example be set to NOK 89 and the weekend price to 109. These prices are simpler than NOK 89.47 and NOK 109.47, and also incorporate the element of psychological pricing and the so-called left-digit anchoring effect (or digit-ending effect). This is a behavioral phenomenon suggesting that judgement of numerical differences is anchored on the left-most digit. In the current example it would mean that movie theater visitors would perceive the difference between NOK 100 and NOK 89 to be closer to 21 than to 11 and would therefore be perceived to be a much better deal compared to if the price was set to NOK 90.

Another possible approach would be to set so-called odd prices of NOK 89.99 or NOK 109.99. The reason why choosing such prices can be a good idea is because consumers tend to round them to the next lowest whole monetary unit. In this case, they would then tend to round the prices down to NOK 89 and NOK 109, respectively. We shall return to more examples of price presentation in Chapter 15.

When the variable pricing scheme has been implemented, the movie theater should monitor and evaluate the performance in accordance with the process described in Figure 1.5. New price/demand data will be available and can be compared with both the estimated demand level and the historical numbers. These data can also be used to update the model and solution and potentially adjust the prices accordingly. The point is that setting the right price is a continuous process that should be monitored and adjusted if needed.

8.8 Limitations and final notes

It is important to end this chapter with some warnings. First, demand for movie theater tickets depends on many other factors than just the day of the week. Examples include, but are not limited to:

- Type of movie.
- Quality of movie.
- Expert reviews.
- IMDB ratings.

Hence, if the movie theater would like to improve its models, one way of doing it could be to incorporate more variables (some of the above) when estimating expected demanded quantity for the various movies they show.

Seasonality on the intra-yearly level is also something that is likely to have an impact on the demand for movie theater tickets and the models can be adjusted to take this into account. Finally, the movie theater can consider price differentiation across other elements of the **PRO** cube. One obvious extension in this matter is to offer differentiated prices to students versus the general public and whether a ticket is purchased online or at the cash desk.

There may also be other limitations or opportunities than those mentioned here. In your own project you should therefore try to think of what opportunities you may have when building your optimization model. At the same time it is important that you are aware of the potential limitations.

8.9 Problems

1. Replicate all the all the analyses presented in this chapter using either (1) the case data following the chapter, or (2) data from your own project.

Notes

1 The KISS (Keep It Simple, Stupid) principle is a good starting point when designing the questionnaire.
2 Note that this is a somewhat tedious calculation as there are 11 unique price difference levels of NOK 10 (weekend NOK 50 – midweek NOK 40, weekend NOK 60 – midweek NOK 50, and so forth), ten unique price difference levels of NOK 20 (weekend NOK 60 – midweek NOK 40, weekend NOK 70 – midweek NOK 50, and so forth). In the Excel file following this chapter an array formula is used to calculate these numbers somewhat more efficiently. The array formula enables us to calculate average difference in demanded quantity at the various price difference levels in one operation (for each price level). To make this formula work we must use the keyboard keys *Ctrl+Shift+Enter* simultaneously, and not just *Enter* when completing it.

Chapter 9

Markdown optimization

When selling perishable goods, it may be necessary to carry out price reductions to move inventory. Finding the timing and magnitude of price reductions to maximize revenues are the key points of markdown optimization. In this chapter we shall focus on what markdown optimization is and how managers can formulate and solve such problems. Several examples on how to implement markdown optimization in Excel will also be presented.

The topics covered are:

- What is markdown optimization?
  - A two-period example.
- Formulating the markdown optimization problem.
- Implementation of markdown optimization in Excel.

9.1 What is markdown optimization?

Many items for sale today either have a specific expiry date (such as groceries) or a product life cycle shape that essentially leads demanded quantity to move towards zero after a certain time period (such as fashion goods). In such cases managers should make active pricing decisions to move inventory and make available the physical space in stores for the latest products or fresh goods.

Markdown optimization is all about finding the optimal timing and magnitude of price reductions for items with a limited time left of their remaining life. Both variable pricing and markdown optimization use the time dimension as a criterion to segment the market. However, an important distinction is that markdown optimization models assume that customers' willingness to pay is either constant or decreases over time. This leads to an important assumption of markdown optimization problems: once the price is reduced, it cannot be increased again. Variable pricing, on the other hand, aims to use price as a mechanism to exploit available capacity. This also typically involves price reductions, but only for limited time periods, and then the price is increased during periods of higher demand.

Figure 9.1 illustrates four price paths, of which two can be categorized as markdowns (can you guess which?). The upper left panel shows a situation where no active pricing decisions are made. The price is constant across all periods. The upper right panel illustrates a price path where the item is marked down by a fixed amount each period and never raised again. The lower left panel shows a price path where the item is marked

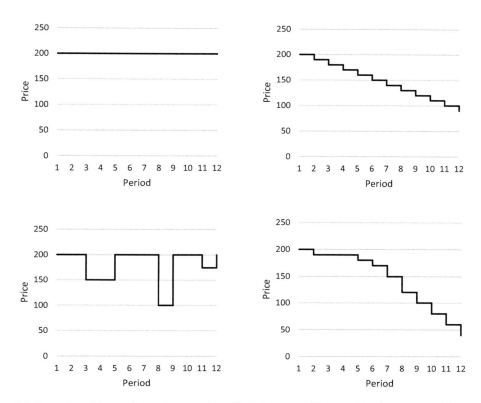

Figure 9.1 Examples of four price paths over time. Markdowns are illustrated in the upper and lower right panels.

down for a period and then marked up to the initial level. The lower right panel shows a markdown price path with random levels of both the markdown amount and the time period the markdown lasts. Formally speaking, only the upper and lower right panel illustrates markdowns. The lower left panel illustrates either a sales promotion or variable pricing, and *not* a markdown.

Phillips (2005) mention perishability, limited supply and constant or decreasing desirability of the item as required criteria for a markdown opportunity to be present. So, which businesses have items that fulfill these? Obviously, all grocery stores and outlets selling fashion goods meet the criteria. But markdowns are not reserved only for them. In fact, any business that has inventory with a certain expiry date or finite lifetime in general, can benefit from marking down remaining items before they reach their salvage value (which could be zero, or even negative – that is, you would have to pay to get rid of it). However, systematically using markdown as a tool in daily operations is mostly needed for businesses that deal in goods with a (relatively) short product life cycle. Two examples of such goods are illustrated in Figure 9.2. The product in the left panel has a longer season length compared with the product in the right panel. In both cases the sales volume reaches a peak and then starts to decline simply because the products are

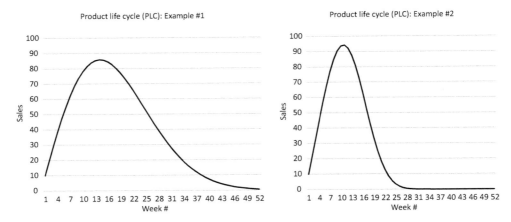

Figure 9.2 Two examples of product life cycles for products with a (relatively) short lifetime. The product in the left panel has a longer season compared with the product in the right panel.

less relevant and, as such, will have less value to consumers. It would make little sense to start marking down these items when the sales volume is increasing (from week 1 to 15, left panel, and from week 1 to 12, right panel). In this area of the product life cycle, customers' willingness to pay is probably increasing. However, from week 15 (left panel) and week 12 (right panel) and for the rest of the season, the desirability of the item is obviously decreasing, and a markdown opportunity is present. An example of an item with a product life cycle like that illustrated in the left panel of Figure 9.2 could be a new iPhone (very fast growing popularity when it arrives). The item in the right panel of Figure 9.2 could be snow shovels. This tool has a lot of value early in the winter season and then the desirability declines as spring arrives.

In many cases, simple rules of thumb are used to manage the markdowns. An example could be to mark down an item by 50%, if there is 50% of the starting inventory left and if the item's life goes into the final 20%. However, such rules of thumb are not guaranteed to maximize the revenues from the remaining items in inventory. This is the objective of markdown optimization: to maximize revenues by adjusting the discount levels dynamically. To get a better understanding of the concept we shall look at a simple two-period example next.

A two-period example

Figure 9.3 illustrates a situation where a seller faces the price–response function $d(p) = 250 - 5p$. The profit-maximizing single-period price can be found by using the techniques from previous chapters.

If we assume that the incremental costs associated with an extra sale are equal to zero,[1] we can simply calculate the marginal revenue and set it equal to zero, to find the optimal single-period price:

$$d(p) = 250 - 5p$$
$$Z = p(250 - 5p) = 250p - 5p^2$$

Markdown optimization 157

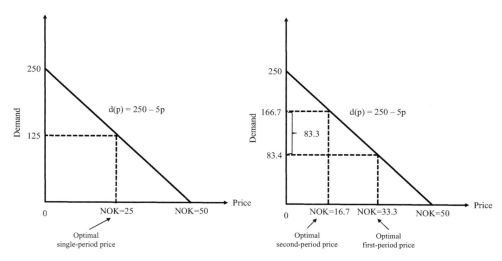

Figure 9.3 Example of optimal price and demand in the single-period (left panel) and two-period (right panel) cases. Adapted from Figure 10.3 in Phillips (2005, p. 245) by permission of the publisher, Stanford University Press.

The derivative of Z with respect to p is then:

$$Z'(p) = -10p + 250$$

Setting this equal to zero and solving for p yields:

$$p^* = \frac{250}{10} = 25$$

At this price, 125 units are sold (plug the optimal price into the price–response function) for a total profit of $Z = 25 \times 125 = 3{,}125$. However, it is apparent from Figure 9.3 that many buyers have a maximum willingness to pay of less than the optimal price of 25. As all buyers with a willingness to pay of NOK 25 or higher have already bought the product at the optimal single-period price, the only way to increase sales, and thus profit, is to reduce the price in the following periods. If splitting the total market into two time period "segments," the objective function can be defined as follows:

$$Z_{\text{Tot}} = Z_{\text{period}_1} + Z_{\text{period}_2}$$
$$Z_{Period_1} = p_1\left(d_1(p_1)\right)$$
$$Z_{Period_2} = p_2\left(d_2(p_2) - d_1(p_1)\right)$$

Plugging in the numbers from the price–response function (assuming identical price–response functions for the two periods), we get:

$$Z_{Tot} = p_1(250 - 5p_1) + p_2((250 - 5p_2) - 250 - 5p_1))$$
$$Z_{Tot} = 250p_1 - 5p_1^2 + 250p_2 - p_2^2 - 250p_2 + 5p_1p_2$$
$$= -5p_1^2 + 250p_1 - 5p_2^2 + 5p_1p_2$$

An expression for the optimal first-period price can then be found by setting the derivative of the profit function with respect to p_1 equal to zero:

$$\frac{\partial Z_{Tot}}{\partial p_1} = -10p_1 + 250 + 5p_2$$
$$\Rightarrow 10p_1 = 250 + 5p_2$$
$$\Rightarrow p_1 = 25 + \frac{1}{2}p_2$$

The expression for the second-period price is obtained in a similar way:

$$\frac{\partial Z_{Tot}}{\partial p_2} = -10p_2 + 5p_1$$
$$\Rightarrow 10p_2 = 5p_1$$
$$\Rightarrow p_2 = \frac{1}{2}p_1$$

We now have two equations with two unknowns and can calculate the optimal price for both periods:

$$p_1 = 25 + \frac{1}{2}p_2$$

inserting the for p_2:

$$p_1 = 25 + \frac{1}{2}\left(\frac{1}{2}p_1\right) = 25 + \frac{1}{4}p_1$$
$$\Rightarrow p_1 - \frac{1}{4}p_1 = 25$$
$$\Rightarrow \frac{3}{4}p_1 = 25$$
$$\Rightarrow p_1 = \frac{25}{\frac{3}{4}} = 33.33$$
$$p_2 = \frac{1}{2}p_1 = \frac{1}{2} \times 33.33 = 16.67$$

Table 9.1 The results of the price optimization using single versus multiple-period pricing

# of periods	Total profit	%-change from single period
1	3,125.0	0.0%
2	4,166.7	33.3%
3	4,687.5	50.0%
4	5,000.0	60.0%
5	5,208.3	66.7%

Note: The results are based on the assumptions of a single linear price–response function $(d(p)250 - 5p)$ and based on the other assumptions given in the text.

Table 9.2 The results of the price optimization when there is cannibalization between the periods

Cannibalization fraction	First-period price	Second-period price	Total revenue	%-change in revenue
0	33.3	16.7	4,166.7	0.0%
20%	34.4	18.7	3,906.2	-6.3%
40%	35.3	20.6	3,676.5	-11.8%
60%	36.1	22.2	3,472.2	-16.7%
80%	36.8	23.7	3,289.5	-21.1%
100%	36.8	25.0	3,125.0	-25.0%

Source: Adapted from Phillips (2005, p. 247).

Plugging the optimal price in the first period, p_1, into the price–response function for this period, we obtain an optimal quantity sold of 83.3. To find the corresponding optimal quantity sold for period two, we first calculate the total quantity that would have been sold using the optimal second-period price, $250 - 5 \times 16.67 = 166.6$. However, those who have already purchased the product (willingness to pay > 33.33) will not buy it again. The quantity sold in the second period will therefore be $d_2(p_2) - d_1(p_1) = 166.6 - 83.3 = 83.3$ units, leading to a total profit for the two periods of $33.33 \times 83.3 + 16.67 \times 83.3 = 4165$, an increase of more than 33% compared to the single-period pricing approach.

By segmenting the market into more periods, we can increase the profit further. Table 9.1 shows the results of the optimization problem by using from one to five separate time periods. The numbers speak for themselves. By increasing the number of separate periods for which you offer a unique discounted price, the total profit also increases, although at a slower and slower pace.

It is important to note, however, that the solutions we have obtained thus far is based on some assumptions, which is unrealistic in real life. First, they assume that no customers expect a second period (or third period, fourth period, etc.) markdown to occur. If some customers expect later period markdowns, it is reasonable to assume that at least some of them would wait to get the item at a discounted price. This phenomenon leads to cannibalization as customers who wait have a willingness to pay high enough to buy the item at the early periods' prices but refuse to do so as they expect a price reduction later. This effect can be directly implemented in the model. By adjusting the demand $(d(p))$ in the first period(s) according to the cannibalization fraction, and hence moving these customers over to the lower-priced later period(s), we can recalculate the optimal prices. For the same example as used above, the new optimal first and second-period prices are presented in Table 9.2 for various cannibalization fractions.

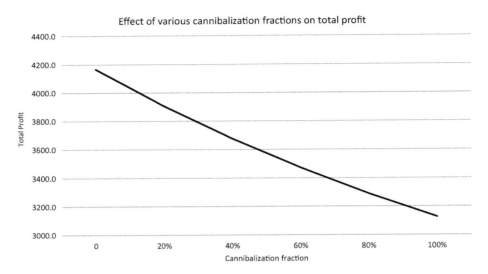

Figure 9.4 Illustration of cannibalization effect on total profit.

The effect of cannibalization on the total revenue is also presented in Figure 9.4. Clearly, when the cannibalization fraction goes up, the total profit from the two-period pricing approach goes down. In the most extreme case, when all customers wait for the lower price, the total profit equals that obtained from the single-period optimization problem (NOK 3,125) with the same single-period optimal price (NOK 25). However, you may notice that for all cannibalization fractions below 100%, the total profit is higher in the two-period pricing approach compared with charging one single price.

Another assumption of the simple two-period model presented above is that the total pool of customers is indifferent between having the item right away and waiting. Put differently, we assume that time does not affect the shape of the price–response function. This is not realistic in real life as we know that at least some customers are willing to pay a higher price to have the item of interest right away. The value of having short-life items right away is also indirectly illustrated in the shape of the product life cycle curves in Figure 9.2. We shall relax this assumption when we move forward to formulating and solving the markdown optimization problem in the next two sections.

9.2 Formulating the markdown optimization problem

Figure 9.5 illustrates how the outcome of a markdown optimization problem may look in practice. In this figure, we have an initial inventory level of x_1 units that are sold at the initial list price of p_1. During the first period a total of $x_1 - x_2$ units are sold at this price (p_1). In period two the price is reduced from p_1 to p_2 and $x_2 - x_3$ additional units are sold, and so forth. The price–response functions corresponding to the various periods are denoted with the number at the beginning of the period of interest. Hence, $d_1(p_1)$ is the demand/sales in period one, which amounts to $x_1 - x_2$ units. Similarly, $d_T(p_T)$ is the demand/sales in the last period. If using the same notation as before, this is the demand/sales between T and $T+1$. In period $T+1$, y is the number of units which are left

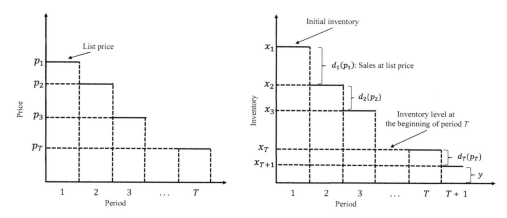

Figure 9.5 Development of price and inventory levels in the case of a markdown optimization problem. Adapted from Phillips (2005, Figure 10.4, p. 251) by permission of the publisher, Stanford University Press.

unsold after the last markdown and is sold at a given salvage value (r) for the product or service of interest. For many service items, the salvage value is zero as the service take place at specific time points and have no value after this (i.e., movie theater tickets, tour operators, concerts, etc.).

The figure indirectly also shows the assumptions markdown optimization models build upon. First, the price of the item sold is initially at list price and can only be reduced over the remaining lifetime. Second, the item cannot be reordered and the inventory/capacity level is therefore declining (or at the same level in the case of no sales) over time. Third, the inventory/capacity has a fixed expiry date. After this date, unsold items or capacity are either sold at a small salvage value or must be removed from the inventory. The latter could also involve disposal costs.

The markdown optimization problem illustrated in Figure 9.5 can be formulated mathematically as follows:

$$\max_{p_1, p_2, \ldots, p_T} Z = \sum_{i=1}^{T} p_i d_i(p_i) + ry$$

s.t. \hfill (9.1)

Restriction #1: $\sum_{i=1}^{T} d_i(p_i) \leq x_1$

Restriction #2: $p_i \leq p_{i-1}$ for $i = 1, 2, \ldots, T$

Restriction #3: $p_T \geq r$

Equation (9.1) states that the objective is to maximize the total revenue ($p_i d_i(p_i)$) over the remaining lifetime plus (if any) the total salvage value (ry) of the product/service of interest.

162　Markdown optimization

In addition, all the assumptions of markdown optimization as mentioned earlier are accounted for in the restrictions. The first constraint simply tells us that we cannot sell more than we have on inventory at the beginning of the first period. This is related to the assumption that it is not possible to reorder the item. The second constraint takes care of the assumption that only price reductions are allowed. The price in this period must be equal to or lower than the price in the previous period. The third and final constraint says that the price in the final period must be equal to or greater than the salvage value.

In the next section we shall examine how we can translate the markdown optimization problem presented in Equation (9.1) into a solvable problem in Excel.

9.3　Implementation of markdown optimization in Excel

Solving the deterministic markdown management model in Excel

Assume that we have an item that satisfies the assumption provided in the previous section. Assume further that we have very good estimates of how the demanded quantity for this item behaves over time for various price levels. These estimates are reflected in distinct price–response functions for the various phases of the remaining life of the item and are given in Table 9.3, together with information about the initial stock and salvage value (r) per unit left unsold at the end of the last period. This information is also provided in Example 9.6 in the Excel file following this chapter.

To solve this problem in Excel we need to carefully prepare the spreadsheet with all the relevant functions. An overview of the key features when setting up the spreadsheet is provided in Figure 9.6 and a detailed illustration of all the relevant functions needed to solve the problem can be found in Figure 9.7 and the Excel file following this chapter. We shall go through the various steps in detail next.

Step 1: Set starting values of the decision variables

The decision variables are the price levels in the various sub-periods and shall be included in the range B19:B22. These values can be set to just a random number at this stage. When we solve the problem later, Excel will give us the price levels that maximizes the objective function. Note that the price in cell B23 is the salvage value given in cell B11.

Table 9.3　Estimates of price–response functions for the various remaining periods of the items lifetime (upper section) and information about the initial stock level and the salvage value (lower section)

Period	d(p)	Constant	Slope	d(p)
1	d1(p1)	200	-2	200-2p
2	d2(p2)	150	-2	150-2p
3	d3(p3)	100	-2	100-2p
4	d4(p4)	50	-4	50-4p
Initial stock	400			
r	10			

Markdown optimization 163

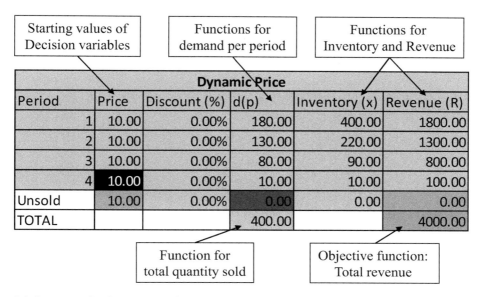

Figure 9.6 Setting up the dynamic markdown optimization problem in Excel.

Step 2: Implement the function for demanded quantity per period

The demanded quantity for the various sub-periods in the markdown problem is given by the price–response functions. We use the VLOOKUP function to make sure we use the correct price–response functions for each of the sub-periods. However, we must make sure that demanded quantity for each period is nonnegative. In Excel, we ensure this by simply using a MAX function (max of the demanded quantity for the given price and zero). The complete function combining VLOOKUP and MAX is implemented in the range D19:D22 in Figure 9.7.

Step 3: Implement the functions inventory levels and revenues for all the periods

The inventory level for the first period is set to the initial stock level given in cell B10. The inventory level for the subsequent periods is calculated by simply taking the inventory level in the previous period and subtracting the demanded quantity of the previous period. The functions for calculating inventory levels for the various periods are implemented in the range E19:E23. The calculation of revenues for each period is straightforward: *price × demanded quantity*. These calculations are implemented in the range F19:F23.

Step 4: Formulate the objective function

The objective function is the total revenues stemming from the sales of the remaining inventory. This consists of the regular sales in each of the four periods and the salvage value of the items left unsold at the end of the last period. Note that revenue and gross

164 Markdown optimization

	A	B	C	D	E	F
1				DYNAMIC PRICING		
2						
3						
4	Period	d(p)	Constant	slope	d(p)	
5	1	d1(p1)	200	-2	=CONCAT(C5;D5)&"p"	
6	2	d2(p2)	150	-2	=CONCAT(C6;D6)&"p"	
7	3	d3(p3)	100	-2	=CONCAT(C7;D7)&"p"	
8	4	d4(p4)	50	-4	=CONCAT(C8;D8)&"p"	
9						
10	Initial stock	400				
11	r	10				
12						
13	Profit with static price:			10337.5		
14	Difference:			=F24-D13		
15	%-change in profit:			=D14/D13		
16						
17				Dynamic Price		
18	Period	Price	Discount (%)	d(p)	Inventory (x)	Revenue (R)
19	1	10	=($B$19-B19)/$B$19	=MAX(VLOOKUP(A19;$A$5:$D$8;3;FALSE)+VLOOKUP(A19;$A$5:$D$8;4;FALSE)*B19;0)	=B10	=B19*D19
20	2	10	=($B$19-B20)/$B$19	=MAX(VLOOKUP(A20;$A$5:$D$8;3;FALSE)+VLOOKUP(A20;$A$5:$D$8;4;FALSE)*B20;0)	=E19-D19	=B20*D20
21	3	10	=($B$19-B21)/$B$19	=MAX(VLOOKUP(A21;$A$5:$D$8;3;FALSE)+VLOOKUP(A21;$A$5:$D$8;4;FALSE)*B21;0)	=E20-D20	=B21*D21
22	4	10	=($B$19-B22)/$B$19	=MAX(0;VLOOKUP(A22;$A$5:$D$8;3;FALSE)+VLOOKUP(A22;$A$5:$D$8;4;FALSE)*B22)	=E21-D21	=B22*D22
23	Unsold	=B11	=($B$19-B23)/$B$19	=B10-SUM(D19:D22)	=E22-D22	=B23*E23
24	TOTAL			=SUM(D19:D22)		=SUM(F19:F23)

Figure 9.7 Detailed illustration of functions used to set up the dynamic markdown optimization problem in Excel.

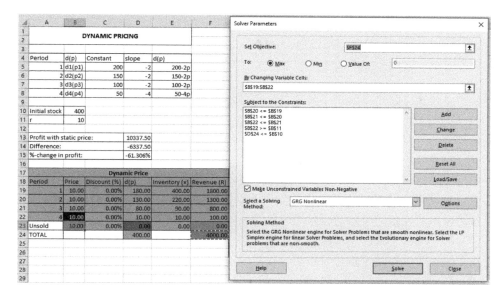

Figure 9.8 Setting up the problem correctly in Excel's Solver.

margin are equivalent when the merchant already owns the inventory of the item, in which case the inventory cost is sunk. We calculate the sum of all the revenues in cell F24.

Step 5: Define the problem in Solver

When the spreadsheet is set up with all the relevant functions, the problem can be defined in Solver. Figure 9.8 provides a detailed description of this.

Step 6: Solve the problem and analyze the results

Once you hit Solve, Excel will do exactly that: solve the problem. The objective is to maximize the total revenues (cell F24) by changing the price levels of the various periods (range B19:B22). The results of the optimization model are illustrated in Figure 9.9.

The results of the optimization model show that the initial (list) price for period one should be set to $55. For period two a price of $42.50 (discount of 22.73%) is suggested. For period three the profit-maximizing price is $30 and the fourth period price should be set to only $11.25 (corresponding to a discount of almost 80%). If following these suggestions, the total sales over the four periods amount to 200 units, leaving 200 units unsold (to regular customers), but that still will induce a revenue of $2,000 (the salvage value of $10/unit times the number of units left unsold). The total revenues from the dynamic markdown as presented in this analysis are $10,969. This is an increase of more than 6% compared with the static pricing approach using the profit-maximizing single price of $42.50 for all four periods.

A so-called step chart is a nice way of illustrating the markdown policy and the inventory development over time. To create this type of chart in Excel the data must be

166 Markdown optimization

	A	B	C	D	E	F
13	Profit with static price:			10337.50		
14	Difference:			631.25		
15	%-change in profit:			6.106%		
16						
17			Dynamic Price			
18	Period	Price	Discount (%)	d(p)	Inventory (x)	Revenue (R)
19	1	55.00	0.00%	90.00	400.00	4950.00
20	2	42.50	22.73%	65.00	310.00	2762.50
21	3	30.00	45.45%	40.00	245.00	1200.00
22	4	11.25	79.55%	5.00	205.00	56.25
23	Unsold	10.00	81.82%	200.00	200.00	2000.00
24	TOTAL			200.00		10968.75

Figure 9.9 The results of the optimization.

organized in a certain way. The left panel of Figure 9.10 shows one approach to doing this. The key is that the time-variable (period number in column G in our case) must be repeated two times. The corresponding price and inventory values should also be repeated. The first time these values are set they should indicate the values corresponding to the previous period. For example, the price in period one is $55 and the inventory level is at 400. These values are then also used as starting values for period two. When these values are repeated further down (on row 23:26) the correct price/inventory levels should be used for each period number. When the step chart is created, the values of the variables of interest should contain the whole range (from row 19:26) and the X-axis label must be the whole range containing the period number. It is also crucial that the format of this X-axis label is *date*. The result is depicted in the right panel of Figure 9.10 and also included in the Excel file following this chapter.

	G	H	I	J	K
17			Number for Figure: Dynamic		
18	Period	Price	sales	Inventory	Revenue
19	1	55.00	90.00	400.00	4950.00
20	2	55.00	90.00	400.00	4950.00
21	3	42.50	65.00	310.00	2762.50
22	4	30.00	40.00	245.00	1200.00
23	1	55.00	90.00	400.00	4950.00
24	2	42.50	65.00	310.00	2762.50
25	3	30.00	40.00	245.00	1200.00
26	4	11.25	5.00	205.00	56.25

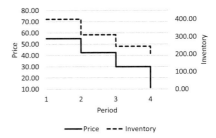

Figure 9.10 Data organization to create step chart in Excel

9.4 Summary

- Markdown optimization is about finding the optimal timing and magnitude of price reductions for items with a limited time left of its remaining life.

- Markdown optimization differs from variable pricing as it assumes that customers' willingness to pay is either constant or decreases over time.
- Only price reductions are allowed in markdown optimization.
- By segmenting the market into several time periods, the firm can increase profit substantially.
- Markdown optimization models must consider the fraction of customers that wait for the sales. This cannibalization effect can be implemented directly in the model.
- The markdown optimization problem is about maximizing the total revenues from regular sales in-store over the remaining lifetime, plus the salvage value, by adjusting the price levels for the various periods. The restrictions are that we do not sell more than what is in the inventory in the beginning of the period (not possible to reorder), that the price in the current period must be the same as, or lower than, the price in the previous period, and that the price in the final period must be higher than or equal to the salvage value.
- By following some distinct steps, the markdown optimization problem can be easily solved in Excel.

9.5 Problems

1. What is markdown optimization and how does it differ from variable pricing?
2. Consider the charts below. Which of these illustrate a markdown? Explain.

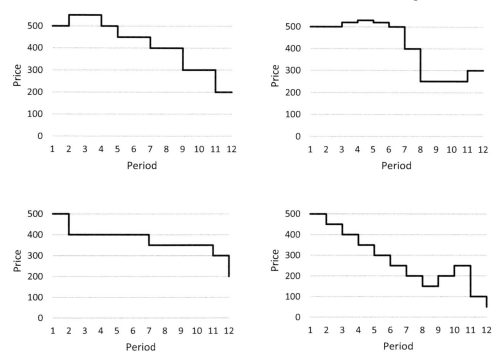

3. Create the step charts illustrated in problem 2 in Excel.

4. What can you say about the sales level and season length of the products below, based on an illustration of their product life cycles?

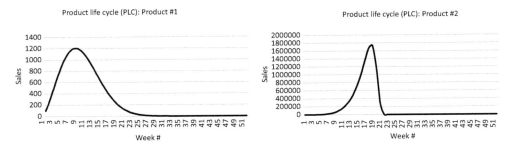

5. Play around with the various shapes of product life cycles and discuss what products or product categories each shape could be in real life.
6. Consider a firm selling swimming shorts. The price–response function can be described by $d(p) = 10,000 - 100p$. Calculate the optimal two-period prices in the cases of no cannibalization, 20% cannibalization, 40% cannibalization, 60% cannibalization, 80% cannibalization and 100% cannibalization. Depict the total profit as a function of the cannibalization fraction. What insight do you get from this?
7. The firm in problem 6 decides to evaluate the possibility to introduce multi-period pricing for its swimming shorts. Calculate the optimal multi-period prices when using two, three, four and five periods. Illustrate how the total profit varies with the number of periods used.
8. Another firm selling a widget with seasonal demand is facing the following price–response functions for the remaining four periods of the widget's season:

Period	d(p)
1	4,000-30p
2	3,000-35p
3	2,000-40p
4	1,800-60p

The salvage value of unsold units at the end of period four is $15. What is the optimal static price for this widget (i.e., the optimal constant price for all four periods)?

9. Use the information from problem 8. What are the optimal dynamic prices of this widget? How much is the total profit improved if dynamically adjusting the price instead of using the static price?

Note

1 In markdown, management revenue and gross margin dollars are often considered equivalent because the inventory cost is considered sunk once the seller owns the items (see e.g., Ramakrishnan 2012).

Chapter 10

The hedonic pricing model

This chapter will introduce you to hedonic price theory, examples of relevant areas where the method has been applied and how we can empirically estimate hedonic pricing models using Excel. In particular the chapter will focus on:

- What is price hedonism?
- The model specification.
- Applications of hedonic pricing:
  - Examples;
  - Step-by-step implementation in Excel.

10.1 What is price hedonism?

The traditional approach of consumer theory was that the product itself was the direct object of utility. Lancaster (1966) introduced a new approach to this theory where the utility of goods is determined by the properties, or characteristics, they consist of. In this seminal paper, he summarized the essence of the approach as follows: (Lancaster, 1966, p. 134):

- *The good, per se, does not give utility to the consumers; it possesses characteristics, and these characteristics give rise to utility.*
- *In general, a good will possess more than one characteristic, and many characteristics will be shared by more than one good.*
- *Goods in combination may possess characteristics different from those pertaining to the goods separately.*

As the most applied measure of utility is money, the theory implicitly states that the price of a product can be viewed as a function of the attributes (characteristics) it consists of. Lancaster thus provides a general model framework that can be used to analyze what contributes to the overall price of a wide range of goods and services. That is, the model framework is not product or problem-specific. We shall return to empirical examples from various products and industries shortly but let us first look at how the model can be defined in a formal manner.

10.2 The model specification

The general specification of the hedonic pricing model assumes that the prices consumers pay for products (or services) are a function of their intrinsic characteristics (Rosen, 1974). The general specification of the model can be presented as:

$$P = f(X_i) \tag{10.1}$$

where P is the price of a good or service and X_i is a vector of various attributes/characteristics of the product/service of interest. Regression analysis is particularly useful when it comes to analyzing variation in one (dependent) variable as a function of other (independent) variables. Hence, in most empirical applications, the hedonic pricing model is analyzed using some sort of econometric specifications. In a general manner, such models can be presented like this:

$$P = \alpha + \sum_{i=1}^{n} \beta_i X_i \tag{10.2}$$

where P is, as before, the price of a specific product, α and the βs are parameters to be estimated (usually by ordinary least squares), and the Xs are characteristics of the product. Hence, the aim in such analysis is to explain variation in the price by the various characteristics of the product/service itself. The concept is illustrated in Figure 10.1. The idea here is that hotel rooms vary in price depending on several characteristics. In the figure a few such attributes that may influence the price are depicted. For example, does the hotel room have a minibar? What is the quality of the restaurant at the hotel? Does the hotel room have a balcony? If yes, what is the size of the balcony? Does the balcony

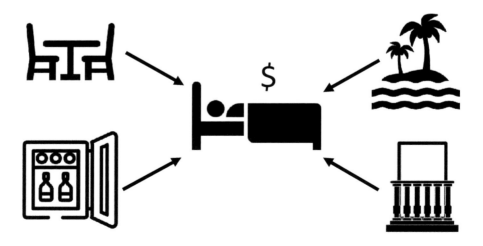

Figure 10.1 Illustration of how a hedonic price model works in the case of hotel room prices.

have an ocean view? What is the distance to the beach from the hotel? What is the distance to the city center?

All these factors may influence the price of a given hotel room. Additionally, non-product-specific factors can also influence the price. Examples of this could be time-of-year, or day-of-week effects. This is particularly true when explaining variation in hotel room prices. The same room can have very different prices depending on the seasonality.

10.3 Empirical applications of hedonic pricing

There are many empirical applications of hedonic pricing, but here we will focus on a select few to familiarize the reader on their use in applied research. We start with applications to real estate pricing where most of the contributions lie. Mok et al. (1995) estimated a hedonic price model for private properties in Hong Kong. They modeled property prices as a function of three kinds of variables: locational variables such as distance from the central business district (CBD), and the floor where an apartment is located; structural variables such as size of the apartment in square feet, and age of the apartment in years; and neighborhood variables such as whether the apartment is located in a school zone, and proximity to a sporting facility. They found that property prices in Hong Kong are sensitive to the specified locational, structural, and neighborhood attributes, with age of the property, distance from the CBD, and the floor where the apartment is located having the largest impacts. Their results provide evidence that buyers are willing to pay more for desirable housing attributes. Factors that affect property prices have also been shown to be important in explaining rental prices. Dunse and Jones (1998) estimated a hedonic price model of office rents in the city of Glasgow in the UK. They specified locational and physical attributes of the commercial properties as determinants of rental prices for the properties, finding that these explained up to 60% of variation in rents across the city. As in the previous study, age and location emerged as the principal determinants of the rental prices.

Apart from identifying the effects of housing attributes on property prices, the hedonic pricing model has also been used to resolve some not so obvious puzzles. Tomkins et al. (1998) sought to find out whether living close to an airport is desirable. On the one hand, residents have easy access to air transport as well as the infrastructure supporting the airport's activities. On the other hand, there is a lot of noise pollution from the airplanes taking off and landing, and there may be a lot of traffic on the roads around the airport. It is not *a priori* evident whether the former outweighs the latter. Tomkins et al. found that the trade-off is in favor of living close to the airport, with a standard property closer to the airport being significantly pricier than one that is farther away. In the U.S.A., hedonic price models that include socioeconomic status and race have been used to investigate whether these variables have an impact on property prices. Richardson et al. (1974) and Ketkar (1992), respectively, found that the lower the social class of the neighborhood and a higher proportion of non-white residents have a negative effect on property prices. However, these results may be subject to omitted variable bias because, on average, non-white residents and lower social class neighborhoods are poorer, according to Gradin (2012), and this may be the determining factor if not controlled for.

Beyond housing prices, hedonic pricing models have been used in the automobile industry. Griliches (1961) specified a hedonic price model to analyze the price–quality relationship of US passenger four-door sedans for the years 1937, 1950 and 1954–1960. He found that a limited number of automobile attributes, including horsepower, weight, length, and the presence of a V-8 engine, explained a very large fraction of the variation of car prices. Combris et al. (1997) specified a hedonic price model of wine from the south-west of France. Their model included both the objective characteristics of the wine, that is, those appearing on the label of the bottle, and the sensory characteristics of the wine. They found that the price of wine is essentially determined by the objective characteristics. Other empirical applications of hedonic pricing can be found in, among others, art, travel and leisure, and the food and hospitality industries. In the Excel file following this chapter you will have access to five unique data sets. These are cognac prices, hotel room prices, apartment prices, motorhome prices and wine prices. All of the data sets also include information about relevant product attributes that can be used in hedonic pricing models. The next section illustrates how one can specify and estimate a hedonic price model, using a scenario for pricing ski lift tickets.

10.4 Implementation of hedonic pricing

In all the applications of hedonic pricing considered in the previous section, the price of the product or service is the dependent variable (Y), and the various characteristics of the product are the independent variables (Xs) used to explain variation in the price. Hence a more general way of presenting the hedonic pricing model is as presented in Figure 10.2.

The idea then is to find the contribution of the various characteristics to the overall price. Housing prices, for example, depend on many factors such as size of the house (in square meters), size of the ground, view, distance to schools, city center, malls, bus stops, etc., whether it has been modified, and so forth. To find the right contribution from each of these attributes we need to model them simultaneously using multiple regression. When doing this, we find the effect from each of the independent variables, controlled for the effects from the other independent variables. For example, if the coefficient for size of the house (in square meters) is NOK 22,000, we can say that for each square meter the house price increases on average by NOK 22,000 when we control for all other measured factors. Put differently, if one house is 100 m² and another house is 101 m², and if the two houses are otherwise exactly similar, the 101 m² house would have a price of NOK 22,000 more than the 100 m² house. Hopefully, this will be even more clear when we examine an empirical example in the next section.

An empirical example

Falk (2008) used a hedonic pricing model to examine the determinants of ski lift ticket prices in Austria. The regression model used in his analysis was expressed like this:

Figure 10.2 General representation of the hedonic pricing model.

The hedonic pricing model 173

$$\ln P_i = \alpha + \beta_1 \ln KM_i + \beta_2 \ln LC_i + \beta_3 LCQUALITY_i + \beta_4 \ln ALT_i$$
$$+ \beta_5 \ln DAYS + \beta_6 ARTSNOW + \beta_7 \ln AVAGE_i + \delta_m \sum_{j=1}^{M} D_m + u_i \qquad (10.3)$$

where ln means the natural logarithm, KM is the total length of slopes in kilometers, LC is the total vertical lift capacity in persons per hour, LCQUALITY is the share of high-speed chairlifts and gondolas, ALT is the average altitude of peak lift stations (excluding T-bar lifts), DAYS is the days of operation in the 2005–2006 ski season, ARTSNOW is the share of ski runs on artificial snow, Ski Arlberg is a dummy variable measuring if the ski pass is valid for interlinked ski resorts in this area.

These variables are used to explain variation in (log) lift ticket prices (one and six-day passes). The main results are given in Figure 10.3 below. What do these results tell us?

First, the general interpretation of the coefficients of all regression models is as follows: The impact (change) in the dependent variable, for a one-unit increase in the independent variable. A one-unit change in the log levels of a variable is not always easy to interpret. Usually, the following approximation is used when interpreting the results when both the independent and dependent variables are log-transformed: For a 1% increase in the given independent variable, the dependent variable changes with a percentage value corresponding to the size of the coefficient. Formally, the change in the dependent variable for any p per cent change in the independent variable can be calculated as follows: Per cent change in the dependent variable = $(1.p^\beta - 1)$.

For example, from the table given in Figure 10.3 above, when the total length of ski runs increases by 50%, the prices for a one-day ski lift ticket increase by 31.439% ($1.5^{0.034} - 1$), on average, and controlled for the other variables that are included in the model.

Similarly, when the number of operational days doubles, the ski lift ticket prices increase by approximately 9.7% on average, everything else equal. The coefficient of a dummy variable presents the percentage impact on the ski lift ticket price when the

Variable	Coefficient
Constant	2.070
lnKM (length of slopes)	0.034*
lnLC (vertical transport metres/hour)	0.042**
LC Quality (share: HS chairlifts and gondolas)	0.120
lnALT (Average altitude of uphill stations)	0.020
lnDAYS (# of operational days)	0.137***
lnARTSNOW (share of slopes with snowmaking facilities)	-0.006
Ski Arlberg (dummy variable)	0.110***

Figure 10.3 The main results from Falk's (2008) hedonic price model for ski lift tickets in Austria. Significance at the 1%, 5%, or 10% level is denoted by ***, **, and *, respectively. N=84 dependent variable is the natural log of the price of a one-day lift ticket in euros.

dummy variable takes the value 1. For example, the Ski Alberg dummy in the analysis of Falk (2008), shows that the ticket prices in this specific region are 11.0% higher compared with ski destinations that are not in this area (i.e, ski resorts that are not in the Ski Alberg category).

Estimating the hedonic price model using Excel

Once we have a data set that contains (1) the prices of a product/service and (2) the various characteristics of that product/service, we can start estimating the hedonic price model. In this section, we will walk you through how such analyses can be carried out using Excel. The data set contains information about prices (in NOK) and various characteristics for 74 hotel rooms in Norway. These data were kindly made available by Professor Christer Thrane at Inland Norway University of Applied Sciences. Descriptive statistics of the variables in the data set are given in the table below. The dependent variable (Y) is the price for one double room and the independent variables (the Xs) are (1) whether there is free parking at the hotel (yes/no), (2) the distance to the city center, (3) whether the hotel room has a minibar (yes/no), and (4) whether there is a hair dryer in the hotel bathroom (yes/no). Hence, our objective is to explain variation in the price using these four independent variables.

	Average	*Std. dev*	*Min*	*Max*
Price double room	1,246.89	360.87	590.00	2,350.00
Free parking (yes=1)	0.50	0.50	0.00	1.00
Distance city (in km)	11.89	14.64	0.25	53.9
Minibar (yes=1)	0.76	0.43	0.00	1.00
Hair dryer (yes=1)	0.84	0.37	0.00	1.00

In Excel, the data should be organized with one variable in a separate column as illustrated as illustrated in Figure 10.4.

	A	B	C	D	E
1	Price	FreeParking	DistanceCityCenter	Minibar	HairDryer
2	1275	0	2.7	1	1
3	1595	1	4.8	1	1
4	2108	1	1.4	1	1
5	895	0	0.8	1	1
6	1825	0	0.25	1	1
7	1395	1	11.3	1	1
8	1575	0	1.5	1	1
9	640	0	3.4	0	0
10	1430	0	0.6	1	1
11	1345	0	2.5	1	1
12	1675	1	4	1	1
13	1355	1	3	0	1
14	1799	1	1.1	1	1
15	1355	0	2.8	1	1

Figure 10.4 Organization of the data in Excel.

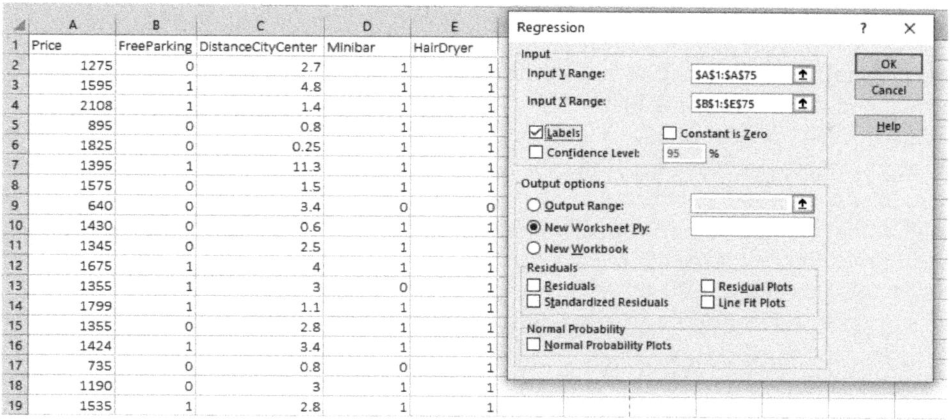

The hedonic pricing model 175

	A	B	C	D	E
1	Price	FreeParking	DistanceCityCenter	Minibar	HairDryer
2	1275	0	2.7	1	1
3	1595	1	4.8	1	1
4	2108	1	1.4	1	1
5	895	0	0.8	1	1
6	1825	0	0.25	1	1
7	1395	1	11.3	1	1
8	1575	0	1.5	1	1
9	640	0	3.4	0	0
10	1430	0	0.6	1	1
11	1345	0	2.5	1	1
12	1675	1	4	1	1
13	1355	1	3	0	1
14	1799	1	1.1	1	1
15	1355	0	2.8	1	1
16	1424	1	3.4	1	1
17	735	0	0.8	0	1
18	1190	0	3	1	1
19	1535	1	2.8	1	1

Regression dialog:
- Input Y Range: $A$1:$A$75
- Input X Range: $B$1:$E$75
- ☑ Labels ☐ Constant is Zero
- ☐ Confidence Level: 95 %
- Output options: ○ Output Range: ⦿ New Worksheet Ply: ○ New Workbook
- Residuals: ☐ Residuals ☐ Residual Plots ☐ Standardized Residuals ☐ Line Fit Plots
- Normal Probability: ☐ Normal Probability Plots

Figure 10.5 Interface for regression analysis in Excel.

	A	B	C	D	E	F	G	H	I
1	SUMMARY OUTPUT								
2									
3	*Regression Statistics*								
4	Multiple R	0.766064188							
5	R Square	0.58685434							
6	Adjusted R Square	0.562903867							
7	Standard Error	238.5853148							
8	Observations	74							
9									
10	ANOVA								
11		df	SS	MS	F	Significance F			
12	Regression	4	5579093.418	1394773.355	24.50282874	1.21017E-12			
13	Residual	69	3927683.717	56922.95242					
14	Total	73	9506777.135						
15									
16		Coefficients	Standard Error	t Stat	P-value	Lower 95%	Upper 95%	Lower 95.0%	Upper 95.0%
17	Intercept	628.2077939	81.54524384	7.703794413	6.95665E-11	465.5294836	790.8861042	465.5294836	790.8861042
18	FreeParking	247.5612214	60.91892034	4.063782155	0.000125989	126.0313005	369.0911422	126.0313005	369.0911422
19	DistanceCityCenter	-7.350529392	2.066356744	-3.557241224	0.000682693	-11.4727983	-3.22826048	-11.4727983	-3.22826048
20	Minibar	314.4755146	73.74532618	4.264345022	6.24674E-05	167.3576142	461.593415	167.3576142	461.593415
21	HairDryer	410.9967349	86.17087863	4.769554906	9.94101E-06	239.0905377	582.9029361	239.0905377	582.9029361

Figure 10.6 Output from hedonic price regression model run in Excel.

When we have the data in this format, the rest is straightforward. Go to *DATA* → *Data analysis* → *Regression*, and the *regression analysis* interface appears:

The input *Y* range is the column where the dependent variable is and the *input X range* is the range for which the independent variables are recorded. If the variable names are included in the defined range, the *Labels* option must be checked before you run the regression.

After hitting the OK button, the output presented in Figure 10.6 appears in a new worksheet.

So, what does this output tell us? There are a few important things to notice. First, the adjusted R square tell us how much of the variation in hotel room prices we can explain with the variables used in our model. In our case this number is 0.587. This means that we explain almost 59% of the variation in hotel room prices by the use of the four independent variables: (1) parking, (2) distance to city center, (3) minibar, and (4) hair dryer.

Second, the tables tell us that all four independent variables have a significant effect on hotel room prices. That is, the t-values for all coefficients are greater than 2 (in absolute terms), and the p-values are below 0.05.

And how should the various coefficients be interpreted? The FreeParking variable is a dummy variable assuming the value 1 if there is free parking at the hotel, and zero otherwise. In this case, the coefficient of the variable tells us how much the price of a hotel room differs if this characteristic is present compared with if it is not present. That is, for hotels that offer free parking, the price of a hotel room is NOK 247.56 higher compared with hotels that do not offer free parking, on average, and everything else equal.

The variable DistanceCityCenter tells us by how much the price of a hotel room changes when the distance to the city center increases by one kilometer. From the table in Figure 10.6 we see that the coefficient takes a value of −7.35, which means that for each kilometer the hotel is located away from the city center, the price of a room goes down by NOK 7.35, on average, and everything else equal. Hence a hotel located 50 km away from the city center will on average have a price that is approximately NOK 350 lower than one which is located exactly in the city center.

The effect of having a minibar in the hotel room is fairly strong in this model. That is, the coefficient for the Minibar variable is 314.48. This means that hotels that offer a minibar in the room on average have a price of NOK 314.48 higher than those that do not have a minibar in the room, and everything else equal.

Finally, hotels that have a hair dryer in the room have a price of NOK 411 NOK higher than those that do not. All the effects are statistically significant at the 1% level.

This analysis shows that the various characteristics of hotel rooms can help us explain why some rooms cost more than others. The analysis can also help us predict the price of a given hotel room. How? We just plug in the values we want to examine for the independent variables. For example, let us figure out what the expected price for a room at a hotel that has free parking, is located 15km away from the city center, has no minibar, but has a hair dryer:

$$Price = 628.2 + 247.56 \times 1 - 7.35 \times 15 + 411 \times 1 = 1,176.51$$

That is, the expected price for a hotel room with the given characteristics is NOK 1,176.51.

In the Excel file following this chapter, four other data sets that can be used to perform hedonic pricing analyses are included. The steps involved are identical to those illustrated for the hotel room prices above.

10.5 Summary

- Price hedonism assumes that the utility of goods or services is determined by the characteristics they consist of.
- The general hedonic pricing model is formulated such that the price of a product or service is a function of their intrinsic attributes/characteristics.

- Hedonic pricing models can be estimated using ordinary least squares regression where price is the dependent variable and the attributes/characteristics are the independent variables.
- There exists a vast amount of literature on empirical applications of hedonic pricing. Examples include property price modeling, automobile price modeling, alpine ski lift pass price modeling, and more.
- Estimating a hedonic price model in Excel is straightforward using regression analysis.

10.6 Problems

1. The Excel file following Chapter 10 contains five data sets (one of them being the data on hotel room prices analyzed in this chapter). You shall use these data sets to do the following tasks:
   a) Create a table with descriptive statistics. The table should include the following: Mean, standard deviation, min, and max for all variables in the data set.
   b) Create a histogram of the dependent variable with bin intervals of your own choice.
   c) List three hypotheses that you would like to test using a regression model later.
   d) Perform bivariate regression models using price as the dependent variable and each of the characteristics as the independent variables.
   e) Report and interpret the results from these analyses.
   f) Experiment with various multiple regression models. Report and comment on the results from the model you have chosen.

Acknowledgment

Andrew Musau has contributed to the content of this chapter.

Chapter 11

Revenue management

Revenue, alongside costs, represents the only available channel for firms to effect profits. Still, not all firms have control over their revenues. In regulated industries such as electric utilities assigned to a given service territory, there is little that the single utility can do to influence its revenues. Firstly, the service territory defines the demand area, and there is no possibility to expand beyond this zone. Secondly, regulations establish the maximum prices that can be charged to customers and the firm cannot exceed these. Therefore, for such firms, efficiency in managing costs is what determines how profitable they are. In industries where controlling revenue is possible, for example airlines, hotels, ski resorts and amusement parks, among many others, revenue management refers to the strategy and tactics employed by the firm to maximize revenues.

You will be familiar with the fare classes Y, J and F in airlines, corresponding to full fare economy class, business class and first class, respectively. Within each service class are further discounted fare classes. As discussed in Chapter 3, this form of segmentation is designed to maximize revenues since airlines attempt to identify passengers with different willingness to pay, and charge different prices to each of these segments rather than charging a flat price to everyone. In this chapter, we will review the history and process of revenue management and how technology and algorithms are fundamental in facilitating this. We will also explore the characteristics of industries that implement revenue management.

11.1 History and applicability of revenue management

A brief history of revenue management

According to the survey by McGill and van Ryzin (1999), revenue management can trace its origins to the airline industry in the early 1970s. Prior to this, airlines focused on overbooking and different statistical methods of predicting the number of passenger show-ups, cancellations and go-shows (passengers who show up and stand by to see whether a flight is full). However, some commercial airlines such as BOAC (now British Airways) started offering options to book up to three weeks in advance at discounted prices. This undertaking set out a challenge: given the implementation of different fares, what proportion of airline seats should be allocated to the early-bird passengers vis-à-vis the full-fare, late-booking passengers? If too many seats were allocated to the early-bird passengers, the airline would lose out on valuable revenue because it could have sold some of those seats at full fare. On the other hand, if too many seats are allocated to full-fare paying passengers, the airline would fly with empty seats that could have been sold at a discount to the early-bird passengers. There was no straightforward rule to resolve this trade-off. Ken Littlewood, a former employee of BOAC, proposed that low-fare bookings should be continually accepted if their revenue value exceeded the expected revenue of future high-fare bookings. His solution, known as *Littlewood's rule*, marked the beginning of what was referred to as yield management (and later revenue management).

Meanwhile, in North America, revenue management systems emerged following the deregulation of the airline industry in the USA in the late 1970s. American Airlines, which was facing fierce competition, introduced discounted fares in April 1977 to segment its market between leisure travellers and business travellers. Over the ensuing years, the development of revenue management systems shifted from single-journey control to segment control and eventually to origin–destination control. This was also accompanied by increased sophistication in information systems. By the early 2000s, most of the world's major airlines had adopted revenue management. The success of airline revenue management spurred the development of such systems in other forms of transport such as railways, as well as in other sectors such as hotels and car rentals.

Applicability of revenue management

Table 11.1 summarizes the conditions under which revenue management is applicable. The first requires that capacity is fixed, implying that there are limited resources to deliver a given quantity of services. For example, airlines have a fixed number of seats, hotels a fixed number of rooms and rental car companies a fixed number of cars. This attribute is invariant, at least in the short term. Secondly, the costs associated with serving an additional customer are lower in comparison to marginal-capacity-costs (i.e., costs required to increase capacity by one unit). For a car rental company, the costs associated with acquiring an extra car or hiring an additional marketing and customer service representative would be much higher than those associated with renting out a car to a customer. The latter entails very little beyond fuelling the car, whereas the former entails covering the purchase price or lease cost of the car, or a salary package for the employee. Thirdly, it should be possible for the firm to segment the market based on aspects such as price sensitivity and time sensitivity. In the airline industry, business travellers often book at the last minute and are not very sensitive to price whereas leisure travellers can book weeks in advance and are more price-sensitive. Likewise, some Apple iPhone customers *must have* the latest version of the iPhone, whereas others are patient enough to wait until a newer model is released, so that they can get the previous model at a lower price. Fourthly, perishable service capacity implies that inventory cannot be stored to be sold at a later point in time. An empty seat in an airline, for example, cannot be carried

Table 11.1 Characteristics of revenue management industries

Capacity is relatively fixed
Small marginal-cost to marginal-capacity-cost ratio
The market can be segmented
Service capacity is perishable
Advance selling of product is possible

forward to the next flight once the airline has taken off. The potential revenue from the seat cannot be stored if not utilized and is lost forever. The same applies to an empty hotel room or a rental car that is parked at base for the night. Finally, the firm should have the ability to sell a product in advance to implement revenue management. This allows the firm to be able to charge different prices based on when a reservation is made.

11.2 Implementing revenue management

Revenue management is implemented at the strategic level and at the booking control level. We review these below.

Revenue management strategy

The first step for the firm is to divide customers into segments. For a rental car company, these could be business clients who arrive at the airport and sign the rental car agreement on the spot, or a few hours before that, versus holidaymakers or leisure clients who commit to agreements weeks in advance. As we saw in Chapter 3, these two groups should have different characteristics for the segmentation to work. Business clients will be less price-sensitive compared to leisure clients. In addition, they will have less flexibility regarding changes to the signed agreement, for example, being allocated a different car (especially if perceived to be of lesser quality) from that specified in the contract, delays in receiving the car, etc. The car rental company therefore must design a product that appeals to one segment, but place restrictions that make it unappealing to the other segment. Thus, on the appeal side, business clients may have priority on newer, better service record and higher-end cars, and can sign agreements on the spot, whereas leisure clients will pay a lower rate and must book some days in advance. For business clients whose schedules are unpredictable, the time lag in booking and the possibility of ending up with an older car, or delays in waiting, make the leisure segment unattractive. On the other hand, the higher prices make the business segment unattractive to leisure clients who have time to plan their trips in advance.

Booking control

Booking control refers to limiting the amount of capacity that can be sold to a particular class at a point in time. For example, a booking limit of 48 in economy fare class Q of an airline indicates that at most, 48 seats can be sold to customers in that class. If the number of tickets sold reaches 48, the economy fare class Q is then closed to additional customers. Note that this number of 48 could be well below the plane's physical capacity; for example, the airline may want to protect seats for future demand from economy fare class Y customers (full-fare economy class tickets). Booking can either be managed using an allotments approach, or nesting. An allotments approach partitions capacity into blocks representing classes, and units within a block can only be sold off to customers of that class. For example, an airline with 100 seats may set a booking limit of ten for economy fare class Y, 25 for economy fare class B, and 65 for economy fare class H. If 65 seats are sold in fare class Y, the class would be closed regardless of how many seats are remaining in the other classes. With a nested booking limit, higher-ranked

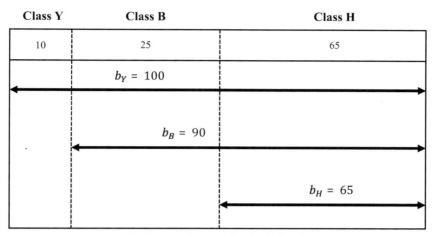

b_i denotes the booking limit for class i

Figure 11.1 Nested booking limits.

classes have all capacity reserved for lower-ranked classes, where rank is defined in terms of revenue per unit sold.

Figure 11.1 illustrates how this works for our example. Fare class Y would have a booking limit equal to the entire capacity of the airline, that is 100 seats. Similarly, fare class B will have all the capacity available to fare class H and thus a booking limit of 90: 25 pre-allocated to this class, plus 65 from fare class H. Finally, the lowest class, fare class H, will have a booking limit equal to the number of seats pre-allocated to this class. Formally, given N booking classes where class 1 is the highest and class N is the lowest, the following relation holds:

$$b_1 \geq b_2 \geq \cdots \geq b_N$$

Protection levels

These specify the amount of capacity to protect for a given class and can be determined using either an allotments approach, or nesting. The allotments approach protection level is equivalent to the fixed capacity allocated to the class of interest. Hence, in Figure 11.1 the protection level in classes Y, B and H would be 10, 25 and 65, respectively. This approach has an obvious problem: if the highest-priced fare classes are filled up quickly these will be closed and we will turn away customers with a high willingness to pay, or they will be forced to choose lower-priced tickets.

In the nested case, protection levels are defined not only for one class, but also for sets of classes where hierarchical ordering (from highest to lowest class) applies. Thus, in our example, we have a protection of ten seats for fare class Y (implying that ten seats would be protected for sale only to fare class Y customers), a protection of 35 seats for fare class Y and fare class B combined, and a protection of 100 seats for fare class Y, fare class B and fare class H combined. The latter is trivial and is usually not specified because it represents the entire capacity available.

11.3 Optimal protection levels in a single period model

As we highlighted at the beginning of this chapter, revenue management models started with Littlewood and have evolved in terms of both complexity and scope resulting from advances in computing and information technology. In this book, we only cover the most basic single period static model. We begin with the two-class model.

The two-class model

We can mathematically formulate the seat inventory problem in the previous section as follows: Given two fare classes with R_H and R_L denoting the value of high-fare class and low-fare class, respectively, C denoting capacity and D_j denoting demand for class $j \in (L, H)$, the question is how much demand for the low-fare class should be accepted so that total revenue is maximized? Littlewood's rule states that we accept demand for the low-fare class if

$$R_L \geq R_H \times Prob(D_H \geq x) \tag{11.1}$$

where x denotes the capacity left. Because the right-hand side of Equation (11.1) is decreasing in x, there exists an optimal protection level y_H^* such that we accept customers of fare class L if x exceeds y_H^* and reject them if x is y_H^* or less. Therefore, y_H^* satisfies

$$R_L < R_H \times Prob(D_H \geq y_H^*) \quad \text{and} \quad R_L \geq R_H \times Prob(D_H \geq y_H^* + 1) \tag{11.2}$$

Assuming a continuous distribution is used to model demand, y_H^* can be simply expressed as

$$R_L = R_H \times Prob(D_H \geq y_H^*), \tag{11.3}$$

which equivalently can be written as

$$y_H^* = F^{-1}\left(1 - \frac{R_L}{R_H}\right). \tag{11.4}$$

Thus, a protection level of y_H^* for fare class H is an optimal policy following Littlewood's rule. This is the same as setting a booking limit of $b_L^* = C - y_H^*$ on fare class L. Note that the fare class L demand is not included in Littlewood's rule and the calculated protection levels and booking limits are therefore totally independent of what the low-fare demand looks like.

Revenue management 183

Finding optimal booking limits and protection levels

Example 1

New Day is a car rental service that has 100 cars that can be offered to business customers and leisure customers. Business customers pay a higher rate of NOK 4,500 per day to rent a car whereas leisure customers are offered a special, non-refundable rate of NOK 3,000 if they book two weeks in advance. Forecasts by New Day's market analyst show that demand for the business class segment follows a normal distribution, with a mean of 65 and a standard deviation of 15. According to Littlewood's rule, at what level should management set out protections for the business class segment?

Solution

Littlewood's rule states that the optimal protection level for the business class segment is given by $y_H^* = F^{-1}\left(1 - \dfrac{R_L}{R_H}\right)$. Thus, we have a critical fractile of

$$\left(1 - \dfrac{3,000}{4,500}\right) = 0.333.$$

Given that demand for the higher-class segment follows a normal distribution, that is, $D_H \sim (65, 15^2)$, from the standard normal table, we look for the value of z for a cumulative probability of 0.333. This value is $z = -0.4307$. The optimal protection level for the business class segment, y_H^*, is given by

$$y_H^* = \mu + z\sigma, \tag{11.5}$$

yielding a value of $65 + (-0.4307(15)) \approx 59$ cars.

Example 2

Demand for Norway's rail service (NSB) full-fare class for the Oslo to Lillehammer route follows a continuous uniform distribution with minimum demand equal to 75 seats and maximum demand equal to 120 seats. A full-fare class ticket costs NOK 349 compared with NOK 249 for a discounted class ticket. Determine the optimal protection level for the full-fare class segment in this route according to Littlewood's rule.

Solution

The optimal protection level for the full-fare class segment is given by $y_H^* = F^{-1}\left(1 - \dfrac{R_L}{R_H}\right)$. This results in a critical fractile of

$$\left(1 - \dfrac{249}{349}\right) = 0.287.$$

184 Revenue management

Given demand is uniformly distributed, the optimal protection level for the full-fare class segment is given by

$$y_H^* = F^{-1}(0.287) = D_{min} + (D_{max} - D_{min}) \cdot 0.287$$
$$= 75 + (120 - 75) \cdot 0.287 \approx 88.$$

The railway operator should therefore protect 88 full-fare class seats on this route.

The N-class model

The two-class model can be generalized to N classes where $N \in \mathbb{Z}$ such that $2 \leq N \leq \infty$. The approach, referred to as expected marginal seat revenue (EMSR), was devised by Belobaba (1987). There are two versions of the EMSR: EMSR-a and EMSR-b. Here, we focus our attention on the former. Under EMSR-a, the protection level for a given class is obtained by applying Littlewood's rule to successive classes. Suppose that we expand the two-class example of the previous section to include two more fare classes with the values R_M and R_Q, respectively, where $R_L < R_Q < R_M < R_H$. There will not be a protection level for the lowest class L, like in the two-class model. The protection level for the highest class H just applies Littlewood's rule to the two highest classes and is given by:

$$y_H^* = F_H^{-1}\left(1 - \frac{R_M}{R_H}\right). \tag{11.6}$$

The protection level for the second highest class M will apply Littlewood's rule to that class and the immediately successive class, added to the highest class and the immediately successive class, that is, respectively,

$$y_{QM} = F_M^{-1}\left(1 - \frac{R_Q}{R_M}\right), \text{ and}$$

$$y_{QH} = F_H^{-1}\left(1 - \frac{R_Q}{R_H}\right).$$

therefore, $y_M^* = y_{QM} + y_{QH}$ implying

$$y_M^* = F_M^{-1}\left(1 - \frac{R_Q}{R_M}\right) + F_H^{-1}\left(1 - \frac{R_Q}{R_H}\right).$$

For the second lowest class, Q, the protection level applies Littlewood's rule to that class and the lowest class, added to the second highest class and the lowest class, and the highest class and the lowest class. These are given by:

$$y_{LQ} = F_Q^{-1}\left(1 - \frac{R_L}{R_Q}\right),$$

$$y_{LM} = F_M^{-1}\left(1 - \frac{R_L}{R_M}\right), \text{ and}$$

$$y_{LH} = F_H^{-1}\left(1 - \frac{R_L}{R_H}\right).$$

thus, $y_Q^* = y_{LQ} + y_{LM} + y_{LH}$ implying

$$y_Q^* = F_Q^{-1}\left(1 - \frac{R_L}{R_Q}\right) + F_M^{-1}\left(1 - \frac{R_L}{R_M}\right) + F_H^{-1}\left(1 - \frac{R_L}{R_H}\right). \tag{11.8}$$

In summary, for $j = 1, 2, \cdots, N$ classes, where class 1 is the highest class and class N is the lowest class, the EMSR-a protection level for class j is obtained by solving Littlewood's rule for class $j+1$ and each of the higher classes separately, and then summing these.

Example 3

Consider the following data from Talluri and van Ryzin (2004) relating to a flight with four fare classes. Demand across each of the fare classes is assumed to follow a normal distribution with the following means and standard deviations:

Class	Fare	Mean	Standard dev.
1	$1,050	17.3	5.8
2	$950	45.1	15.0
3	$699	39.6	13.2
4	$520	34.0	11.3

Compute the EMSR-a protection levels for the three highest classes.

Solution

The EMSR-a protection level for Class 1 is given by

$$y_1^* = F_1^{-1}\left(1 - \frac{950}{1,050}\right).$$

This results in a critical fractile of 0.0952. Given $D_1 \sim (17.3, 5.8^2)$, from the standard normal table, we look for the value of z for a cumulative probability of 0.0952. This value is $z = -1.3093$. Therefore,

$$y_1^* = \mu + z\sigma = 17.3 + (-1.3093) \cdot 5.8 \approx 9.706$$

The EMSR-a protection level for Class 2 is given by

$$y_2^* = F_2^{-1}\left(1 - \frac{699}{950}\right) + F_1^{-1}\left(1 - \frac{699}{1,050}\right).$$

These result in the critical fractiles 0.2642 and 0.3343, respectively. Given $D_2 \sim (45.1, 15.0^2)$ and $D_1 \sim (17.3, 5.8^2)$, the values of z for cumulative probabilities 0.2642 and 0.3343 are −0.6305 and −0.4281, respectively. Therefore,

$$y_2^* = (\mu_1 + z_1\sigma_1) + (\mu_2 + z_2\sigma_2) = (17.3 + (-0.4281) \cdot 5.8) + (45.1 + (-0.6305) \cdot 15) \approx 50.45$$

Finally, EMSR-a protection level for Class 3 is given by

$$y_3^* = F_3^{-1}\left(1 - \frac{520}{699}\right) + F_2^{-1}\left(1 - \frac{520}{950}\right) + F_1^{-1}\left(1 - \frac{520}{1,050}\right).$$

These result in the critical fractiles 0.7439, 0.4526 and 0.5048, respectively. Given $D_3 \sim (39.6, 13.2^2)$, $D_2 \sim (45.1, 15.0^2)$ and $D_1 \sim (17.3, 5.8^2)$, the values of z for cumulative probabilities 0.2561, 0.4526, and 0.5048 are, respectively, −0.6554, −0.1191 and 0.0120. Therefore, $y_3^* = (\mu_1 + z_1\sigma_1) + (\mu_2 + z_2\sigma_2) + (\mu_3 + z_3\sigma_3) = (17.3 + (0.0120) \cdot 5.8) + (45.1 + (-0.1191) \cdot 15) + (39.6 + (-0.6554) \cdot 13.2) \approx 91.63$.

In the Excel file following this chapter all three examples in the text are implemented and solved. We have also included one more example of optimal protection levels in the case of multiple fare classes and an example of how the optimal protection level changes with the level of the low fare in the two-class model.

11.4 Summary

- Revenue management refers to the practice of optimally allocating existing capacity to various fare classes to maximize expected revenue.
- Revenue management is applicable when capacity is relatively fixed, there are small marginal costs, the market can be segmented, the service capacity is perishable and advance selling is possible.
- Ken Littlewood of BOAC introduced a rule to resolve a simple capacity allocation problem in the 1970s. This is known as *Littlewood's rule* and it marked the beginning of revenue management.
- Revenue management is implemented at the strategic level and at the booking control level.
- Protection levels specify the capacity to protect for a given class and can be determined using either an allotment approach or nesting.

11.5 Problems

1. Not all firms can implement revenue management. Evaluate this statement.
2. List and discuss characteristics of revenue management industries.
3. Highlight the difference between a partitioned booking system and a nested booking system.
4. Consider a hotel chain that has four different booking classes denoted P, Q, R and S. Total capacity stands at 1,000 rooms and a quarter of all rooms are reserved for booking class P. A third of the remainder is reserved for booking class Q and 200 rooms are reserved for booking class R. Given that P is the highest class and S is the lowest class with $P > Q > R > S$, draw a diagram such as in Figure 11.1 and determine the booking limits for each class under a nested booking system.
5. Consider the example of the railway company given earlier in this chapter and now suppose that on a different route, demand follows a continuous uniform distribution with minimum demand equal to 140 seats and maximum demand equal to 280 seats. If a full-fare class ticket costs NOK 499 on this route compared with NOK 399 for a discounted class ticket, determine the optimal protection level for the full-fare class segment following Littlewood's rule.
6. Demand for an airline's seats on a short-haul route follows a normal distribution with a mean of 80 and a standard deviation of 20. If the price of an economy fare class Y seat is $200 and that of an economy fare class B seat is $120, calculate the optimal protection level for economy fare class Y seats following Littlewood's rule.
7. Consider a hotel with a 100 rooms capacity that has four different nightly rates for its standard rooms. If the demand for a room across all segments follows a normal distribution with the following means and standard deviations, determine the EMSR-a protection levels for the three highest segments.

Segment	Nightly rate	Mean	Standard dev.
1	$850	22.2	16.2
2	$700	15.1	8.1
3	$600	19.7	6.4
4	$450	30.0	10.0

Acknowledgement

This chapter is written by Andrew Musau.

Chapter 12

Big Data and pricing analytics

Big Data has become one of the hottest buzzwords over the last years. Figure 12.1 illustrates this by displaying the popularity of the terms "Big Data" and "Big Data Analytics" in Google searches from 2004 to 2020. It is probably not an exaggeration to state that its development has been massive, starting first and foremost in 2011. In 2012, which could be labeled the early days of the "Age of Big Data," Steve Lohr described the future as being very bright for those who are good with numbers and are fascinated by data: "The sound you hear is opportunity knocking," he wrote in the introduction of a New York Times article (Lohr, 2012). Even though some of the hype may have overestimated these opportunities, there is no doubt that the enormous amount of data becoming available each day, hour, minute, second, or even hundredth of a second, can be used to create business value if utilized correctly.

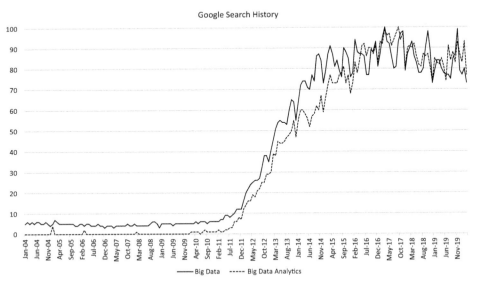

Figure 12.1 Google searches for terms related to Big Data and Big Data Analytics from 2004 to 2020 (as of March 23, 2020). Source: trends.google.com.

In this chapter we shall focus on what Big Data is and how it can be used in combination with pricing analytics to create business value. We will also examine its applications in various industry sectors, introduce you to specific data analytics techniques that can be useful in pricing analytics, and go through a relevant case from real life. The chapter will also focus on how Excel can be used efficiently for pricing analytics when working with big data sets.

12.1 What is Big Data?

Laney (2001) proposed using three Vs to characterize the key features of Big Data. These Vs stand for *Volume, Velocity, and Variety,* and are now included in most definitions of the term. They are illustrated in Figure 12.2 and described in more detail below.

- *Volume:* Large data sets as measured by their actual volume (terabytes, petabytes, exabytes, zettabytes).
- *Velocity:* New data arriving continuously with a high refresh rate. Examples include high-frequency transaction data (from stock exchanges, e-commerce, supermarkets, etc.), streaming data (YouTube, Spotify), sensor-driven data (weather sensors, traffic data), among others.
- *Variety:* Data come from various sources and in a number of different formats. Examples include structured (database tables), semi-structured (XML data) and unstructured data (text, images, video- and audio streams, etc.).

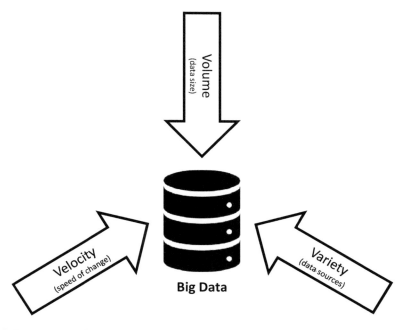

Figure 12.2 The three Vs of Big Data.

Hence, the size (volume) of the data set itself is not enough to justify the use of the term Big Data. It should also be continuously updated and/or stem from different sources with a varying degree of structure/complexity. As stated by Holmes (2017), *V* has become the letter of choice, and new or alternative terms starting with this letter have been added to the original three mentioned above. Some of these are briefly described below:

- Veracity: The quality of the data being collected and used.
- Value: The quality of the results derived from big data analyses.
- Visualization: Interactive graphics with automatic updates/high refresh rates (in contrast to more static charts/graphics that are usually applied to small data sets).

However, one of the most widely used definitions in the industry is that proposed by Beyer and Laney (2012), and they focus on the original three Vs in their definition:

"Big Data is high-volume, high-velocity and/or high-variety information assets that demand cost-effective, innovative forms of information processing that enable enhanced insight, decision-making and process automation."

The awake reader may also notice that, given this definition, it is not strictly needed to have all three Vs present at the same time for a data set to be labeled as Big Data. The point is that the traditional tools for information processing are no longer enough to transform the data into its full potential business value.

12.2 The business value of Big Data in pricing analytics

In many cases, the big data sets private or public companies have access to are often collected without any specific (research) questions in mind. One challenge is then to figure out how one can take advantage of these huge amounts of data to create business value for the firm. Data in general only provides value once it is analyzed in one way or another. The same holds for Big Data, but the complexity, speed of change and size of the data (the three Vs) can make it even harder for many organizations to create insight from them.

There are several examples of businesses that have struggled with creating business value from Big Data when it comes to pricing decisions. One such is mentioned by LaValle et al., (2011) who cited a manager they interviewed as saying that "…they had a very good understanding of the impact of price changes on single products and channels, but that they were blindsided once the company shifted strategy to dynamic pricing across channels (among other things)." LaValle et al. (2011, p. 30) explained:

"Because their data marts had been developed de facto over time, they found themselves struggling to understand which tools and information were needed to go forward."

Barton and Court (2012) stated that another reason why many big data implementation projects fail is because they are not in sync with the firm's day-to-day processes and decision-making norms. That is, if big data projects are initiated without a clearly defined business problem that should be solved, it is likely to be of little use. In their own words: "A pure data mining approach often leads to an endless search for what the data really say." (Barton and Court, 2012, p. 81).

However, these authors mention specifically an example of a *successful* implementation that focused on optimizing complex product pricing. Here the objective was clearly defined and the variables to be included in the analyses were carefully selected based on how likely they were to deliver the needed insight to make better business decisions.

Hence, to benefit from (big) data when it comes to pricing decisions, it seems like a good idea to start with specific research questions, and not the (big) data, tools, or techniques in general.

Examples of research questions that can be useful for pricing decisions are:

- How can customers be segmented based on certain criteria?
- How sensitive are our customers to price changes?
- What are the biggest drivers of sales?
- How can demand for our product and services be forecasted?
- What is the expected demand versus the capacity over the next week?
- What tools can be used to enhance our employees' understanding of how the business is performing on a daily basis?

Most of these questions can be answered with modest amounts of data with a simple structure, but additional insights (and thus value) could be obtained when we have access to continuously updated information and/or when information from different data sources can be combined. What insights we can extract from the (big) data also depends on the analytical techniques used to process the (vast amount of) information we have available. Within the literature on Big Data and business analytics the techniques typically fall into one of three broad categories: *descriptive*, *predictive*, or *prescriptive analytics*. A brief description is given below.

Descriptive analytics focus on summarizing and describing what has happened. Examples are:
- Average number of visitors on Mondays over the past year.
- Total daily sales visualized in a line plot over the past five years.
- Which country lost the most existing customers last quarter.

Predictive analytics is about using historical data to foresee what will happen in the future.
- What will the number of visitors be next Monday?
- What will the total daily sales be next week if the price is set to $5?
- Which country will lose most existing customers next quarter?

Prescriptive analytics provides specific suggestions for what to do in order to optimize business performance:
- What is the optimal price to maximize profits from visitors on Mondays?
- What is the optimal product mix to maximize sales profit?
- What is the profit-maximizing strategy in terms of what countries to enter with a new product?

Some scholars claim that the availability of Big Data has also led to a shift in analytical focus from descriptive to predictive and prescriptive. However, in many cases, the descriptive analyses are crucial to build good predictive or prescriptive models, and often the true gain in business value is obtained when both various techniques *and* various data are combined.

A ski resort may, for example, be able to predict visitation frequency for the next week based solely on historical visitation records (mainly descriptive analysis). However, these predictions would likely be improved if the historical visitation data were combined with continuously updated weather forecasts for the next week (precipitation, wind, cloudiness, temperature, etc.). If also including information about marketing campaigns, competitors' marketing activities (including their pricing tactics), and other information that may affect skiing attendance in one way or another, the predictions would likely be improved further still. Such improved visitation predictions could lead the ski resort to better dynamic pricing decisions (prescriptive analysis).

Further, *dynamic pricing* is one of the most frequently mentioned areas for which the use of Big Data can enhance business value of firms. In a systematic review article, Akter and Wamba (2016) examined the use and potentials of big data analytics within e-commerce. In this study, the words "pricing" and "price" were mentioned a total of 36 times. The word "pricing" is, in addition to being combined with "dynamic," mentioned together with such terms as "optimize," "differential," and "on-demand." Hence, according to this study, pricing seems to be one of the most important areas to create value within the field of big data analytics. As an example of the use of Big Data in pricing analytics, they mention Amazon.com's dynamic pricing system, which monitors competing prices and alerts Amazon every 15th seconds. This enables them to continuously adjust their own prices to avoid lost sales.

Other examples of the combination of Big Data and pricing analytics are found in professional sports. Erevelles et al. (2016) described how Major League baseball teams improved revenue management by dynamically adjusting prices frequently during the season. They do so by integrating many variables and sources of information including weather, construction around the ball park, teams on the rise, the potential for a record-setting event (hit, homeruns, or play), amount of chatter about a game on social media, and more (Erevelles et al. 2016).

Big Data can be used to make better pricing decisions and, as such, create additional business value. To do so we must start with a business problem and apply the relevant techniques. Many of the tools and techniques presented in previous chapters can also be applied on big data sets (at least when it comes to the two Vs, volume and velocity). Examples include the estimation of price sensitivity, willingness to pay, and price–response functions using historical transaction data, and optimal markdown and revenue management using high-frequency sales and inventory data. However, in some cases, we may be interested in solving business problems for which these techniques cannot be used. In the next section we shall therefore focus on some other well-known data analytics techniques that could be particularly useful in the case of Big Data for pricing decisions.

12.3 Big Data analytics techniques for pricing decisions

Many techniques used on big data sets today have been around for a long time and were originally developed before the era of Big Data. Examples are database querying and regression analysis. The latter is commonly applied to predict numerical values of a given variable; for example, how much demanded quantity changes for a given price change. There is nothing stopping us from running this regression on a small data set (we have already done that many times in this book). However, with big data sets available, we may either get some additional insight from the simple fact that we have more observations, or because the technique can be used in other ways. One potential problem with big data sets is that the meaningful insight could be somewhat hidden. The focus of many techniques is therefore on extracting the meaningful information in an efficient manner. A full description of all relevant applications, techniques, or algorithms is beyond the scope of this text. We shall therefore focus on how some of the most common techniques can be used to discover patterns or predict outcomes that are (or could be) useful when it comes to make better pricing decisions.

Supervised versus unsupervised methods

In modern data analytics the various techniques often fall into either *supervised* or *unsupervised* (learning) methods. The main difference between these two broad categories is that supervised methods are used when we wish to predict the outcome for a given variable. The unsupervised methods, on the other hand, are more explorative, and the aim is to find patterns in data without concrete guidance on what to find. Examples of supervised learning methods are *classification techniques* and various *regression methods*. When applying such methods, the data set always contains information on a target (dependent) variable that we wish to predict the outcome of.

Examples of unsupervised methods are *cluster analysis* and *co-occurrence grouping*. Cluster analysis is about finding cases in the data (for example, customers) which exhibit similar characteristics and, as such, can be grouped together. Cluster analysis can therefore for example be used for segmentation. Co-occurrence grouping is also known as frequent itemset mining, association rule discovery and market-basket analysis. You may guess what the aim of this technique is, then. It is about identifying relationships among products or services that are usually purchased together. Such relationships can be used in many ways, but for pricing decisions, the most interesting area of application is probably to offer customers bundles of products services with a unique price.

Next, we shall describe the basics of classification techniques, cluster analysis and co-occurrence grouping more formally. Then we shall examine a few simple examples with implementations in Excel.

Basics of classification using k-nearest neighbor algorithm

Classification can be used in pricing decision to, among other things, predict the likelihood of customers taking advantage of a specific offer or not. For example, if a company wants to run a campaign on a new product or service, and they have historical data on the actions of customers on other, similar campaigns, they can use this information to predict how likely new customers, or customers outside the data currently available, would be to take advantage of the offer. There are many available algorithms that can be used for classification modeling. We shall briefly examine the k-nearest neighbor (k-NN) algorithm and show how this can be implemented in practice. To understand how the k-NN algorithm works, see Figure 12.3. In this figure the existing customers of a

194   Big Data and pricing analytics

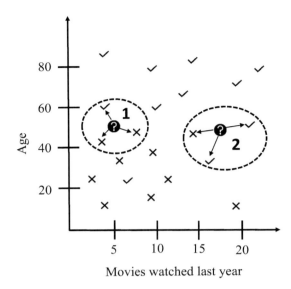

Figure 12.3 Illustration of k-NN algorithm. The two question marks indicate new customers or customers to whom we consider sending an offer. × indicates that a given customer did not take advantage of a similar offer earlier. ✓ indicates that a given customer did take advantage of a similar offer previously.

movie theater are depicted in a scatter plot. The two characteristics of the customers are (1) their age, and (2) how many movies each of them watched in the movie theater last year. The scatter plot also indicates whether the customers took advantage of the previous offer they received, or not. Those who did are assigned a check mark, and those who did not are assigned a cross. Assume now that we are considering running a new campaign (for example, a special offer with price reduction), but that we want to offer this only to customers with a high probability of accepting to target the campaign. In our database we have two customers who have previously not received an offer. These are highlighted by a question mark in Figure 12.3. The question then is: Can we use the existing data to predict how likely it is that these two customers will accept the offer? The answer is: Yes! And we can use the k-NN algorithm to do so. The way we do it is to calculate the distance from the k-nearest (for example $k=3$) neighbors to customer 1. These neighbors are highlighted by a dashed circle in the figure. We see that two out of the three nearest neighbors of customer 1 declined the previous offer, while the opposite is the case for customer 2. Based on these facts, we may jump right to the conclusion that customer 2 is likely to accept the offer and customer 1 is not. Given the information in the figure, this seems reasonable. However, as we usually want to include information about more characteristics of the customers, it is a good idea to calculate the distance in a more formal manner.

One way of doing this is to calculate the so-called *Euclidian distance*. With two dimensions (also called characteristics or variables), as in the above example, the distance is equivalent to the Pythagorean theorem:

$$d(C_1, C_y) = \sqrt{(M_1 - M_y)^2 + (A_1 - A_y)^2}. \tag{12.1}$$

In Equation (12.1), $d(C_1, C_y)$ refers to the Euclidean distance between customer 1 (C_1), as indicated with the question mark in Figure 12.3, and the nearest customer who had previously accepted a similar offer (C_y), as indicated with a check mark within the dashed circle in the same figure. M_1 and M_y is the number of movies watched by customer 1 and the nearest (check mark) neighbor over the last year and A_1 and A_y is the age of the same two customers. In Figure 12.4 the coordinates of the nearest neighbors of customer 1 and 2 are included, and all customers who are not the nearest neighbors of either customer 1 or 2 are removed for expository purposes. Customer 1 has watched five movies over the last year and is about 50 years old. The nearest "Yes" customer (C_y) has the coordinates (4,60), which means that he or she watched four movies over the last year and is 60 years old.

With this information available we can calculate the Euclidean distance by simply plugging the numbers into Equation (12.1):

$$d(C_1, C_y) = \sqrt{(5-4)^2 + (50-60)^2} = \sqrt{26} = 10.05.$$

The same exercise can be done for the other customer we are interested to predict the likely outcome for, as indicated by the other question mark in Figures 12.3 and 12.4. Focus on the nearest neighbor who responded "No" to a similar offer (indicated by

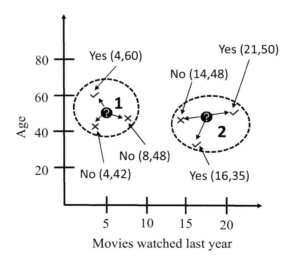

Figure 12.4 Illustration of k-NN algorithm. The two question marks indicate new customers or customers to whom we consider sending an offer. × indicates that a given customer did not take advantage of a similar offer earlier. ✓ indicates that a given customer did take advantage of a similar offer previously. The coordinates are included for all neighbors of the two customers.

196 Big Data and pricing analytics

a cross within the dashed circle surrounding customer 2). This customer has watched approximately 14 movies over the last year and is about 48 years old. Customer 2 has watched 17 movies and is 52 years old. The Euclidean distance between these two is then:

$$d(C_2, C_y) = \sqrt{(17-14)^2 + (52-48)^2} = \sqrt{25} = 5.000.$$

In general, for n-dimensions (customer characteristics or variables) the Euclidian distance can be calculated as:

$$d(C_1, C_c) = \sqrt{(C_{1,D1} - C_{c,D1})^2 + (C_{1,D2} - C_{c,D2})^2 + \ldots (C_{1,Dn} - C_{c,Dn})^2}, \quad (12.2)$$

where $C_{1,D1}$ represents the value of the first dimension (i.e., customer characteristic: for example, age) for customer 1 and $C_{c,D1}$ represents the value of the same dimension for the customer we want to compare it to (in our example, the nearest neighbor who responded "Yes" to a similar offer previously). $C_{1,D2}$ is the value for customer 1 on the second dimension (customer characteristic: for example, number of movies watched) and $C_{c,D2}$ is the value of the same dimension for the customer we would like to compare customer 1 with, and so forth.

To further illustrate how the algorithm works we can include a third dimension – income – in the movie example, and calculate the Euclidean distance between customer 1 and three neighbors. The results are illustrated in Figure 12.5 where we also show the same calculations for customer 2 and three neighbors.

You may notice that the scaling of the various variables used in the calculations may induce some problems. In Figure 12.5 income has a much higher impact than any of the

CALCULATING EUCLIDEAN DISTANCE BETWEEN CUSTOMER 1 AND 3 NEAREST NEIGHBORS					
Customer	Movies watched	Age	Income	Euclidean Distance
Customer 1	5	50	100000	0.0
Yes(4,60)	4	60	125000	25000.0
No(4,42)	4	42	80000	20000.0
No(8,48)	8	48	55000	45000.0

CALCULATING EUCLIDEAN DISTANCE BETWEEN CUSTOMER 2 AND 3 NEAREST NEIGHBORS					
Customer	Movies watched	Age	Income	Euclidean Distance
Customer 2	17	52	100000	0.0
No(14,48)	14	48	125000	25000.0
Yes(16,35)	16	35	80000	20000.0
Yes(21,50)	21	50	55000	45000.0

Figure 12.5 Calculation of Euclidean distance from customer 1 (upper table) and 2 (lower table) to their three nearest neighbors, respectively.

two other variables, simply because the variation and scale of income is much higher than for movies watched and age. We purposely set the income level of the various customers as equal for customer 1, customer 2 and the neighbors surrounding them in the upper and lower part of the figure. The result is obvious; income is the *only* driver of the Euclidean distance, as the scale and variation of the other variables are so low in comparison. Consequently, the ranking of which customers are nearest customer 1 and 2 are affected by only this one single variable. If we included another dimension measuring the distance from the movie theater, it would also play a big role if it was measured in miles, kilometers, meters, or something else. You see the point: to avoid the Euclidean distance being affected too much by the scale and variation of one or more variables, we should normalize the numbers before computing the similarity between cases. We do this by computing the z-score of the various variables for each observation. The z-score is given as:

$$z_{C_{1,D1}} = \frac{\left(C_{1,D1} - \bar{D}_{1,n}\right)}{\sigma_{D_{1,n}}}. \tag{12.3}$$

That is, customer 1's observed value on dimension 1 (for example, movies watched) minus the average value of dimensions 1 for the whole (training) sample divided by the standard deviation of that dimension. If we assume that the average number of movies watched is 12 with a standard deviation of five, the z-score (i.e., the normalized value) of this dimension for customer 1 would be:

$$z_{C_{1,D1}} = \frac{(5-12)}{5} = -1.4.$$

If we have information on the mean and standard deviation of *age* and *income* as well, we can update the calculations presented in Figure 12.5. It turns out that the average and standard deviation of the age variable are 50 and 10, respectively. For the income variable the average and standard deviation have been estimated to $80,000 and $30,000. With this information the z-scores for all variables can be calculated. These are presented in Figure 12.6. We see that the ranking of the distances from customer 1 to their neighbors stays the same as before the normalization. However, this is not the case for customer 2, and in general, the relative importance of the income variable is now equal to the two other variables.

When all these calculations are done, the only thing remaining is to classify the new observations (i.e., customer 1 and customer 2). To do this, we need to decide how many neighbors to include when assigning the new observations to a class. If we set $k=1$, we use only the nearest neighbor of the new customer and assign them to the same class as that neighbor. Using the information from Figure 12.6 we would then simply assign customer 1 to the class "No" (nearest neighbor has a Euclidean distance of 1.06 and is labeled No(4,42)). Customer 2 would also be assigned to the class "No" as the nearest neighbor (No(14,48)) is in the "No" class.

NORMALIZED VALUES FOR THE VARIOUS DIMENSIONS - CUSTOMER 1				
Customer	Movies watched	Age	Income	Euclidean Distance
Customer 1	-1.40	0.00	0.67	0.00
Yes(4,60)	-1.60	1.00	1.50	1.32
No(4,42)	-1.60	-0.80	0.00	1.06
No(8,48)	-0.80	-0.20	-0.83	1.63

NORMALIZED VALUES FOR THE VARIOUS DIMENSIONS - CUSTOMER 2				
Customer	Movies watched	Age	Income	Euclidean Distance
Customer 2	1.00	0.20	0.67	0.00
No(14,48)	0.40	-0.20	1.50	1.10
Yes(16,35)	0.80	-1.50	0.00	1.84
Yes(21,50)	1.80	0.00	-0.83	1.71

Figure 12.6 Calculation of Euclidean distance using z-scores from customer 1 (upper table) and 2 (lower table) to their three nearest neighbors, respectively.

If using more than one neighbor, we simply calculate the proportion of the k-nearest neighbors that fall into the class. Then we define a cutoff value (typically 0.5) that we use to classify the new observation. If setting $k = 3$, customer 1 would be assigned to the "No" category. We see this clearly if setting Yes=1 and No=0. The average of the three nearest neighbors is then 0.33 ((1+0+0)/3). As 0.5 is defined as the threshold, this customer will be classified as "No." For customer 2, using $k = 3$, the corresponding value would be 0.67 ((0+1+1)/3) and this customer would therefore be classified as "Yes." A natural question arising from the above exercise is: *How many neighbors should be used in the classification of new observations?* There is no concrete answer to this question. In general, small values of k are more exposed to noise in the data while large values of k could fail to capture the relevant relationships between the various dimensions and the class. Values of k between 1 and $\sqrt{n}/2$ could be considered and the best value can be found by dividing the data into a *training set* and a *validation set* and then choose the k resulting in the smallest classification error. We shall return to various performance measures for evaluating the classification of categorical outcomes when we go through the implementation in Excel later in this chapter. The k-NN algorithm can also be used without the aim of classifying customers in distinct classes, but instead trying to find customers with similar patterns more generally. This is often referred to as *cluster analysis* and is a typical example of a technique that can help us extract valuable information from Big Data. We shall briefly explain the main ideas behind this technique next, building on the insights we now have on the k-NN algorithm.

Basics of cluster analysis using k-nearest neighbor algorithm

We can use the same framework as introduced in the previous section to calculate clusters of customers who are similar to each other in terms of the characteristics we have recorded about them. For pricing decisions this can be useful first and foremost to segment the market to subsequently approach them more efficiently with unique marketing activities and pricing offers. Now, we are not interested in assigning customers to distinct classes, but rather various clusters (segments) where the customers within each segment are similar to each other based on the various characteristics we have recorded about them in our database.

Again, there are many different approaches to calculate similarities between observations and to assign them to clusters. We focus on the Euclidean distance to calculate similarities and the k-Means clustering technique to allocate observations to clusters. The Euclidean distance measure was thoroughly introduced in the previous section. We then knew what to calculate the distance from (the distance from a given customer to their nearest neighbors). In cluster analysis we do not readily have any such starting points. The solution is then to randomly generate such starting points of the cluster centers, which we call *centroids,* and then assign each observation to the nearest one. The locational values of the centroids should then be recomputed based on an objective, such as minimizing the total (Euclidean) distance between observations and the centroid they belong to. We shall return to the details of the steps involved in this procedure when we go through various implementations in Excel, but Figure 12.7 illustrates how the results of a k-Means cluster analysis could look after the locations of the centroids have been optimized.

Basics of co-occurrence grouping

If we have access to historical transaction data, we can identify products or services commonly purchased together to create promotions, or special offers. This technique uses *if-then* statements to calculate various measures that contain information about the relation of various items in a (potential) market basket. However, unlike *if-then rules,*

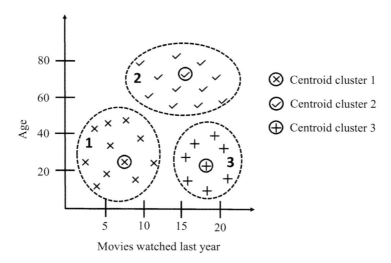

Figure 12.7 Illustration of how the result of a k-Means cluster analysis may look.

the if-then statements in the co-occurrence grouping algorithm are probabilistic. This means that we find the probability of the *then* part to be satisfied given the *if* statement. Or, if simply calculating the number of occurrences using historical data, the *then* part would refer to the actual fraction in the data satisfying the *if* statement. One example of a co-occurrence grouping rule from a movie theater kiosk could be:

$$\{popcorn, chocolate\} \Rightarrow \{big\ soda\}[30\%, 70\%]$$

This rule states that if customers bought popcorn and chocolate at the movie theater kiosk, 70% of them also purchased a big soda. Additionally, the rule states that of all the historical transactions in the movie theater kiosk, 30% bought all three items together. This fraction of 30% is called *support* while the fraction of 70% is referred to as *confidence*. A general representation of the co-occurrence grouping algorithm is as follows:

$$\{X\} \Rightarrow \{Y\}[Support, confidence] \tag{12.4}$$

where X is the item set corresponding to the *if* part of the rule and is often referred to as the *antecedent*. The item or item set on the right-hand side, Y, is related to the *then* part of the rule and is called the *consequent*. The *support* is the *support count* divided by the total number of transactions. We can calculate the support for both the antecedent, the consequent, and for the two combined as follows:

$$Support(X) = \frac{\#of\ baskets\ that\ contain\ X}{total\ \#of\ baskets} \tag{12.5}$$

$$Support(Y) = \frac{\#of\ baskets\ that\ contain\ Y}{total\ \#of\ baskets} \tag{12.6}$$

$$Support(X \Rightarrow Y) = \frac{\#of\ baskets\ that\ contain\ both\ X\ and\ Y}{total\ \#of\ baskets} \tag{12.7}$$

The *confidence* is defined as:

$$Confidence(X \Rightarrow Y) = \frac{support(X \Rightarrow Y)}{support(X)} \tag{12.8}$$

that is, the fraction of transactions with the antecedent (LHS) that also contains the consequent (RHS). Formally speaking, this is the conditional probability of seeing the consequent item set given that the antecedent item set is there. For example, out of all the transactions in the movie theater 43% bought popcorn and chocolate together (this is the support of the antecedent measure – i.e., $support(X)$), while 30% bought all three items together (popcorn, chocolate and big soda). This is the $support(X \Rightarrow Y)$ measure. The confidence can then be calculated as 30% / 43% ≅ 70%. You should note at this stage that the confidence measure can be somewhat misleading. The reason is that it is calculated as a relative measure of two fractions. However, both fractions in Equation (12.8) can be very low while still obtaining a high confidence. If $support(X \Rightarrow Y)$ is 1% and $support(X)$ is 1%, the confidence is 100%. We can account for this by calculating what is called the *lift ratio*:

$$Lift(X \Rightarrow Y) = \frac{support(X \Rightarrow Y)}{support(X) \times support(Y)} \tag{12.9}$$

The *lift ratio* or just the *lift* tells us more about the strength of the co-occurrence rule as it measures association between the item sets in the antecedent and consequent, compared to what would be expected by chance alone. A lift value greater than 1 indicates that there is a level of association beyond what would be expected if the two item sets were totally independent of each other.

It is important to note that co-occurrence analysis in many cases reveals obvious relationships that may not be very useful in pricing decisions. For example, customers who bought hamburgers also, to a large extent, bought fries and soda. These items are typically already grouped together in a menu and will yield little new insight for the firm. Hence, for a rule to be valuable it should contain some new or surprising information. To extract this from the (big) data it is useful to have a plan or algorithm stating how one should go about to discover the potentially fruitful associations. One such step-by-step algorithm is the *Apriori* algorithm illustrated in Figure 12.8. An example of how this algorithm can be implemented is provided in the Excel file following Chapter 12.

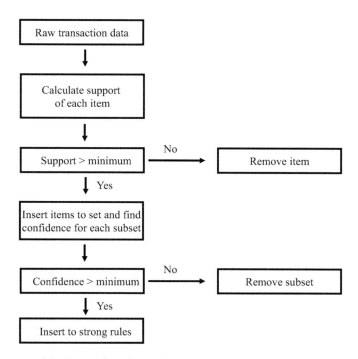

Figure 12.8 Illustration of the *Apriori* algorithm to discover strong co-occurrence (or association) rules.

12.4 Implementation in Excel

This section will focus on how the techniques described in the previous section can be implemented in Excel. We shall focus on specific business problems that should be solved and use small data sets for expository purposes. However, Excel has a lot of new features that will enable you to implement many big data projects that would have been impossible just a few years ago. We shall therefore go through Excel's role in big data pricing analytics in the final section.

Business problem #1: Classify customers into high and low reservation prices

We start with a case where the objective of a movie theater is to perform classification of five new customers' reservation price (RP) level. We shall use data containing information about various characteristics of 50 existing customers to predict the (likely) reservation price level of the five new customers. A snapshot of the data is given in Figure 12.9 and included in the Excel workbook following this chapter.

The data consist of information about whether the customer is a member of a movie club or not (Y/N), how many movies the customer has watched over the last year, the annual net income and whether the RP (given in column E) of the customer is above (high) or below (low) $10 for a ticket. This information will be used to create offers specifically tailored to the new customers and the objective is thus to predict which reservation price class they belong to. Those with a high reservation price will get an offer of a little more exclusive show than those with a low reservation price. Below is a step-by-step description of how we can classify the new customers using the *k*-NN algorithm.

Step 1: Create numerical values and normalize the data

The first step is to transform string variables into numerical variables and to normalize all values. The member variable is an example of a string that should be converted into numerical values. We do this with a simple if statement (see Excel file), assigning the value

	A	B	C	D	E
1	\multicolumn{5}{c}{DATA ON VARIOUS CHARACTERISTICS OF EXISTING MOVIE}
2	\multicolumn{5}{c}{THEATER CUSTOMERS}
3	Member	Member-#	Movies watched	Income	RP
4	Y	1	20	$ 11,320	High
5	Y	1	9	$ 7,200	low
6	Y	1	11	$ 20,000	High
7	N	0	15	$ 12,800	low
8	N	0	12	$ 5,700	low
9	Y	1	22	$ 9,000	High
10	N	0	7	$ 35,200	High
11	N	0	5	$ 22,800	low
12	Y	1	17	$ 16,500	low
13	Y	1	24	$ 9,200	High

Figure 12.9 The data used in the classification problem.

1 if the customer is a member and 0 otherwise. Other string variables can be converted in similar ways, but if you have many categories it may be useful to have a lookup table with all the categories and the corresponding numerical values. Once all the variables are in a numerical format, we can normalize them using Equation (12.3).

Step 2: Calculate the Euclidean distances between existing and new customers

To calculate the similarities between existing and new customers we need information about the new customers on the same variables as we have in the data set of our existing customers (the training data). This is given in Figure 12.10. The upper part reflects the raw values, while the lower part shows the corresponding normalized values. The normalization must be done using the data of our existing customers (the training data). Two of the customers are members of a movie club, the number of movies watched last year ranges between two and 11 and their annual net income ranges from $2,500 to $21,000.

To calculate the Euclidean distance in Excel we can use the =SUMXMY2 function. This function calculates the squared difference of each dimension and sums these. The only thing remaining then is to take the square root of this quantity and we have the Euclidean distance. The results are given in Figure 12.11. For example, when considering only the first five observations in the training data, the new customer number 1 (ED-1) is most similar to existing customer number 3 (Euclidean distance of 0.51). The new customer number 2 is most similar to existing customer number 5 (Euclidean distance of 1.65), and so forth.

Step 3: Rank observations according to similarity

When we have the distances from the existing customers to the new customers who shall be classified, we need to rank them in order to know which neighbors to use in the classification. We do this in Excel with the =RANK function and choose ascending order, such that the neighbor closest to the new customers achieves a rank of 1, and so forth.

	V	W	X	Y	Z	AA
1	INFORMATION ABOUT NEW CUSTOMERS THAT SHOULD BE CLASSIFIED INTO					
2	HIGH/LOW RP					
3	Customer #	1	2	3	4	5
4	Member	Y	N	Y	N	N
5	Member #	1	0	1	0	0
6	Movies watched	8	2	11	9	2
7	Income	$21,000	$4,000	$8,500	$16,300	$2,500

	V	W	X	Y	Z	AA
10	Customer	1	2	3	4	5
11	Member	Y	N	Y	N	N
12	Member #	0.91	-1.07	0.91	-1.07	-1.07
13	Movies watched	-0.53	-1.51	-0.04	-0.36	-1.51
14	Income	0.78	-1.10	-0.60	0.26	-1.27

Figure 12.10 The data on the new customers that shall be classified into either high or low RP.

	I	J	K	L	M
1	\multicolumn{5}{c}{CALCULATION OF EUCLIDEAN DISTANCES BETWEEN EACH}
2	\multicolumn{5}{c}{OBSERVATION AND NEW CUSTOMERS}
3	ED-1	ED-2	ED-3	ED-4	ED-5
4	2.24	3.65	1.51	2.74	3.69
5	1.54	2.32	0.36	2.23	2.35
6	0.51	3.05	1.28	2.05	3.15
7	2.47	2.35	2.15	1.06	2.42
8	2.69	1.65	2.02	1.28	1.68

Figure 12.11 The Euclidean distance from the five new customers (ED-1 – ED-5) to each of the first five observations in the (training) data.

Step 4: Choose value of k and predict class of new customers

When we have the rank of all existing customers (in terms of how close they are to the new customers), we only need to decide how many neighbors to use in the classification. As previously mentioned, the best value of k can be found by building models with various ks and then use performance measures to evaluate how many neighbors (i.e., ks) to use in the final model. We shall briefly illustrate how a *confusion matrix* can be used to evaluate the performance of classification models shortly, but for now we shall use $k=3$ when predicting the class of the new customers. If you have many new customers to be classified (100s, 1,000s, or more) it is a good idea to set up a model that does the job automatically. There are as many approaches of doing this as there are readers of this book. However, one possible approach is illustrated in Figure 12.12 and given in the Excel file following this chapter. Focus on the upper part of the figure. Here the VLOOKUP function looks up the nearest neighbor in row 16 ($k=1$) and returns the corresponding class of that neighbor, the class of the second nearest neighbor ($k=2$) is returned in row 17 and the third nearest ($k=3$) in row 18. The results are illustrated in the middle part of the figure. Clearly, only the nearest neighbor of this customer has a high reservation price (remember high RP = 1, and low RP=0). In row 19 we then calculate the average class of the three nearest neighbors. As only one out of the three nearest neighbors has a high RP, the average is equal to 0.33. In row 20 we create a simple if statement that will return the predicted class of the new customers. In this case a cutoff value of 0.5 is used. This means that if the majority of the nearest neighbors have a high RP, the new customer of interest will also be classified with a high RP and vice versa.

However, at this stage we do not know whether our predicted classes of the new customers are correct or not. The reason is that we have no information about their true reservation prices. When we obtain this information at a later stage, we can evaluate how well the model is working. In practice, business analysts rarely wait for the real values of the target value to be available before assessing the performance of various models. Instead, they split the data into one *training (data) set* used to build candidate models, for example using various values of k or other alternative methods to predict classes, and

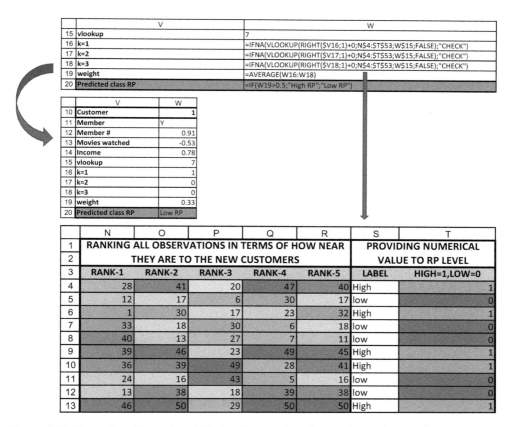

Figure 12.12 Illustration of how the k-NN classification algorithm can be implemented in Excel.

one *validation (data) set* used to evaluate the performance of the various models. This is not done in the current example, but you can use the available data and split it into a training set (e.g., n=40) and validation set (e.g., n=10).

Step 5: Evaluate performance of classification models

If we have organized the data into a training set and a validation set, or if we have obtained the real values of the target variable (after a little waiting), we can evaluate the performance of the classification model and eventually compare it to some alternatives. We shall here compare the predictions we did in the last step with the real classes of the five customers. The starting point for evaluating the performance of the classification models is usually a *confusion matrix*, which simply displays the number of correct and incorrect classifications performed by the model of interest. A general presentation of such a confusion matrix is given in the upper panel of Figure 12.13 and the classification results of the five new customers from the example problem is in the lower panel (also available in the Excel file following the chapter). From this matrix we can calculate

206 Big Data and pricing analytics

Actual class	Predicted class	
	0	1
0	n_{00}	n_{01}
1	n_{10}	n_{11}

Actual class	Predicted class	
	0 (Low RP)	1 (High RP)
0 (Low RP)	2	0
1 (High RP)	2	1

Figure 12.13 General presentation of a confusion matrix (upper panel) and the results from the example problem (lower panel).

performance measures such as *the overall error rate, the accuracy of the model, class 1 error rate, and class 0 error rate*:

$$Overall\ error\ rate = \frac{n_{10} + n_{01}}{n_{00} + n_{01} + n_{10} + n_{11}} \quad (12.10)$$

$$Model\ accuracy = 1 - overall\ error\ rate \quad (12.11)$$

$$Class\ 0\ error\ rate = \frac{n_{01}}{n_{00} + n_{01}} \quad (12.12)$$

$$Class\ 1\ error\ rate = \frac{n_{10}}{n_{11} + n_{10}} \quad (12.13)$$

The class 0 error is also often referred to as a *false positive* and the class 1 error as a *false negative*. The reason is that we falsely predict an actual 0 observation as a 1 and vice versa. The corresponding correct 0 and 1 predictions are referred to as *true negative* and *true positive*.

By plugging the numbers from the confusion matrix into the formulas given in Equation (12.10) – (12.13) we obtain the following results for the classification model using $k=3$:

Performance measures	
Overall error rate	40.0%
Model accuracy	60.0%
Class 0 error rate	0.0%
Class 1 error rate	66.7%

The question then is whether these results are good or bad. The answer is, *it depends*. First, we generally would need to compare the performance measures across alternative models to say if a model is good or bad. Second, for some classification problems the costs associated with making a lot of class 0 errors may be higher than making a lot of class 1 errors and vice versa. Without such information it is hard to evaluate how well or poorly the model performs. However, on a general basis we can say that the overall error rate is 40%, which corresponds to an accuracy of 60%. What does it mean? In 60% of the classifications the model was able to assign the new customers to the right reservation price class (three out of five customers). Moreover, it was able to correctly classify all customers belonging to the *low reservation price* group, but failed to classify the *high reservation price customers* in two out of three cases (66.7%).

If the costs associated with wrongly classifying the high reservation price customers are higher than wrongly classifying the low RP customers, we should consider adjusting the cutoff value used in the classification. In the current example we set a cutoff value of 0.5, meaning that if two or three out of the three nearest neighbors were in the high RP class the new customer would be classified as high RP. If we adjusted this cutoff down, we would automatically reduce the class 1 error rate. It is beyond the scope of this book to go into the details of this, but it is still important that you are aware of the trade-offs between the various classification errors when you run your own project.

Business problem #2: Segment the market based on certain criteria

Assume now that instead of classifying new customers with respect to their reservation prices, we want to segment our current customer into homogeneous groups using the same criteria as in the previous business problem. We can do this using the *k*-Means algorithm. In this case, *k* refers to the number of clusters and *not* the number of neighbors. Each cluster needs a cluster center – that is, a centroid. As a starting point we choose random values for each centroid. One approach is to use the =PERCENTILE.INC function in Excel. This ensures that there is some distance between the starting values of the centroids. The upper part of Figure 12.14 shows the percentiles used and the corresponding starting values of all the four customer characteristics that will be used in the cluster analysis. Alternatively, you could set the starting values based on your own experience or expectations. As seen in this figure, we use three clusters in this analysis.

Once we have the starting values of the centroids, we can calculate the Euclidean distance between each customer and the centroid, and assign each customer to the cluster with the lowest distance. As the calculation of the Euclidean distance is the same as for the *k*-NN algorithm the implementation of this part will not be repeated, but an illustration of the allocation of customers to clusters is given in Figure 12.15. The assignment rule is straightforward: the customer is allocated to the cluster with the smallest (Euclidean) distance to the cluster centroid. The first customer is closest to the centroid of cluster 3 (0.96) and is therefore assigned to this cluster. The next customer is closest to cluster 2 (0.60) and is placed there, and so forth.

However, these initial values of the centroids' positions should be recalculated such that the total (Euclidean) distance between all observations and their respective centroids is minimized. We do this using the Solver in Excel. The objective function is the total distance and the decision variables are the positions of the centroids. Note that we should

	V	W	X	Y	Z	AA
2		Starting values centroids				
3	Cluster	Percentile	Member	Movies	Income	RP
4	Cluster 1	0.25	-1.07	-0.82	-0.67	-0.91
5	Cluster 2	0.5	0.91	-0.04	-0.25	-0.91
6	Cluster 3	0.75	0.91	0.74	0.37	1.07
7		Optimal values centroids				
8	Cluster	Percentile	Member	Movies	Income	RP
9	Cluster 1		-0.66	-0.44	-0.02	-0.83
10	Cluster 2		0.92	0.07	-0.35	1.07
11	Cluster 3		0.91	1.49	-0.19	1.08
12						
13		Starting values centroids		Optimal values centroids		
14	Cluster	Distance	# of cases	Cluster	Distance	# of cases
15	1	1.320	20	1	1.645	29
16	2	1.538	8	2	0.551	13
17	3	1.099	22	3	0.446	8
18	SUM	3.957	50.000		2.642	50.000

Figure 12.14 Starting values of centroids (upper part), optimal values of centroids (middle part) and summary measures of the average distance between the actual observations and the centroids using the starting values of the centroids (lower left part) and the optimal values of the centroids (lower right part).

use the "Evolutionary" solver method in this case and for this work we need to impose some restrictions on the values the centroids position can take. As all the variables are normalized (z-scores) it is usually sufficient to set the range between −3 and +3. It could also be smart to set a maximum number of iterations for very big problems.

The middle part of Figure 12.14 shows the results of the optimization. All the centroids' positions changed from their starting values. As the customers are automatically allocated to the cluster nearest a cluster centroid, many customers have also in this process been reallocated to a new cluster. This can be clearly seen in the lower part of Figure 12.14 where the average distance between the customers and their respective centroid, and the number of customers in each cluster, are presented both using (1) the original starting values of the centroids and (2) the optimized values. The sum of the (average Euclidean) distance is reduced by 33% (from 3.957 to 2.642) and the number of customers belonging to clusters 1, 2 and 3 is changed.

So, what can we say about the various clusters after the recalculations of the centroids? Focus on the middle panel of Figure 12.14. We use the formula for calculating the z-scores to transform the centroid values back to meaningful quantities. If doing so, we see that the real-life values of cluster 1 are [0.2, 8.5, $13,839, 0]. This means that cluster 1 is characterized by non-members, watching relatively few movies (8.5),

	K	L	M	N	O
1	\multicolumn{5}{c	}{EUCLIDEAN DISTANCE - FROM STARTING VALUES OF}
2	\multicolumn{5}{c	}{CLUSTERS}
3	ED-1	ED-2	ED-3	ROW	CLUSTER
4	3.62	2.48	0.96	51.00	3.00
5	2.04	0.60	2.54	50.00	2.00
6	3.21	2.19	0.84	49.00	3.00

Figure 12.15 Euclidean distance between the first three customers and the centroids (cluster centers) of the three clusters. Column O indicates the initial assignment of a customer to a cluster.

having an income of $13,839, and a low reservation price (0 vs 1). The corresponding values of cluster 2 are [1.0, 11.7, $10,874, 1.0]. Hence, these customers are members, watch 11.7 movies, have income of almost $11,000, and high reservation prices. The centroids of cluster 3 are [1.0, 20.3, $12,304, 1.0]. Hence, apart from movie consumption, this cluster is very similar to cluster 2. From the analysis it seems like income is not an important variable to use in the segmentation of customers, but we can obviously use the other results to create offers that are likely to be appealing to each group. For example, we may approach cluster 1 with a special loyalty discount if watching ten movies or more (remember the centroid is 8.5 movies and they have low reservation prices). We could also consider offering them a special deal on memberships. Clusters 2 and 3 may be triggered by more exclusive offers (high reservation prices) and potentially some perks only available to those with a minimum of, for example, 20 movies watched. Special loyalty programs with pricing schemes and other benefits as part of the programs could also be considered.

To get a quick overview of the similarities between clusters, we can calculate the Euclidean distances between cluster centroids as shown in Figure 12.16. This information helps us evaluate the distinctness of the clusters and provide some guidance on how many clusters to construct from the data. Clusters 1 and 3 are clearly (not surprisingly) most distinct from each other, while clusters 2 and 3 are most similar. Maybe clusters 2 and 3 in the current analysis are so similar that they could be merged into one?

Business problem #3: Create a special offer menu in a movie theater kiosk

This business problem is about using raw transaction data on purchases of popcorn, chocolate and soda at a movie theater to detect strong associations that can be used to

\multicolumn{4}{c	}{Distances between centroids}
Cluster	1	2	3
1	0.00	2.54	3.15
2	2.54	0.00	1.43
3	3.15	1.43	0.00

Figure 12.16 Distances between cluster centroids.

Transaction ID	Popcorn Small	Popcorn Medium	Popcorn Large	Chocolate Small	Chocolate Medium	Chocolate Large	Soda Small	Soda Medium	Soda Large
1	0	1	0	0	0	0	1	0	0
2	0	1	0	1	0	0	0	0	0
3	0	0	1	0	1	0	0	1	0
4	0	1	0	0	0	1	0	0	1
5	1	0	0	0	0	1	0	0	1
6	1	0	0	1	0	0	1	0	0
7	1	0	0	1	0	0	0	1	0
8	0	0	0	1	0	0	0	1	0
9	0	0	1	0	0	0	1	0	0
10	1	0	0	0	1	0	1	0	0

Figure 12.17 The ten first transactions of movie theater kiosk purchase data.

Product	Size	Support
Popcorn	Small	46.0%
Popcorn	Medium	25.0%
Popcorn	Large	18.0%
Chocolate	Small	46.0%
Chocolate	Medium	33.0%
Chocolate	Large	9.0%
Soda	Small	41.0%
Soda	Medium	34.0%
Soda	Large	14.0%

Figure 12.18 Support of each item/size combination of all transactions.

put together valuable menus. All three items come in three sizes: small, medium, and large. The ten first transactions are illustrated in Figure 12.17. As seen from this figure, if the item was purchased, it takes the value 1 and 0 otherwise. For example, the customer behind the first transaction bought a medium popcorn, no chocolate, and a small soda. The customer behind the second transaction bought a medium popcorn, a small chocolate, and no soda, and so forth.

When we have the raw transaction data organized this way, it is straightforward to calculate measures of interest as presented in Equations (12.5) to (12.9) and used in the steps of the *Apriori* algorithm presented in Figure 12.8. The first step is to calculate the support of each item. In our case each product/size combination is treated as one item. The results of the simple support calculations (which is the count divided by the total of transactions) are presented in Figure 12.18. The numbers tell us, for example, that out of all the transactions, 46% contain a small popcorn, 25% a medium popcorn, and 18% a large popcorn, and so forth. Based on these initial results, the management are first

X {Popcorn, Chocolate}	Y {Soda}	Support (X)	Support (Y)	Support (X->Y)	Confidence	Lift
Small, small	Small	18.00%	41.00%	7.00%	38.9 %	0.949
Small, medium	Medium	18.00%	34.00%	5.00%	27.8 %	0.817
Small, large	Large	4.00%	14.00%	1.00%	25.0 %	1.786
Medium, small	Small	17.00%	41.00%	6.00%	35.3 %	0.861
Medium, medium	Medium	4.00%	34.00%	2.00%	50.0 %	1.471
Medium, Large	Large	2.00%	14.00%	1.00%	50.0 %	3.571
Large, small	Small	6.00%	41.00%	2.00%	33.3 %	0.813
Large, medium	Medium	8.00%	34.00%	5.00%	62.5 %	1.838
Large, Large	Large	3.00%	14.00%	1.00%	33.3 %	2.381

Figure 12.19 Support of each item/size combination of all transactions.

and foremost interested in antecedents containing combinations of various popcorn and chocolate sizes and using soda (and various sizes of this product) as consequent.

Based on this information, we can formulate the business problem in Excel and perform the necessary calculations to advise the managers of potential actions. An illustration of the implementation of the problem is provided in Figure 12.19. The results can be summarized as follows. First, among the various antecedent combinations (popcorn/chocolate), small/small (18%), small/medium (18%), and medium/small (17%) are most frequently occurring in the transaction data. None of these have a very high support. The least popular combinations of the antecedent are medium/large (2%) and large/large (3%). As a rule of thumb, a cutoff value of 20% is sometimes applied in order to consider using the item set in a co-occurrence grouping rule. However, in our case, the aim is to put together a menu that could boost sales if priced correctly. This therefore represents a valuable opportunity and the support cutoff can be set lower. The consequent has three possible outcomes and we clearly see that it is the small soda (41%) that is most popular followed by the medium size (34%) and large (14%).

The *Support*$(X \Rightarrow Y)$ measure shows the fraction of the transactions containing both the antecedent and the consequent and is used to calculate the confidence measure. Out of all the considered combinations, the small/small/small is most popular as 7% of all transactions includes these item/size combinations. The medium/small/small (6%) and the large/medium/medium (5%) follow in popularity, but these various combinations have totally different confidence measures. Recall that the confidence measure says something about how often the consequent (Y) goes together with the antecedent (X) and can be viewed as the conditional probability of Y occurring given that X occurs. A high value of the confidence could indicate a strong rule, but it could also be very misleading. To see why, consider again the computation of this measure: *Support*$(X \Rightarrow Y)/ support(X)$. That is, it depends heavily on the size of the antecedent. In cases where we have low support of the antecedent, the confidence would be high in most cases if the consequent is a frequent item. The effect of the size of the antecedent is seen clearly in Figure 12.19 for some of the combinations. To account for the potential misleadingness of the confidence we also compute the lift measure. This quantity reveals the level of "surprise" of the co-occurrence rules. A level higher than 1 suggests a relation between the antecedent and consequent that is stronger than one would expect by chance alone. We see that many of the combinations in these data have a lift measure higher than 1. Most prominent are the medium/large/large combination (3.571), followed by large/large/large (2.381), and large/medium/medium (1.838).

Based on these analyses, what could be our advice to the management when it comes to pricing/promotion decisions? Perhaps the movie theater could consider special offer menus consisting of medium/large/large, large/large/large, and large/medium/medium combinations. Even though the antecedents do not have high support individually, the co-occurrence grouping analysis suggests that there may be some valuable opportunities in these combinations.

12.5 Excel's role in big data pricing analytics

Recall that one of the most widely used definitions of Big Data by Beyer and Laney (2012) states that Big Data "...*demand cost-effective, innovative forms of information processing.*" Another definition provided by Mills et al. (2012) state explicitly that new technology and techniques are required to capture, store and analyze the data.[1] The big question then is: Can Excel be used at all when we talk about big data analytics? The answer is, fortunately, yes. First, the phrasing that Big Data requires *new technology and techniques* will always be relative to the time point at which the definition is made. Yes, the traditional version of Excel has narrow limits on the number of rows and columns that a spreadsheet can be filled with. However, Microsoft is a big company that focuses on innovative solutions, and a quick Google search on "Excel and big data" reveals a range of potential solutions when it comes to efficiently using the analysis tools available in Excel against new data stores.

For example, the weather forecasting system provided by the Norwegian Meteorological Institute offers continuously updated weather forecasts in XML format for more than 10 million locations worldwide that can be directly linked to Excel via Power Query. The link to the weather forecasting system can then simply be refreshed to update the forecasts you are interested in using in your own models. This could be potentially very fruitful in many pricing analyses that aim at optimizing prices with a very high frequency based on certain algorithms where the weather forecast is a key input variable. We know that the weather heavily affects the demand for a wide range of goods and services. Think of amusement parks, movie theaters, alpine ski resorts, ice cream producers, snow shovel dealers, and more. All these businesses regularly experience the weather and weather forecast affecting the demanded quantity. Hence, building a model using historical weather data and connecting it to the weather forecasting system can improve your own modeling and price optimizations substantially.

To get you started on your own project, we briefly illustrate how such dynamic weather forecast data for New York City can be accessed in Excel via yr.no in Figure 12.20.[2] The process is very simple. We only need the link to the XML file for the location we are interested in the weather forecasts for and paste it into the URL text box.[3] We then choose all the data items we are interested in, and choose Load. After a little manipulation of how the data is displayed the result could be as illustrated in the lower panel

Big Data and pricing analytics 213

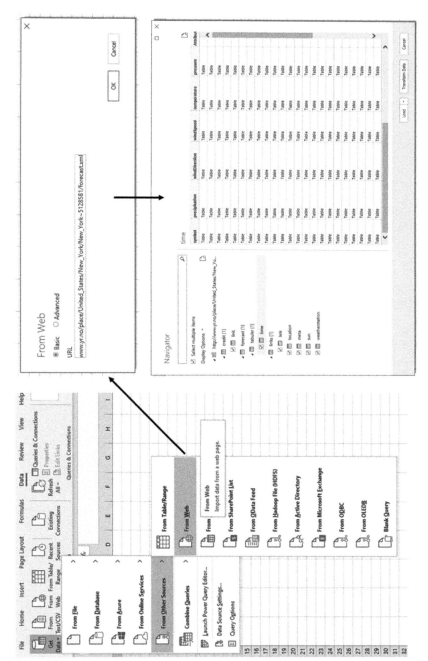

Figure 12.20 Dynamic weather forecast for New York City (USA) obtained from yr.no via Excel's Power Query. Weather forecast from Yr, delivered by the Norwegian Meteorological Institute and NRK.

#	symbol.Attribute:name	precipitation.Attribute:value	temperature.Attribute:value	pressure.Attribute:value	Attribute:from	Attribute:to
1	Light rain	0.2	10	1015.8	06/04/2020 01:00:00	06/04/2020 06:00:00
2	Clear sky	0	8	1017.0	06/04/2020 06:00:00	06/04/2020 12:00:00
3	Clear sky	0	14	1017.6	06/04/2020 12:00:00	06/04/2020 18:00:00
4	Fair	0	14	1014.0	06/04/2020 18:00:00	07/04/2020 00:00:00
5	Cloudy	0	7	1014.9	07/04/2020 00:00:00	07/04/2020 06:00:00
6	Partly cloudy	0	8	1013.7	07/04/2020 06:00:00	07/04/2020 12:00:00
7	Partly cloudy	0	14	1012.3	07/04/2020 12:00:00	07/04/2020 18:00:00
8	Fair	0	12	1007.3	07/04/2020 18:00:00	08/04/2020 00:00:00
9	Light rain	0.6	10	1004.3	08/04/2020 00:00:00	08/04/2020 06:00:00
10	Cloudy	0.4	11	998.2	08/04/2020 06:00:00	08/04/2020 12:00:00
11	Fair	0	19	997.0	08/04/2020 14:00:00	08/04/2020 20:00:00
12	Partly cloudy	0.9	10	1003.1	08/04/2020 20:00:00	09/04/2020 02:00:00
13	Light rain showers	0	8	1003.2	09/04/2020 02:00:00	09/04/2020 08:00:00
14	Rain showers	3.9	9	997.3	09/04/2020 08:00:00	09/04/2020 14:00:00
15	Clear sky	0	8	991.3	09/04/2020 14:00:00	09/04/2020 20:00:00
16	Clear sky	0	9	994.4	09/04/2020 20:00:00	10/04/2020 02:00:00
17	Clear sky	0	6	995.9	10/04/2020 02:00:00	10/04/2020 08:00:00
18	Partly cloudy	0.1	5	998.0	10/04/2020 08:00:00	10/04/2020 14:00:00
19	Partly cloudy	0	8	1000.8	10/04/2020 14:00:00	10/04/2020 20:00:00
20	Fair	0	6	1007.1	10/04/2020 20:00:00	11/04/2020 02:00:00
21	Fair	0	4	1012.7	11/04/2020 02:00:00	11/04/2020 08:00:00
22	Partly cloudy	0	3	1017.5	11/04/2020 08:00:00	11/04/2020 14:00:00
23	Cloudy	0	11	1017.4	11/04/2020 14:00:00	11/04/2020 20:00:00
24	Cloudy	0	7	1019.3	11/04/2020 20:00:00	12/04/2020 02:00:00
25	Cloudy	0	8	1020.1	12/04/2020 02:00:00	12/04/2020 08:00:00
26	Heavy rain	5.0	8	1018.8	12/04/2020 08:00:00	12/04/2020 14:00:00
27	Heavy rain	29.8	9	1011.1	12/04/2020 14:00:00	12/04/2020 20:00:00
28	Cloudy	0.4	10	994.6	12/04/2020 20:00:00	13/04/2020 02:00:00
29	Partly cloudy	0.1	9	993.7	13/04/2020 02:00:00	13/04/2020 08:00:00
30	Fair	0	9	1000.1	13/04/2020 08:00:00	13/04/2020 14:00:00
31	Partly cloudy	0.1	14	1000.5	13/04/2020 14:00:00	13/04/2020 20:00:00
32	Partly cloudy	0	11	1002.1	13/04/2020 20:00:00	14/04/2020 02:00:00
33	Clear sky	0	6	1007.0	14/04/2020 02:00:00	14/04/2020 08:00:00
34	Fair	0.3	5	1009.7	14/04/2020 08:00:00	14/04/2020 14:00:00
35	Fair	0.3	10	1007.7	14/04/2020 14:00:00	14/04/2020 20:00:00
36	Fair	0	8	1011.6	14/04/2020 20:00:00	15/04/2020 02:00:00

Figure 12.20 Cont.

of Figure 12.20. This information can be used in combination with other relevant data (such as marketing activities, sentiment analysis of social media feeds and more) directly in a model to forecast demanded quantity of a range of products and services. Another great feature is that the information in the data table is very easy to update. We simply choose Refresh all and the most recent forecasts are updated "on the fly."

We shall not go into all the details of the potential Excel has when it comes to Big Data and pricing analytics. The important thing is that you are aware that Excel aims at taking a leading role in the era of Big Data and that you can probably use your favorite tool (Excel) to perform most of the tasks even if the volume, variety, and velocity of the data are increasing rapidly.

12.6 Summary

- The three Vs, volume, velocity and variety, are often used to characterize the key features of Big Data.
- The vast amount of data that has become available to companies over the world can create insight and business value if utilized correctly.
- To benefit from Big Data in pricing decisions we should start with certain research questions and not with the data themselves, tools, or techniques.
- The analytical techniques we can use to process and analyze Big Data are usually either descriptive, predictive or prescriptive.
- Techniques can also be categorized as supervised or unsupervised methods. The main difference between the two is that supervised methods predict the outcome of a given variable, while unsupervised methods are more explorative and aim at finding patterns in the data with limited guidance.
- Regression analysis and classification techniques are examples of supervised methods, while cluster analysis and co-occurrence grouping are examples of unsupervised methods.
- Excel has many features specifically designed to handle and analyze big data sets. One example is Power Query, which allows you to combine and analyze data from a range of data sources.

12.7 Problems

1. How can the term Big Data be formally defined? Explain.
2. How can big data sets create business value when it comes to pricing decisions? Give a few examples.
3. Provide examples of supervised and unsupervised methods and explain the main difference between the two.
4. What is meant by the term Euclidean distance? Explain.
5. Give a brief explanation of how the k-nearest neighbor algorithm can be used for classification problems.
6. What is the main objective of cluster analysis?
7. Calculate the Euclidean distance between customer 1 and the following neighbors:

Customer	Haircuts per annum	Age	Distance from city (km)
Customer 1	8	32	3.0
Neighbor 1	2	22	25.0
Neighbor 2	6	60	5.0
Neighbor 3	12	79	0.5

8. Use the same data as in problem 7, but now you shall normalize all the values before calculating the Euclidean distances. The means and standard deviations of the various attributes are given below:

	Mean	Standard Dev.
Haircuts per annum	8.56	2.76
Age	43.45	12.43
Distance from city (km)	7.67	5.23

Does the ranking of the various neighbors (in terms of how close they are to customer 1) change when using normalized numbers?

9. Use the results from problem 8 in combination with the following information about whether the three customers have previously taken advantage of a direct mail offer or not: Neighbor 1 → Yes, Neighbor 2 → No, Neighbor 3 → Yes. Based on this information, what class would you assign customer 1 to if using k=1, k=2, and k=3 and a threshold of 0.51 (where 1=yes, and 0=no)?

10. In the Excel solution file accompanying this chapter, a data set on hairdresser customers is included (sheet named P-12-10-Data). The data contain information about the various characteristics of existing customers and whether they responded positively to a previously given offer (Yes/No). The hairdresser now has information about five new customers and wants your help in determining which of these new customers are likely to respond "Yes" to a similar offer. Use the k-nearest neighbor algorithm (with k=3 and a threshold of 0.5) to classify these five new customers. Also assess the performance of your classification results using the metrics described in the chapter.

Information about new customers that should be classified into yes/no

Customer #	1	2	3	4	5
Hair cuts/yr	6	8	2	15	12
Age	25	65	52	79	16
Distance city (km)	5.80	16.05	2.14	0.60	0.75

11. In the Excel solution file accompanying this chapter, a data set on hairdresser customers is included (sheet named 'P-12-11-Data'). The data contain information about various characteristics of existing customers and whether they responded positively to a previously given offer (Yes/No). These data are identical to those used in the previous problem. However, now the hairdresser wants you to segment the customers into three segments. Use the technique examined in this chapter and

evaluate and discuss the results. Does the number of clusters seem appropriate? Why/why not?
12. Replicate Business problem #3 from the main text of this chapter: *Business problem #3: Create a special offer menu in a movie theater kiosk*. The data you need are provided in a sheet named "P-12-12-Data."
13. Link weather forecasts for a location of your own choice via Excel's Power Query. Follow the steps as provided in the main text. You can also try to connect the weather forecast to a prediction model of a product or service you may have data for.
14. Search the web for access to big data sets and examine if it is possible to get access to these using Excel. Create your own project using some of the techniques provided in this chapter.

Notes

1 Mills et al. (2012, p. 10): "*Big Data is a term that is used to describe data that is high volume, high velocity and/or high variety; requires new technologies and techniques to capture, store, and analyze it; and is used to enhance decision-making, provide insight and discovery, and support and optimise processes.*"
2 Note that the use of the weather forecasts from yr.no in your own services shall be marked by the following statement: Weather forecast from Yr, delivered by the Norwegian Meteorological Institute and NRK.
3 For example: www.yr.no/place/United_States/New_York/New_York~5128581/forecast.xml. See the following link for an overview of more than 16,000 locations worldwide: http://fil.nrk.no/yr/viktigestader/verda.txt

Chapter 13

Monte Carlo simulation for pricing decisions

In most cases, managers or other decision-makers do not have perfect information about what the actual consequences of various pricing decisions will be like. Additionally, the properties of the various variables going into a pricing model may be hard to describe with smooth functions, and the pricing problem itself could be so complex that it is impossible to find analytical solutions. In such situations, Monte Carlo simulation is a valuable tool that can be used to get an overview of the potential outcome of various pricing decisions. Examples of applications include, but are not limited to:

- Estimating the probability of breaking-even from a given price change.
- Estimating the market response from a range of pricing decisions.
- Estimating competitors' response from a range of pricing decisions.
- Setting prices under uncertainty in general.
- Setting dynamic prices under uncertainty with a special focus on some variables:
  - Weather, cannibalization, competitor actions.
- Setting mark-down levels under uncertainty with a special focus on:
  - Response to various mark-down levels, cannibalization fraction.

We shall, in this chapter, focus specifically on what Monte Carlo simulation is, how it can be used when making pricing decisions, and how this powerful technique can be implemented in Excel. Specifically, the chapter will cover the following topics:

- What is Monte Carlo simulation?
- How can simulation be used for pricing decisions?
- The basics of Monte Carlo simulations in Excel.
- Examples of simulation models for pricing problems.

13.1 What is Monte Carlo simulation?

Monte Carlo simulation is all about using the computer to draw random numbers in order to replicate elements of the real world. The term Monte Carlo is used because of the similarities between many gambling devices and the process behind simulation using the computer. A device such as the roulette wheel, for example, produces random numbers from a defined range (from 0 to 36). In practice, we could use a roulette wheel to perform simulation of many interesting real-life applications. There is only one drawback, though: It takes a very long time to obtain the random numbers we need. Many

FREQUENCY TABLE AND PROBABILITY DISTRIBUTION OF DEMAND FOR COFFEE		
Cups Sold	Days with this demand	Probability
20	3	0.8%
40	45	12.3%
60	120	32.9%
80	95	26.0%
100	75	20.5%
120	20	5.5%
140	7	1.9%
Sum	365	100.00%

Figure 13.1 Frequency table and probability distribution of demand for cups of black coffee at a coffee shop.

simulation projects require thousands of trials, and if you spend on average 30 seconds on each trial, it will take many hours, at best, to run one simple simulation experiment. This is the reason why we use the computer (using Excel for example) to draw the random numbers we need.

To illustrate the concept further, consider the frequency table presented in Figure 13.1 containing a record of cups sold per day over the last year (365 days) at a local coffee shop.

The table should be interpreted as follows: For three out of the last 365 days, the coffee shop sold 20 cups per day. For 45 of the last 365 days, the coffee shop sold 40 cups per day, and so forth. When we have the historical sales data organized in this way, it is easy to calculate the probability of a given demanded quantity: We simply take the number of days with the given demand and divide it by the total number of days in a year the coffee shop is open (assumed to be 365). Hence, the probability of selling 80 cups on any given day is then 26% (95/365).

We can use this information to simulate the demand on any given day. We simply create a roulette wheel consisting of 365 pockets. Then we split the wheel into slices with sizes equal to the number of days with a certain demand for coffee. Figure 13.2 illustrates the concept. In this roulette wheel, the size of a given slice equals the probability of the demanded quantity for black coffee on a given day. When spinning this wheel, we simulate a day at the coffee shop. It may stop at 20 cups (i.e., we sell 20 cups of coffee), or it may stop at 100 cups. The probability of the wheel stopping at a given level depends on the size of the slice. Spinning this wheel enough times will enable us to say something about expected daily demand for coffee and can be used as input in further analysis, such as whether to invest in a new coffee machine or not. If we have additional information on historical price variations, or promotions and corresponding sales data, we can use this information to simulate the effect of pricing decisions on demanded quantity.

Note that in the given example, we can also calculate the expected daily demand analytically using the following formula:

$$E(x) = \sum_{i=1}^{n} P(x_i) x_i \qquad (13.1)$$

220 Monte Carlo simulations

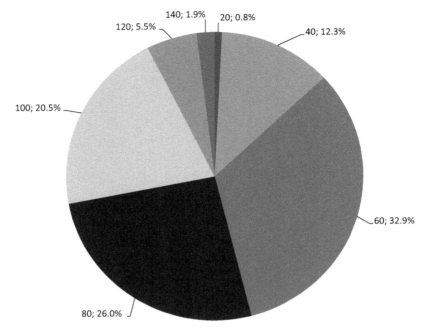

Figure 13.2 Roulette wheel with slices equal to the probability of the various demanded quantities for coffee on a given day. In the data labels, the demanded quantity is given first and then the associated probability of this demand. For example, the numbers 100; 20.5% mean that there is a 20.5% probability of a demanded quantity of 100 cups.

Where x_i is the various levels of demanded quantity given in the leftmost column of Figure 13.1 (e.g., 20, 40, 60, and so forth), $P(x_i)$ is the probability of the demanded quantity occurring given in the rightmost column of Figure 13.1. If we do these calculations correctly (see the Excel file following Chapter 13), we end up with an expected daily demand of 75.45 cups. If we run enough trials (for example, 1,000), we would end up with an average simulated daily demand close to this analytical result. However, in many cases, the analytical solution to a problem is very complex, or may not be available. In such cases, building a simulation model is the only way of analyzing the problem. In general, there are many applications of computer-based simulation within pricing analytics. We shall go through some of these next.

13.2 How can simulation be used for pricing decisions?

The effect of almost any pricing decision can be simulated. We simply need a set of input variables and the properties of these, based on either historical data or (expert) judgements. However, we should bear in mind at this stage that the KISS principle is always a good starting point when it comes to Monte Carlo simulation using the computer. KISS stands for *Keep it simple, stupid*. Even though you have the opportunity to include almost "everything you can think of" in the simulation model, the noise/

uncertainty of all the variables you include as input to your model will soon enough also induce a lot of noise/uncertainty in the output. Put differently: garbage in = garbage out.

Therefore, when building the simulation model, just like building any other model, we should have a special focus on the business problem we want to solve and KISS.

Within a pricing context, the number of business problems that can be analyzed and solved with computer-based simulation is almost unlimited. A few examples are listed below:

- What is the probability of a reduced profit of $1,000,000 or more for a price increase of 5%?
- What is the optimal price to set when also considering potential (uncertain) pricing reactions from competitors?
- What is the probability of breaking even given a price change when accounting for uncertainty in the input variables?
- The maximum affordable loss in profits from implementing a new price is $20,000. What is the probability that we will exceed this loss?
- What price do we need to set in order to be 95% sure to break even given uncertainty in demand and fixed costs?
- What price do we need to set in order to be 90% sure to break even given uncertainty in variable unit costs?
- What is the optimal (profit-maximizing) price when there is uncertainty in how our customers will react to a price change, and the price response cannot be easily described by a simple function?
- What is the optimal variable price to set for low versus high demand periods when we account for uncertainty in demand shifting/cannibalization?
- How should our products be dynamically marked down when we account for the uncertainty in the future price response?

These problems, and many, many more, can be answered by running simulation experiments. Next, we shall go through the basics of Monte Carlo simulation using Excel before illustrating how some of the problems above can be solved.

13.3 The basics of Monte Carlo simulation in Excel

Drawing random numbers and sample from a discrete probability distribution

As Monte Carlo simulation is all about replicating elements of the reality by drawing random numbers, we simply need an efficient way of generating such random numbers with the help of the computer. Excel has two main functions to do this: (1) the RAND function; and (2) the RANDBETWEEN function. Strictly speaking, these functions only generate what are called pseudo-random numbers because they are both built on a certain algorithm to come up with the next number. In this sense, if we know the details of the algorithm used, we could (in theory) predict the next random number and then it would not be random anymore. However, for almost all practical applications, the RAND and RANDBETWEEN functions in Excel work very well. The RAND function generates a random number greater than or equal to 0 and less than 1 based on the

EXAMPLES OF THE RAND() AND RANDBETWEEN FUNCTIONS		
TRIAL	RAND	RANBETWEEN
1	0.430733	73
2	0.139473	449
3	0.38101	702
4	0.255874	567
5	0.29509	328
6	0.689991	141
7	0.825548	428
8	0.727362	1000
9	0.902334	599
10	0.51107	689

Figure 13.3 The results from running 10 trials using the RAND() and RANDBETWEEN() functions in Excel.

Marsenne Twister algorithm. If you type =RAND() into a given cell in the spreadsheet, one possible outcome is the number 0.732592921. Every time you update the calculations in the spreadsheet (using the F9 key) a new random number will appear. The RANDBETWEEN function uses the same pseudo-number generator as the RAND function. The difference is that you specify an upper and lower boundary, for example 1 and 1,000. And, this function returns integers only. If you, for example, specify =RANDBETWEEN(1;1000), the result is one number in this range (greater than or equal to 1 and less than or equal to 1,000) where all the 1,000 possible numbers are equally likely to occur (i.e., it follows a uniform probability distribution). An illustration of the results from ten trials of =RAND() and =RANDBETWEEN(1,1000) is given in Figure 13.3.

In most practical situations, all possible outcomes within a specified range are *not* equally likely to occur. If we want to simulate the change in demanded quantity based on a range of price changes, we expect the impact to be greater from a big price change (say 20%) compared to a small price change (say 5%). The way we solve this is to first generate random numbers with either the RAND or the RANDBETWEEN function, and then sample from a given probability distribution that best describes the properties of the variable we are interested in simulating.

Consider again the simple example presented in both Figures 13.1 and 13.2. In this scenario, we can define certain ranges corresponding to the probabilities of each demand level and use the RAND function to simulate the demand from this probability distribution. To do so, it is useful to define a table consisting of the probability of each outcome $P(x_i)$ and the cumulative probabilities. One way of doing this is illustrated in Figure 13.4. The left panel presents the numbers as percentages and the right panel using decimal points.

CUMULATIVE PROBABILITIES OF COFFEE DEMAND			
P(x)	Lower	Upper	Demand
0.8%	0.0%	0.8%	20
12.3%	0.8%	13.2%	40
32.9%	13.2%	46.0%	60
26.0%	46.0%	72.1%	80
20.5%	72.1%	92.6%	100
5.5%	92.6%	98.1%	120
1.9%	98.1%	100.0%	140
100.0%			

CUMULATIVE PROBABILITIES OF COFFEE DEMAND			
P(x)	Lower	Upper	Demand
0.008	0.000	0.008	20
0.123	0.008	0.132	40
0.329	0.132	0.460	60
0.260	0.460	0.721	80
0.205	0.721	0.926	100
0.055	0.926	0.981	120
0.019	0.981	1.000	140
1.000			

Figure 13.4 The results from running 10 trials using the RAND() and RANDBETWEEN() functions in Excel.

The reason for using decimal points is because it makes it easy to illustrate and understand how the RAND function can be used to sample from this probability distribution. Focus on the table in the right panel of the figure. If the random number we draw (using the RAND function) is within the "Lower" and "Upper" bands, we have defined the demand next to this range that should be returned. For example, if we draw one random number equal to 0.265, this falls into the range [0.132, 0.460] and a demand of 60 should be returned. As all random numbers in the range from 0 to 1 are equally likely to occur, there is a 32.9% probability that any given random number using the RAND function will fall in the range between 0.132 and 0.460. Assume now that we have used the RAND function to generate five random numbers: 0.547; 0.643; 0.021; 0.997; 0.278. What corresponding levels of demand should be returned? Using the table in the right panel of Figure 13.4, try to solve the problem just by visual inspection. The answer is in the Excel file following Chapter 14.

The exercise we have done now is called to *sample from a discrete probability distribution*. Each outcome of demanded quantity has a distinct probability of occurring and these are properly defined in the table. When simulating variables with this property, the VLOOKUP function in Excel is particularly useful. This function essentially uses the randomly generated number and searches in the column where the "Lower" boundary of our cumulative probabilities is defined, and then returns the number in a given column to the right of this, which we specify (in our scenario, the third column to the right) if the random number we use to search is above the number in the "Lower" boundary of that row, and below the "Lower" boundary in the next row. This if further illustrated in Figure 13.5. The function displayed is written in cell M5. The lookup value is the example random number given in cell L5, which could have been generated with the RAND function. We use this number and look it up in the "lookup table," which is our table containing the cumulative probabilities of the various demand levels. This is given in the range G5:I11. We must lock this range such that new simulated random numbers are looked up in the same table when copying the formula to new rows. When the VLOOKUP function finds a number that is above a "Lower" boundary in column

224 Monte Carlo simulations

	F	G	H	I	J	K	L	M
1	CUMULATIVE PROBABILITIES OF COFFEE					EXAMPLE: FIVE RANDOM NUMBERS		
2	DEMAND					AND SIMULATED DEMAND		
3								
4	P(x)	Lower	Upper	Demand		Trial	Example	Demand
5	0.008	0.000	0.008	20		1	0.547	80
6	0.123	0.008	0.132	40		2	0.643	80
7	0.329	0.132	0.460	60		3	0.021	40
8	0.260	0.460	0.721	80		4	0.997	140
9	0.205	0.721	0.926	100		5	0.275	60
10	0.055	0.926	0.981	120				
11	0.019	0.981	1.000	140		=VLOOKUP(L5;$G$5:$I$11;3;TRUE)		
12	1.000							

Figure 13.5 Illustration of the VLOOKUP function in Excel.

G and below the number on the next row, it should return the number given in the third column in the lookup table. This is where the demand level associated with this discrete probability is given.

Sample from the normal distribution using the RAND function

In many cases, we may have a feeling of the average or expected value of a given variable, but the actual outcome could be both lower than or greater than this expectation. If our judgement is that outcomes lower than, and higher than, this expectation are approximately equally likely to occur *and* that outcomes close to the expectation are more likely than outcomes far away, we can sample values of the variables using the normal distribution.

Consider again the coffee example, but now assume that daily demand follows a normal distribution. Our expectation about the daily demand is still based on the historical data, which we have already calculated to be 75.45 cups (see section 13.1). Moreover, we believe that there is a probability of approximately 68% that the demand will be between 50 and 100 cups on any given day. That is, the standard deviation is 25 cups. This situation is illustrated in Figure 13.6. The question then is, how can we use Excel to simulate demand levels that have these properties? The answer is a combination of the RAND function and the NORM.INV function. The NORM.INV function needs three input values to return a value. The first is the probability, the second the expected value (the mean), and the third is the standard deviation. The probability is simply the likelihood of seeing a value equal to or less than a certain normally distributed number with a specified mean and standard deviation. Take the standard normal distribution, for example, which is recognized by a mean value of 0 and a standard deviation of 1. In this case, the probability of seeing a value of zero (the mean) or less is 50%. Seeing a value of −1.96 or less is 2.5% and seeing a value of −2.32 is approximately 1%. This means that if we specify the probability to be 1% in the NORM.INV function, and the mean to be zero and standard deviation to be 1, Excel would return the value −2.32. However, this value will be returned every time we update the formula. There is no randomness going

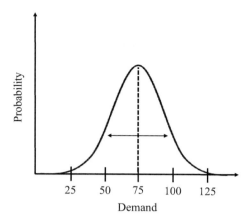

Figure 13.6 Illustration of daily demanded quantity that follows the normal distribution.

on. To fix this, we use the RAND function to generate probabilities. Even though the RAND function follows a uniform distribution (all values in the 0–1 range are equally likely to occur), we will automatically have more values close to the mean of the distribution compared to values far away, because values far away require incredibly small or large (random) probabilities.

In the coffee example, we would have to draw a (random) probability of 0.01 or less to get a simulated demand of 16.8 cups or less. This means that in only 1% of the simulations, the demand will be lower than 16.8 cups. However, if we draw random numbers between 0.25 and 0.75, which will be the case 50% of the time, the simulated demand will be in the range of 58.1 to 91.9 cups. Likewise, in the right tail of the distribution, to obtain a very high simulated demand, the (random) probability must be very close to 1. To get a value of more than 116.1 cups, we need a random probability of 0.95 or higher (occurring 5% of the time). To get a simulated demand of 133.2 or more, we need a random probability of 0.99 or higher (happening 1% of the time), and so forth. Various demand outputs for a range of fixed probabilities are displayed in the Excel file accompanying Chapter 13. In the same example, the use of the NORM.INV function in combination with the RAND function is also implemented.

Efficiently collecting and summarizing the results of a simulation study with Excel

Because we are working with random numbers, the results of a simulation study will be slightly different each time we run the experiment (that is, every time we update the random numbers, for example using the F9 key). How much different the results will be, depends on the number of trials we run. Few trials means big variation in the results, and vice versa. Some business problems may require several thousand trials to get stable results and reach what is often referred to as a *steady state*. In such cases it is important to use the computer efficiently and be able to summarize results such that they can be easily interpreted by managers.

	A	B	C	D
1		APPROACH #1: SIMULATE REVENUE		
2				
3				
4	TRIAL	PRICE	DEMAND	REVENUE
5	1	=NORM.INV(RAND();35;5)	=NORM.INV(RAND();10000;2000)	=B5*C5
6	2	=NORM.INV(RAND();35;5)	=NORM.INV(RAND();10000;2000)	=B6*C6
7	3	=NORM.INV(RAND();35;5)	=NORM.INV(RAND();10000;2000)	=B7*C7
8	4	=NORM.INV(RAND();35;5)	=NORM.INV(RAND();10000;2000)	=B8*C8
9	5	=NORM.INV(RAND();35;5)	=NORM.INV(RAND();10000;2000)	=B9*C9
10	6	=NORM.INV(RAND();35;5)	=NORM.INV(RAND();10000;2000)	=B10*C10
11	7	=NORM.INV(RAND();35;5)	=NORM.INV(RAND();10000;2000)	=B11*C11
12	8	=NORM.INV(RAND();35;5)	=NORM.INV(RAND();10000;2000)	=B12*C12
13	9	=NORM.INV(RAND();35;5)	=NORM.INV(RAND();10000;2000)	=B13*C13
14	10	=NORM.INV(RAND();35;5)	=NORM.INV(RAND();10000;2000)	=B14*C14

	A	B	C	D
1		APPROACH #1: SIMULATE REVENUE		
2				
3				
4	TRIAL	PRICE	DEMAND	REVENUE
5	1	31.8	10533.1	334514.6
6	2	33.0	8774.8	289444.8
7	3	38.8	9526.1	369570.2
8	4	35.9	10793.0	387148.0
9	5	45.3	13301.7	603160.0
10	6	37.1	12696.5	470570.8
11	7	32.7	11345.5	371380.7
12	8	33.0	9999.3	330067.1
13	9	37.4	9238.7	345884.7
14	10	32.4	10933.0	354416.7

Figure 13.7 Illustration of one way of simulating revenue based on uncertain price and demand.

A rule of thumb is to limit the number of projects you perform in the same workbook. The reason is that the computer can freeze if too many complex tasks are carried out simultaneously. Next, we should aim at implementing the simulation in a (stupidly) simple way. A great way of keeping it simple is to collect simulated results in a *data table*. The way this works is that we formulate the simulation model only once in a spreadsheet and then we send the simulated value of the variable we are interested in (such as sales) into a data table that displays simulated values of this for the number of trials we are interested in.

To understand how to use a data table, consider first Figure 13.7. In this figure, the simulation experiment is constructed such that we simulate ten trials of the price variable (sampled from the normal distribution with a mean equal to 35 and a standard deviation of 5), ten trials of the demand (sampled from the normal distribution with a mean equal to 10,000 and a standard deviation of 2,000), and then we calculate the simulated revenue as a function of these two (*price × demand*). It turns out, however, that instead of simulating ten trials of all these three variables, we only need to do it *once* and then send the variable of interest – that is, the revenue in our case – directly into a data table, which will display the ten simulated results based on the input we have defined. One such simulated value that can be sent to a data table is the simulated revenue in cell D5.

Figure 13.8 illustrates the steps involved to create a data table with simulated values. First, we must indicate the cell reference where the revenue has been simulated once, and refer to this in the upper right cell of the data table. Hence, in cell G4, we write a reference to D5. Second, the range in the spreadsheet where the simulated results shall appear must be marked. In our case, this is the range F4:G14. The F column is a simple count of the number of trials in the simulation experiment. In column G the simulated revenue shall appear soon. Once the area F4:G14 is highlighted, we choose the tool data table: Data → What-if-Analysis → Data Table. A small user form then appears. Here, we shall only do one thing and that is to refer to the upper left cell of our data table in the field for the "Column input cell." In our example, this is cell F4. After this, we hit enter and the range G5:G14 will be filled with simulated values of the revenues with the properties specified by D5 (which, again, is based on simulations in B5 and C5).

The use of data tables will be particularly useful if the problems you work on are very complex with many input variables. In such cases, it will be faster to build the simulation

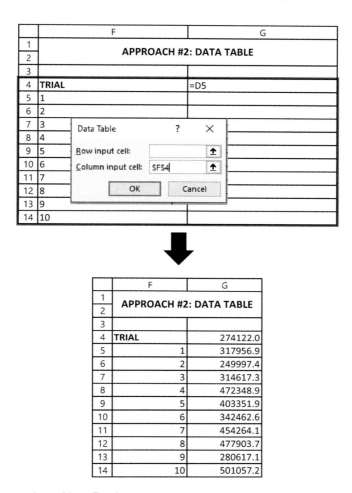

Figure 13.8 Creating a data table in Excel.

model once (one trial), and then send the variable or variables you want to analyze into a data table collecting the simulated results (for 1,000 trials, for example). We shall illustrate more examples on the use of data tables later in this chapter, but let us first examine how we efficiently can summarize and visualize the results of a simulation study for interested parties.

Summarizing and visualizing simulation results using frequency tables and histograms

When you have completed the simulation experiment it is very important that you extract the useful information from all the, potentially thousands of, values in an efficient manner. In many simulation experiments within the area of pricing, we are often interested in the potential impact on profits from price changes. Hence, the variable of interest could be profit and our task would then be to inform management about the key properties of the simulated values of this variable. There are a couple of ways one can go about to summarize results from simulation studies. We could start with something simple: Calculate the mean and standard deviation of the profit from all the trials. This would give us some indication of the expected profit if carrying out the changes defined in the simulation model, and the variation around this mean. Though these measures are somewhat useful, they do not provide information about the general shape of the profit distribution. To illustrate this, we can create a frequency table and then use this to visualize the simulation in a histogram.

To do so, we need to define the intervals the frequency table shall use when counting the number of results within each interval. Sometimes it can be hard to know exactly what the lowest and highest value of the such intervals shall be. The MIN and MAX functions in Excel can be used to find the lowest and highest simulated results, respectively. In this example, we have simulated 500 trials of the revenue using the properties of price and demand as defined in Figure 13.7. Figure 13.9 shows the results of the MIN and MAX functions when applied to the results of the 500 trials. Note that we get a different MIN and MAX value here every time the spreadsheet updates (by hitting F9 or when opening the workbook after being closed). The minimum simulated revenue (out of the 500 trials) is equal to $86,400 and the maximum is $617,565. Based on this information the frequency table could start with a low value of $100,000 and a maximum value of $700,000. The frequency formula we shall apply shortly will then count the number of simulated results below $100,000, between $100,000 and $200,000, and so forth.

Figure 13.10 illustrates the main steps involved to implement the FREQUENCY function. First, we must mark the range where the frequency (count) of the simulated results within the given bin intervals should be placed. In our example, this is the range J5:J11, Once this is done, we can start writing the function =FREQUENCY. Normally,

MIN	86400
MAX	617565

INTERVAL	FREQUENCY
100000	
200000	
300000	
400000	
500000	
600000	
700000	

Figure 13.9 Using the MIN and MAX functions to obtain values for the intervals in a frequency table.

Monte Carlo simulations 229

we would write a function into a single cell, but now we write it into the whole range. This function asks for a data array and a bin array. The data array is the range where all the simulated results are given: D5:D504. The bins array is the range where the bin intervals are placed in the worksheet: I5:I11. When you have done these steps, *it is very important that you hit Ctrl+Shift+Enter, and not just Enter, to complete the function.* The reason is that this is a so-called array formula in Excel and the magic trick to make this work is to hit *Ctrl+Shift+Enter* simultaneously. If done correctly, the result will be a frequency table that contains the number of simulated results within the various bin intervals.

The lower panel of Figure 13.10 shows the results from the example. The interpretation is as follows: One out of the 500 trials ended up below $100,000, 14 out of the 500 trials are between $100,000 and $200,000, 139 out of the 500 trials are between $200,000 and $300,000, and so forth.

	I	J	K
4	**INTERVAL**	**FREQUENCY**	**FORMULATEXT**
5	100000	1	{=FREQUENCY(D5:D504;I5:I11)}
6	200000	14	{=FREQUENCY(D5:D504;I5:I11)}
7	300000	139	{=FREQUENCY(D5:D504;I5:I11)}
8	400000	202	{=FREQUENCY(D5:D504;I5:I11)}
9	500000	115	{=FREQUENCY(D5:D504;I5:I11)}
10	600000	27	{=FREQUENCY(D5:D504;I5:I11)}
11	700000	1	{=FREQUENCY(D5:D504;I5:I11)}

Figure 13.10 Implementation of the FREQUENCY function in Excel.

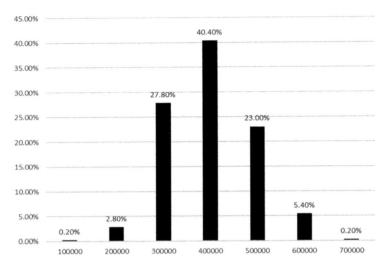

Figure 13.11 Histogram of the simulated results based on bin intervals from the upper panel of Figure 13.10.

It is somewhat easier to interpret the results if presenting the number of occurrences as fractions. This can also be viewed as the probability of the revenue being in each interval. To calculate the fraction, we simply take the count of the number of occurrences within a certain interval and divide it by the total number of trials. These fractions (probabilities) will then summarize to 100% and can be presented in a histogram to visualize the results, making them easier to interpret. This is done in Figure 13.11. The results shall be interpreted as follows: There is a 0.20% probability of revenue being less than $100,000, a 2.80% probability of revenue being between $100,000 and $200,000, a 27.80% probability of revenue being between $200,000 and $300,000, and so forth. Managers can look at this histogram and quickly decide whether the decision or project meets certain criteria. For example, if managers know that the given decision requires increased revenues of at least $300,000 to break even, we can now inform them right away that there is approximately a 70% chance that this will happen. This visualization also has the benefit of quickly revealing any strange outcomes, such as very heavy tails or potential outliers generated by the simulation model. We shall look at more examples of histograms from simulation trials in the next section. However, sometimes we may be more interested in how many of the trials meet certain criteria, or just present a table containing summary statistics of the simulated variable. In such cases we could benefit from being able to count the number of occurrences *if* certain criteria are met, and ask for many summary statistics in one operation. Fortunately, Excel has features for two both and we shall briefly examine these next.

Summarizing results using COUNT, COUNTIF, COUNTIFS, and summary statistics

The COUNT, COUNTIF, and COUNTIFS functions can be useful when summarizing simulation results that meet certain criteria. In Figure 13.12, all three functions are applied to the same revenue example as given in previous section. However, now

Monte Carlo simulations 231

we are interested in calculating the probability that the simulated revenue satisfies the conditions given in column N. The first condition states that revenue should be below $150,000. The business problem in this case could be: *What is the probability that revenue will be below $150,000?*

The COUNTIF function can be used here as it counts the number of cells in a range that satisfies a certain condition. In cell O5 the correct specification of the COUNTFIF is implemented, and in cell P5 the corresponding probability is calculated by taking the number of trials satisfying the condition (given in O5) divided by the total number of trials. The COUNT function is used to find the total number of trials, as it simply counts how many cells in a range that contain numbers. The result in the given simulation is that one out of the 500 trials satisfies the condition of being below $150,000. This corresponds to a probability of 0.20%.

The next condition states that revenue should be less than $500,000 to "count." The direct translation of this to a business problem could be: *What is the probability that revenue will be less than $500,000?* The functions involved are identical to those for the first condition, we only need to change the number from $150,000 to $500,000. The result show that 477 out of the 500 trials satisfy this condition, which means that there is a 95.40% probability that the revenue will be less than $500,000.

In N8 and N9 the conditions become slightly more complicated. Here, we are asked to find the number of trials that fall within a given range. In N8 the condition that should be satisfied for a trial to "count" is that the revenue is between $250,000 and $500,000. In N9, the range is from $350,000 to $550,000. In such cases, when there is more than one condition that should be met for an observation to count, we can use the COUNTIFS function (note the "S" at the end). This allows us to include many conditions before the count is carried out. The correct implementations and the corresponding results are illustrated in Figure 13.12.

	N	O	P
1		COUNT, COUNTIF, & COUNTIFS	
2			
3			
4	CONDITION	COUNT	PROBABILITY
5	R<150000	=COUNTIF($D$5:$D$504;"<150000")	=O5/COUNT($D$5:$D$504)
6	R<500000	=COUNTIF($D$5:$D$504;"<500000")	=O6/COUNT($D$5:$D$504)
7	R>500000	=COUNTIF($D$5:$D$504;">500000")	=O7/COUNT($D$5:$D$504)
8	250000<R<500000	=COUNTIFS($D$5:$D$504;">250000";$D$5:$D$504;"<500000")	=O8/COUNT($D$5:$D$504)
9	350000<R<550000	=COUNTIFS($D$5:$D$504;">350000";$D$5:$D$504;"<550000")	=O9/COUNT($D$5:$D$504)

	N	O	P
1		COUNT, COUNTIF, & COUNTIFS	
2			
3			
4	CONDITION	COUNT	PROBABILITY
5	R<150000	1	0.20%
6	R<500000	477	95.40%
7	R>500000	23	4.60%
8	250000<R<500000	409	81.80%
9	350000<R<550000	224	44.80%

Figure 13.12 Illustration of the COUNT, COUNTIF, and COUNTIFS functions in Excel.

232 Monte Carlo simulations

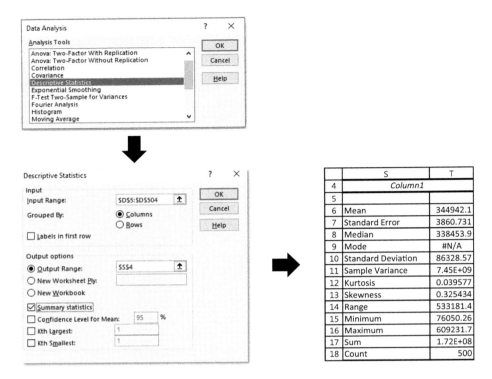

Figure 13.13 Obtaining descriptive statistics in Excel.

Sometimes it can be useful to summarize the simulation results using several measures of central tendency and variation. In such cases we can use Excel to provide the most important descriptive statistics in one operation. Figure 13.13 shows the steps involved and the output.

Choose Data and then Data Analysis and then Descriptive Statistics to get to the user form. Define the Input Range to be the cells where the simulated results are given and ask for Summary Statistics. The results are given to the right. The mean value of the simulated revenue is almost $345,000 with a standard deviation of 86.328. The median is almost equal to the mean, which indicates a fairly symmetric distribution. This is also confirmed by the skewness (close to zero). The range is a little more than $500,000, which can be understood as the difference between the "worst case" and "best case" scenario. We also get information about the sum of all the trials. This number is not very meaningful when running simulation experiments as it would always depend on how many trials we choose to run.

Simulation using other distributions and Excel's random number generator

In this chapter, we have focused on simulating variables that follow either a discrete probability distribution that we define ourselves, or the normal distribution. Though

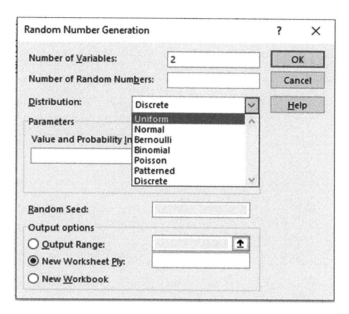

Figure 13.14 Random Number Generation dialogue box in Excel.

these distributions are very flexible, you may want to simulate variables that follow other distributions in your own projects. You can do this in a simple way by using Excel's built-in *Random Number Generator*. Go to Data → Data Analysis and choose Random Number Generation.[1] The dialogue box depicted in Figure 13.14 then appears. In the dropdown menu, you can choose between six different distributions and specify the properties of the parameters.

However, you should note that most of the things you can specify from this dialogue box can also be implemented directly in cells in the spreadsheet itself. This way it is somewhat easier to stay in control of the simulation experiment. Another benefit of writing the functions directly into the spreadsheet is it allows you to update the simulation experiment (to examine whether a steady state is reached, for example) by hitting the F9 key.

13.4 Example of simulation models for pricing problems

Simulating changes in profit from a price change

In many cases, managers or other decision-makers do not have perfect information about what the actual impact from a price change on sales volume will be. However, they may have estimates of expected impact *and* the uncertainty associated with it. In such cases it may be very useful to simulate how profit is affected by the price change to get better decision support for whether to implement it. The business problem could for example be: *For a given price change, what is the probability that we will reach the volume required to break even?*

234 Monte Carlo simulations

	A	B	C
1	INFORMATION ABOUT PRODUCT/SERVICE AND		
2	PRICING DECISION		
3			
4		Baseline	Change
5	Price	$100.00	$75.00
6	% Price change	0.00%	-25.00%
7	Variable costs	$25.00	$25.00
8	Contribution	$75.00	$50.00
9	% contribution	75%	67%
10	Break-even (%)		50.00%
11	Break-even (units)		25000
12	Total volume	50000	75000
13	Total contribution	$3,750,000.00	$3,750,000.00

Figure 13.15 Information about prices, costs, sales volume for a given product.

Consider a business that wants to run a one-week price campaign for one of its products. The information about the price and costs associated with producing and selling the product, and calculations of new prices, contribution margins, and break-even numbers is presented in Figure 13.15. The current price of the product is $100, but the pricing manager wants to run a 25% reduction in price for one week to boost sales. The required sales increase to break even from this price reduction is 25,000 units, which is equal to an increase of 50% of the current sales volume (see Chapter 4 and the Excel file following Chapter 13).

Managers expect the campaign will generate a sales increase of 65%, but there is a lot of uncertainty associated with this number. Someone in the marketing team says that the expected sales change is approximately 65%, but that it could be anywhere between 0% and 100%. In such cases, sampling from the normal distribution could be a good starting point, using 65% as the expected value with a standard deviation of 20%. Then the maximum sales change will be more than 100% less than 5% of the trials and there is less than a 0.1% probability that the sales change will be negative (use the NORM.INV function in Excel to verify this yourself). As the managers are so sure that the sales change will be positive from the price campaign, we can also ensure this by taking the maximum of 0 and the simulated sales change.

A big sales volume increase will induce changes in the fixed costs associated with producing and selling the item. The changes in the fixed costs for various sales changes are given in the table below.

Information about incremental fixed costs

Sales change	Interval	Change fixed costs
0.0%	0%–50%	$0.00
50.0%	50%–75%	$250,000.00
75.0%	75%+	$500,000.00

Monte Carlo simulations

	A	B	C
14			
15		INPUT FOR SIMULATION	
16	Expected change in sales		0.65
17	Std.dev. For change in sales		0.2
18	% change in sales		=MAX(0;NORM.INV(RAND();C16;C17))
19	Current sales		=B12
20	Change in sales		=C19*C18
21	Required change		=C11
22	Change in contribution		=(C20-C21)*C8
23	Incremental fixed costs		=VLOOKUP(C18;E5:G7;3;TRUE)
24	Total change in profit		=C22-C23

	A	B
26		DATA TABLE
27		
28	Sim #	=C24
29	1	=TABLE(;A28)
30	2	=TABLE(;A28)
31	3	=TABLE(;A28)
32	4	=TABLE(;A28)

	E	F	G
1	INFORMATION ABOUT INCREMENTAL FIXED		
2		COSTS	
3			
4	Sales change	Interval	Change FC
5	0	0%-50%	0
6	0.5	50%-75%	250000
7	0.75	75%+	500000

Figure 13.16 Setting up the simulation experiment in Excel.

Such deterministic changes in a given variable can easily be included in a simulation model. We could also sample the changes in fixed costs or other input variables from various probability distributions, if there is uncertainty associated with what values they will take. We shall return to this later. The complete setup to run the simulation experiment based on the information we have so far is presented in Figure 13.16.

As seen from Figure 13.16, the only variable containing uncertainty in the simulation model at this stage is the change in sales stemming from the price reduction of 25%. This variable takes the maximum of zero and a random normal number with a mean of 0.65 (i.e., 65%) and a standard deviation of 0.20 (i.e., 20%), and is given in C18. Some of the calculations in the range C19:C22 refer to cells from Figure 13.15 and are carried out to obtain the overall change in the profit in cell C24. To obtain the level of the fixed costs associated with the simulated sales volume level, a VLOOKUP function is used. This function uses the simulated sales change (C18) and looks it up in the table depicted in the lower right panel of Figure 13.16.

To efficiently collect the results, we use the data table tool. This is done by following the steps explained in the previous section. The value that should be sent to the data table is the simulated change in profit, which is given in cell C24. We run 1,000 trials in the current example.

The main descriptive statistics (min, max, mean, standard deviation, and count) are summarized in a table using the respective Excel functions. The results are presented in the left panel of Figure 13.17. The minimum and maximum value out of the 1,000 simulation trials are used to define the bin intervals in the frequency table. We start with a low value of −$1,000,000 and a maximum value of $2,000,000. The FREQUENCY function

236 Monte Carlo simulations

SUMMARY OF SIMULATION RESULTS	
MIN	-$1,250,000.00
MAX	$1,549,461.15
MEAN	$104,033.19
STD.DEV	$341,325.23
COUNT	1000

FREQUENCY TABLE		
Bins	Frequency	Prob
-$1,000,000.00	3	0.3%
-$500,000.00	32	3.2%
$0.00	363	36.3%
$500,000.00	498	49.8%
$1,000,000.00	93	9.3%
$1,500,000.00	10	1.0%
$2,000,000.00	1	0.1%

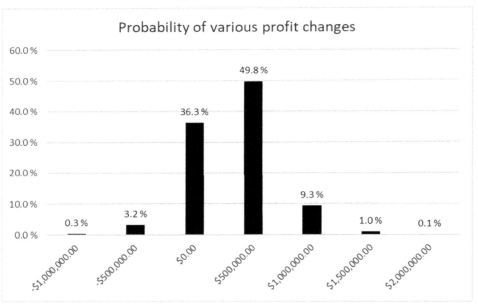

Figure 13.17 Summarizing results using Excel functions for minimum, maximum, mean, standard deviation, count, and frequency (upper panel). Histogram of the calculated probabilities (lower panel).

then returns the number of simulated profit changes that fall in the range between the value on the same row and the immediately preceding value on the row above. For example, three out of 1,000 trials assume a value of less than −$1,000,000, 32 out of 1,000 trials are assume values of between −$500,000 and −$1,000,000, and so forth. The corresponding probabilities are calculated in the column to the right and presented in a histogram in the lower panel of Figure 13.17. Note again that these numbers will change slightly when you update the simulation model.

From the information in the frequency table, we can answer the business problem (and more): The (approximate) probability of breaking even from the price campaign is 60% $(49.8\% + 9.3\% + 1.0\% + 0.1\% = 60.2\%)$, given the information we have and the choice of sampling distribution of the sales change.

As you have probably already understood, the results we obtain depend heavily on the properties of the variables used in the simulation model. If we, for example, change the standard deviation of the sales change from 20% to 50%, the probability of breaking even is reduced to approximately 50%.

To further see how the results of a simulation study are totally dependent on the input, we shall update the model slightly based on the latest new information. Assume now that after a meeting among the managers, the following list of things to be considered has emerged:

- Our main competitor has heard about our campaign and there is:
  - a 65% chance that this competitor will match our price reduction;
    - The expected sales increase will then be 20% with a standard deviation of 20%.
  - a 25% chance our main competitor will reduce prices more than us;
    - The expected sales increase will then be only 5% with a standard deviation of 20%.
  - a 10% chance that the competitor will do nothing.
    - The expected sales increase is then best described by a Poisson distribution with a mean of 75%.

The changes needed in the simulation model based on the list above are implemented in the Excel file accompanying the chapter (Example 13.7.2). Figure 13.18 summarizes the updated results. The new information about the potential actions of the main competitor heavily affects the distribution of changes in profit from the price campaign. The frequency table and histogram show that there is now only about 9% chance of breaking even from a price reduction of 25%. Moreover, there is now a substantial risk of a loss of $1,000,000 or more (approximately 35%). It would be hard, if not impossible, to quantify this risk, or the probability of breaking even, if we did not set up this pricing problem as a simulation experiment. However, a final note of caution is in place here: The last update of the model show that the results are highly sensitive to the input of the model. This is the reason why we often refer to the saying "garbage in = garbage out" when it comes to simulation using the computer.

Simulating willingness to pay and corresponding price–response functions

The techniques we have been through in this chapter can also be used to simulate our customers willingness to pay (WTP). Simulation of willingness to pay will also allow us to quickly illustrate the shape of the price–response function for the product or service of interest. This information can again be used in price optimization following the techniques examined in earlier chapters (e.g., Chapter 7). To get started we only need to consider a likely shape of our customers' willingness to pay. Assume that a small

238 Monte Carlo simulations

SUMMARY OF SIMULATION RESULTS	
MIN	-$2,556,642.69
MAX	$625,000.00
MEAN	-$776,060.81
STD.DEV	$567,664.89
COUNT	1000

FREQUENCY TABLE		
Bins	Frequency	Prob
-$3,000,000.00	0	0.0%
-$2,500,000.00	1	0.1%
-$2,000,000.00	11	1.1%
-$1,500,000.00	84	8.4%
-$1,000,000.00	250	25.0%
-$500,000.00	344	34.4%
$0.00	217	21.7%
$500,000.00	90	9.0%
$1,000,000.00	3	0.3%
$1,500,000.00	0	0.0%

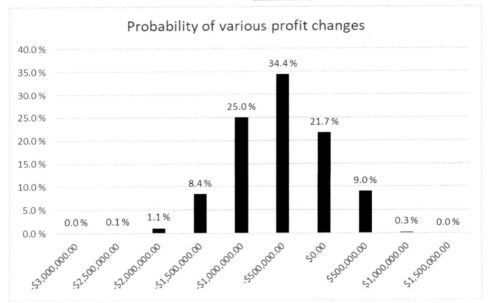

Figure 13.18 Summarizing the updated results based on the new information about the potential actions of the main competitor.

survey has revealed an average willingness to pay of $50 with a standard deviation of $10 for the product or service of interest. Moreover, the fraction of customers with a willingness to pay above and below the average seems to approximately the same, meaning that the distribution is symmetric. As a starting point we could therefore consider simulating willingness to pay by sampling from the normal distribution, with a mean and standard deviation as obtained from the survey. Again, we can make sure

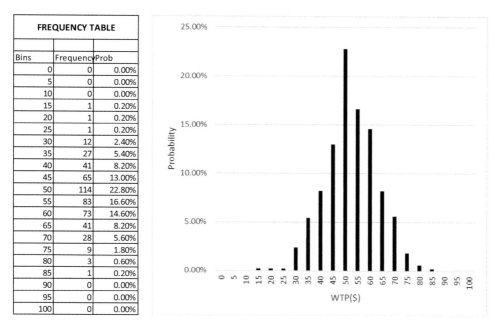

Figure 13.19 Summarizing the results form simulating willingness to pay from the normal distribution with a mean of $50 and standard deviation of $10.

that only non-negative values are possible by taking the max of zero and the simulated willingness to pay.

Figure 13.19 shows the results from running 500 trials of the willingness to pay, given the above-mentioned inputs. The frequency table and histogram now show the number of trials and/or the fractions of customers with willingness to pay in the various intervals.

To illustrate how the corresponding price–response function looks, we simply create a table where we count the number of trials where the simulated willingness to pay is at or above the same levels as those used in the frequency table. This amounts to the number of trials with a reservation price equal to or higher than the given level on each row. The corresponding fraction is calculated as the number of trials satisfying $RP \geq p$ divided by the total # of trials (500 in the given example). The results using a normal willingness to pay distribution with mean of $50 and standard deviation of $10 are presented in Figure 13.20.

Figure 13.21 illustrates how the shape of the price–response function is affected by the standard deviation of the willingness to pay distribution. The mean is $50 in all four cases, but the standard deviation takes a value from $5 (upper left panel) to $30 (lower right panel). Clearly, the higher the standard deviation, the lower the price sensitivity. This makes sense, as a higher *variation* in willingness to pay essentially says that we have more people with reservation prices away from the mean.

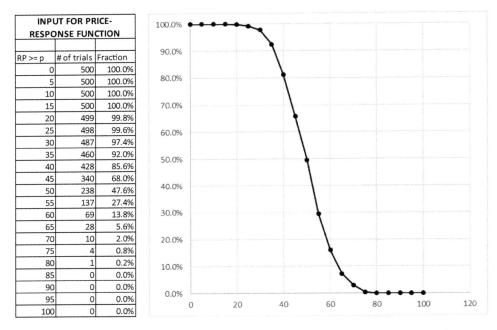

Figure 13.20 Illustration of how to obtain the price–response function from simulated willingness to pay data.

Simulation-based optimization

Simulation can also be combined directly with optimization techniques. Think of the price optimization problem as defined in Equation (7.1) in Chapter 7 and given again below:

$$\max_{p} Z = (p - c_v) d(p) - c_f \tag{13.2}$$

In Chapter 7 we assumed that the variables or functions used in the optimization model were deterministic. That is, there was no uncertainty associated with variable and fixed costs, or the price–response function $(d(p))$. . However, it is possible to add uncertainty to all these variables/functions and still solve the optimization model. Consider the basic optimization problem presented in Example 7-1, but now we have some more information about the variables/functions going into the model:

Basic optimization: Linear PRF with uncertainty

	Deterministic	*Uncertain*
INTERCEPT	250.00	250, p=50%; 300, p=50%
SLOPE	−10.0	−10, p=75%; −15, p=25%
cv	2.25	2.25, p=40%; 3.00, p=60%
cf	0.00	0.00, p=20%; 300, p=80%

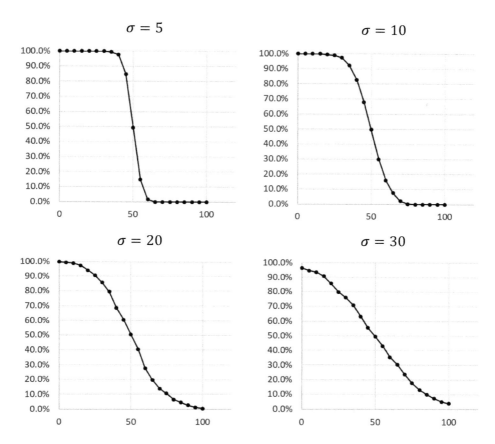

Figure 13.21 Illustration of how the standard deviation of the willingness to pay distribution affects the shape of the price–response function. The standard deviation used to simulate the willingness to pay is given above each chart. The mean is equal to $50 in all four cases.

The table above shows that there is uncertainty in both the intercept and slope of the price–response function. There is a 50% chance that the intercept of the price–response function is 250 and a 50% chance that it is 300. The slope takes a value of −10.0 with a 75% probability and −15.0 with a 25% probability. There is a 40% chance that the variable costs will be $2.25/unit and a 60% chance that they will be $3.00 per unit. Finally, the fixed costs will be $0 with a probability of 20% and $300 with a probability of 80%. The objective function must now be based on a summary of many simulated trials of the profit. An example could be the average profit from 1,000 trials. Or, if we are more concerned about downside risk, we could choose to maximize the minimum profit level from all simulated trials. The optimal price will be very different depending on what summary statistic we choose as the objective function. This simulation-based optimization problem is given as an exercise following Chapter 13. It is important to note that the Evolutionary solver should be used when solving simulation-based optimization problems and that complex simulation models could make it difficult to evaluate the objective function. Therefore: KISS!

13.5 Summary

- Monte Carlo simulation is about replicating elements of the real world by drawing random numbers using the computer.
- We can sample simulated numbers from any given probability distribution.
- Sampling from the discrete probability distribution can be done in Excel by looking up random numbers in a table with cumulative probabilities.
- The use of the NORM.INV function in combination with the RAND function lets you sample from the normal distribution with a mean and standard deviation of your own choice.
- Simulation results can be efficiently collected and summarized using: (1) Data table; (2) frequency tables; (3) histograms; (4) COUNT; COUNTIF, COUNTIFS; and (5) summary statistics.
- There are many interesting applications of simulation for pricing decisions. Some of these are illustrated with examples in this chapter.

13.6 Problems

NB! To avoid your computer freezing, you should set up each simulation problem in its own workbook and close other workbooks while working on the specific problem.

1. What is Monte Carlo simulation?
2. List at least five business problems within the field of pricing a firm can use Monte Carlo simulation to solve and/or get decision support for.
3. Evaluate the saying "garbage in = garbage out" in a simulation context.
4. Run ten trials of random numbers using (1) the RAND() function and (2) the RANDBETWEEN() function with a minimum value of 0 and maximum value of 99. Multiply the ten trials using the RAND() function by 100 in a new column next to the second random number. What can you say about the properties of these simulated numbers?
5. The demand for a given product next year will be 150,000 units with a 70% probability. However, there is a 30% chance that demand could drop to 100,000 units because of the uncertainty associated with one big customer. Simulate 500 trials where the demand is sampled from this probability distribution. In this, and all the following problems, you shall use the "Data Table" tool in Excel to efficiently collect the simulated results.
6. New information arrives for the company above. Now the demand could also be as low as 10,000 because two other big clients are considering choosing another supplier. The probability of this is low, though: 10%. Updated probabilities for the other two levels are 80% for a demand of 150,000 and 10% probability for a demand of 100,000. Simulate 500 new trials. Compare the results with those obtained in problem 5 using appropriate metrics.
7. The company must also report expected revenues for budgeting. In that process the management has also asked for the probability of revenues reaching certain thresholds to create bonus payment schemes for the sales team. The market price is expected to be $7.60, but there is some uncertainty associated with it. One analyst

says that a good estimate of one standard deviation would be $2.00. Simulate 500 new trials and summarize the results in a frequency table and histogram. Include also a summary of the results using the COUNTIF and COUNTIFS functions. Choose the conditions to be satisfied yourself.

8. Another analyst states that the firm has some market power and suggests that they could set the price higher without losing all demand. Assume now that the demand depends solely on the price the business sets. For every $1 increase/decrease in the price from $7.60, the analyst expects demand to go down/up by 50,000 units from a base demand level of 100,000 units. The expected change of 50,000 units has a standard deviation of 10,000 units. Inform management about how the distribution of the revenue looks with these changes when sampling the price variable from a normal distribution with a mean equal to $7.60 and a standard deviation of $2.00. You shall make sure that demand can never be negative in the simulation model.

9. A company is considering a price increase for one of its products because of increased production costs. The current sales volume is 100,000 units and the expected change in sales volume from the price increase given in the table below is −10% with a standard deviation of 5%. The company is certain of a negative impact on demand resulting from the price increase, so the simulation model should take this into account. The other relevant information about the decision they consider is given in the table below. Perform 1,000 simulation trials of the impact this decision will have on the profit. What is your advice to the management based on your simulated results?

	Baseline	Change
Price	$15.00	$16.50
% Price change	0.00%	10.00%
Variable costs	$5.00	$6.00

10. The company Cool Chairs is producing and selling designer chairs. It is now considering introducing a new chair and has carried out a small survey asking about potential customers' willingness to pay. Based on this, the mean willingness to pay has been estimated at $162 with a standard deviation of $25. Use this information to simulate 1,000 trials of potential customers' maximum willingness to pay (i.e., reservation prices) and illustrate the results in a price–response function.

11. This problem was introduced in the text towards the end of the chapter. The information you need to solve this problem is included in the table below.

	Deterministic	Uncertain
INTERCEPT	250.0	250, p=50%; 300, p=50%
SLOPE	−10.0	−10, p=75%; −15, p=25%
cv	2.25	2.25, p=40%; 3.00, p=60%
cf	0.00	0.00, p=20%; 300, p=80%

Interpretation: There is a 50% chance that the intercept of the price–response function is 250 and a 50% chance that it is 300. The slope takes a value of −10.0 with a 75% probability and −15.0 with a 25% probability. There is a 40% chance that the variable costs will be $2.25/unit and a 60% chance that they will be $3.00 per unit. Finally, the fixed costs will be $0 with a probability of 20% and $300 with a probability of 80%. The objective function must now be based on a summary of many simulated trials of the profit. You shall now maximize (1) the average simulated profit from 1,000 trials and (2) the minimum profit level from all simulated trials. To solve this problem you must use the Evolutionary solver in Excel.

Note

1 "Data Analysis" is only available if the Analysis ToolPak is installed. See the Appendix of Chapter 6.

Chapter 14

Conjoint analysis for pricing decisions

Conjoint analysis is a measurement technique for quantifying buyer trade-offs that can be directly used in pricing decisions. In this chapter we briefly introduce you to the conjoint method and show, in a step-by-step manner, how it can be applied to estimate reservations prices and then calculate optimal prices in practice. The data used for illustration purposes in this chapter is based on a survey among existing alpine skiers at a major Norwegian ski resort. Interested readers can consult Haugom et al. (2020) for more information about the survey and data of interest.

14.1 Conjoint analysis

Broadly speaking, conjoint analysis is about revealing customers' preferences for product or service attributes by having them choose between various options. Consider the illustration of a conjoint questionnaire in Figure 14.1. This is an example of a rating-based conjoint questionnaire in which alpine skiers must assign a number between 0 (would definitely not go skiing) and 100 (would definitely go skiing) for a range of alternative scenarios.[1] These ratings can then be used to estimate: (1) Part-worth utilities of the various attributes (such as waiting time, weekday, and price); (2) the relative importance of various attributes; and (3) determine price elasticities and optimal prices, among other things. In this chapter, we focus on how conjoint analysis can be used for pricing decisions. Specifically, we show how you can estimate price–response functions and calculate optimal prices using the conjoint method. Readers interested in other areas of applications of the conjoint method are referred to Rao (2014).

14.2 Estimate price–response functions with conjoint data

To be able to follow the approach presented here, you need conjoint data on a product or service such as those obtained using the questionnaire design presented in Figure 14.1. In this example we have $k = 3$ attributes, where price is one of these. It is very important to note that price must be one of the included attributes for the estimation procedure described in this chapter to work.

The discussion of the analytical underpinnings of the proposed model is based on Kohli and Mahajan (1991). In their approach they assume that the reservation price follows a normal distribution. The starting point of their reservation-price model is the following relation:

$$u_{it|\sim p} + u_i(p) \geq u_i^* \qquad (14.1)[2]$$

For each proposed scenario, please indicate how likely you would be to go skiing in each case, on a scale from 0 ("Would definitely **not** go skiing in that given scenario") to 100 ("Would definitely go skiing in that given scenario"). You may choose any number between 0 and 100. (For example, feel free to use numbers such as 37, 50, 92, etc.).

The given price is for a one-day ski pass in all cases!

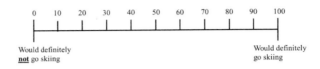

PROFILE	WAITING TIME MAIN LIFTS	WEEKDAY	PRICE (ONE-DAY)	YOUR RATING
1	10 MIN	MID-WEEK (MON-THU)	250	
2	5 MIN	MID-WEEK (MON-THU)	350	
3	5 MIN	MID-WEEK (MON-THU)	450	
4	1 MIN	MID-WEEK (MON-THU)	550	
5	10 MIN	WEEKEND (FRI-SUN)	250	
6	10 MIN	WEEKEND (FRI-SUN)	350	
7	5 MIN	WEEKEND (FRI-SUN)	450	
8	5 MIN	WEEKEND (FRI-SUN)	550	
9	1 MIN	WEEKEND (FRI-SUN)	650	

Figure 14.1 Illustration of conjoint questionnaire. This questionnaire is used to measure preferences of alpine skiers when it comes to waiting time, weekday, lift ticket prices, and weather.

where $u_{it|\sim p}$ is the multiattribute utility of product or service t for consumer i. The subscript $\sim p$ denotes that this estimated utility is *without* the utility contribution of price. $u_i(p)$ is the contribution of price p to individual i's utility for a given product or service, and u_i^* is the highest estimated utility for consumer i (including the contribution from price). The relation in Equation (14.1) then states that the reservation price of individual i can be calculated if treating the inequality as an equation and solving it with respect to p_{it}. The step-by-step procedure for finding this p_{it} is described next.

Step 1: Estimate individual preference functions

The first step in the process of finding the optimal prices for a given product or service is to estimate individual preference functions. This is done using linear regression with the ratings of the respondents as dependent variable, u_i, and the various attributes, including price (specified as a continuous variable), as the independent variables. The linear regression model takes the following form using data from the questionnaire in the example.

$$u_i = \alpha + \beta_{1,i} 5MIN + \beta_{2,i} 10MIN + \beta_{3,i} WEEKEND + \beta_{4,i} PRICE + \varepsilon_i \qquad (14.2)$$

Again, the subscript i indicates that this regression model should be estimated separately for all consumers. We assume that the utility of the consumers is a decreasing function of price. Hence, all estimations where the $\beta_{4,i}$-parameter is either zero or positive should be dropped from the analysis. This is in line with standard economic theory and is not a strict assumption. The estimations of the model in (Equation 14.2) allows us to calculate both $u_{it|\sim p}$ and u_i^*.

Step 2: Set a "status quo" profile alternative and calculate u_i^*

Once the individual preference functions have been estimated, we need to set a common base case or "status quo" for all respondents. We can do this by taking the estimated utility, u_i, for a specific combination of attributes available in all respondents evoked set. An illustration of a questionnaire is given in Figure 14.1. The estimated utility for this combination is then extracted for all consumers and defined as u_i^* in the relation given in Equation (14.1). This can easily be achieved using a simple IF statement in any software, for example Excel.

Step 3: Calculate reservation prices for all consumers

The estimated multi-attribute utility of a product or service alternative, without the contribution of price, $u_{it|\sim p}$, can be calculated from the estimated model in Equation 14.2 by simply extracting the price effect from the utility estimate:

$$u_{it|\sim p} = u_i - \beta_{4,i} PRICE \qquad (14.3)$$

Moreover, the utility contribution from price, $u_i(p)$, is equal to the last term in (14.3), i.e., $\beta_{4,i} PRICE$. We are interested in finding the "unknown" price that satisfies the relation in (14.1) as an equation. Why? Because this is an estimate of each consumer's reservation price. We can calculate $u_i(p)$ for each consumer by re-arranging (14.1) and treating it as an equation (assuming that ϵ from (14.1) is zero):

$$u_i(p) = u_i^* - u_{it|\sim p} \qquad (14.4)$$

For each consumer we now have a vector of $u_i(p)$. As we have this, and we know that the utility contribution from price must be the last term in Equation 14.3, we can put forward this relation:

$$\beta_{4,i} PRICE = u_i(p)$$

and rearrange it to directly calculate the reservation price for each unique combination of attributes in the evoked set of the consumer:

$$PRICE = \frac{u_i(p)}{\beta_{4,i}} \qquad (14.5)$$

Now we have estimates of the reservation price for each consumer for each product or service alternative in his or her evoked set. However, as conjoint preference functions are estimated only over a restricted positive range of prices $[p_{min}, p_{max}]$, we should be careful estimating reservation prices outside this range, without making any adjustments. Kohli and Mahajan (1991) show how to do this, and we describe their approach in the next step.

Step 4: Estimate mean and variance of the normal density of reservation prices

First, let us define the following:

- $\bar{p}_t$ and s_t are the average and the standard deviation of the reservation price observations between p_{min} and p_{max}. p_{min} and p_{max} are the minimum and maximum price included in the conjoint questionnaire.
- q_{1t} and q_{2t} are the fraction of consumers with estimated reservation prices (from Equation (14.5)) below p_{min} and above p_{max} for profile t, respectively. These are found by counting outside the defined range.
- $z_{t,min}$ and $z_{t,max}$ are the standard normal value at q_{1t} and $1-q_{2t}$, respectively.
- $R = \dfrac{f(z_{t,min}) - f(z_{t,max})}{F(z_{t,max}) - F(z_{t,min})}$, where:

  - $F(Z_{t,min}) = q_{1t}$, $F(Z_{t,max}) = q_{2t}$, $f(Z_{t,min}) = 1/\sqrt{2\pi}e^{(-z_{t\min}^2/2)}$, $f(Z_{t,max}) = 1/\sqrt{2\pi}e^{(-z_{t\min}^2/2)}$

- $C = 1 + \dfrac{z_{t,min} f(z_{t,min}) - z_{t,max} f(z_{t,max})}{F(z_{t,max}) - F(z_{t,min})} - R^2$

Once we have the numbers above, we can estimate the mean and the variance of the untruncated normal distribution of reservation prices as follows:

$$\hat{\mu}_t = \bar{p}_t - R\hat{\sigma}_t^2 \qquad (14.6)$$

$$\hat{\sigma}_t^2 = \frac{s_t^2}{C} \qquad (14.7)$$

Step 5: Create the price–response function and optimize prices

As we assume that consumers' reservation prices can be described by the normal distribution, the adjusted mean and variance of the estimated reservation prices given in Equation (14.6) and Equation (14.7) can then be used directly to create the willingness to pay distribution with the properties $N(\hat{\mu}_t, \hat{\sigma}_t)$. The corresponding price–response function is found by the fraction satisfying $RP \geq p$. This is simply the inverse of the cumulative distribution function. In our case, more precisely, starting with the normal distribution, $N(\hat{\mu}_t, \hat{\sigma}_t)$, the cumulative distribution function is represented by $H(p_t)$. The proportion of consumers with a reservation price less than p_t is then the inverse cumulative distribution function, or $1 - H(p_t)$. The price–response function for the given product/service will then be:

$$d(p_t) = m\left[1 - H(p_t)\right] \tag{14.8}$$

where m is the total number of potential consumers for that product/service in the target market. Once we have an estimate of the price–response function, it is easy to define the profit function as we did in Equation (7.4), and given again here:[3]

$$\max_{p_t} Z = (p_t - c_v)d(p_t) - c_{f_t}$$

s.t.

$$d(p_t) \leq C \tag{14.9}$$

We now have all the necessary tools to be able to implement the above analysis in practice. We show how you can do this in Excel next.

14.3 Implementation in Excel

In this section, we will show how you can implement the steps described in the previous section in Excel. Before we start the estimation procedure, the data must be organized properly. An illustration of how this can be done is given in Figure 14.2.

First, the data shall be sorted by respondent ID and the profile number (as defined in the questionnaire). Next, we have to include a vector of "ones" to estimate the intercept of the multiple regression model. This is included together with rest of the independent variables and should therefore be placed next to these. The dependent variable in our analyses is the ratings of the various profiles. These ratings are included in column C. To make Excel "jump down" to the next respondent before doing a new estimation, we need to indicate how many rows Excel should move. This is the reason for including the OFFSET variable in column I in the illustration in Figure 14.2. Once the data is structured this way, we are ready to start the estimation procedure involving the five steps described in the previous section. We will walk you through each of these steps next.

Step 1: Estimate individual preference functions

To estimate the preference functions using OLS for each respondent in Excel we rely on a user-defined function written by Veka (2011). This function, combined with the OFFSET function, allows us to efficiently run unique multiple regression models for all respondents in the sample. To be able to use this function you need to include a module in VBA. This is done in the example file accompanying this text. If you want to start from scratch, you need to hit ALT+F11 to open the VBA interface, then create a new module and insert the VBA code as presented in Figure 14.3.

250 Conjoint analysis for pricing decisions

	A	B	C	D	E	F	G	H	I
1	ID	PROFILE	RATING	CONSTANT	QUE_5	QUE_10	WEEKEND	PRICE	OFFSET
2	1	1	80	1	0	1	0	250	0
3	1	2	85	1	1	0	0	350	0
4	1	3	35	1	1	0	0	450	0
5	1	4	30	1	0	0	0	550	0
6	1	5	80	1	0	1	1	250	0
7	1	6	35	1	0	1	1	350	0
8	1	7	10	1	1	0	1	450	0
9	1	8	0	1	1	0	1	550	0
10	1	9	0	1	0	0	1	650	0
11	2	1	45	1	0	1	0	250	9
12	2	2	50	1	1	0	0	350	9
13	2	3	35	1	1	0	0	450	9
14	2	4	45	1	0	0	0	550	9
15	2	5	45	1	0	1	1	250	9
16	2	6	40	1	0	1	1	350	9
17	2	7	50	1	1	0	1	450	9
18	2	8	35	1	1	0	1	550	9
19	2	9	40	1	0	0	1	650	9
20	3	1	40	1	0	1	0	250	18
21	3	2	35	1	1	0	0	350	18
22	3	3	30	1	1	0	0	450	18
23	3	4	10	1	0	0	0	550	18
24	3	5	55	1	0	1	1	250	18
25	3	6	60	1	0	1	1	350	18
26	3	7	75	1	1	0	1	450	18
27	3	8	60	1	1	0	1	550	18
28	3	9	45	1	0	0	1	650	18

Figure 14.2 Screenshot of how the data shall be organized before starting the estimation procedure in Excel.

Once this is done, you hit Save and move back to the spreadsheet where your data is recorded. Now highlight the area J2:N2 in the spreadsheet as illustrated in Figure 14.4. This is where the parameters shall be placed after the estimation is completed. Once this area is highlighted you write the following function:

=TRANSPOSE(ols(OFFSET($C$2:$C$10;I2;0);OFFSET($D$2:$H$10;I2;0)))

As this is an array formula we must hit *ctrl+shift+enter* simultaneously. The parameter estimates will then be placed in the range J2:N2. The OLS function above estimates the parameters of a multiple regression model directly in the spreadsheet. The only alternative to this, is to do it mechanically by hitting Data → Data Analysis → Regression.[4]

```
Public Function trsp(y As Variant) As Variant
trsp = Application.WorksheetFunction.Transpose(y)
End Function
'trsp returns the transpose of an array

Public Function mult(y1 As Variant, y2 As Variant) As Variant
mult = Application.WorksheetFunction.MMult(y1, y2)
End Function
'mult returns the matrix product of two arrays

Public Function minv(y As Variant) As Variant
minv = Application.WorksheetFunction.MInverse(y)
End Function
'minv returns the inverse of a matrix

Public Function ols(y As Range, x As Range) As Variant
vy = y.Value
vx = x.Value

b1 = minv(mult(trsp(vx), vx))
b2 = mult(trsp(vx), vy)
ols = mult(b1, b2)
End Function
```

Figure 14.3 Screenshot of the user-defined VBA function to estimate parameters of a multiple regression model written by Veka (2011).

The problem of using this approach when it comes to conjoint analysis, however, is that we must do as many estimations as we have respondents in our sample. Hence, implementing the above-described user-defined function saves you a lot of time.

To copy the formula down to all rows you pull or double-click the Fill handle. Due to the OFFSET formula, the parameter estimates will update for every new respondent in the sample (nine observations per respondent). An illustration of how the spreadsheet shall look after you have completed the estimations is in Figure 14.5.

It is important to note here that one assumption of the subsequent analysis is that the utility of a product or service alternative is a decreasing function of price. Hence, if any of the estimated parameters for the price variable (given in column N) assume positive values (or a value of zero), we should drop these observations from the data and rerun all the estimations. To check whether this is the case, you can write a simple IF formula. We will not go through this in more detail here, but it is important to be aware of this assumption and make the necessary adjustments if this is not the case.

The final task in Step 1 is to calculate predicted utilities, for each respondent and for each profile in the respondent's evoked set, based on the estimations. This is easily done with the =SUMPRODUCT function, as illustrated in Figure 14.6.

The result can be seen in the screenshot presented in Figure 14.7. First, for columns J:N, we see that the parameters for the various independent variables and the constant, are staying fixed per respondent, as they should do. Further, in column O we see that the predicted utilities differ for each profile and also for each respondent, as they should do. We have now completed Step 1 in the procedure of finding optimal prices using a conjoint analysis.

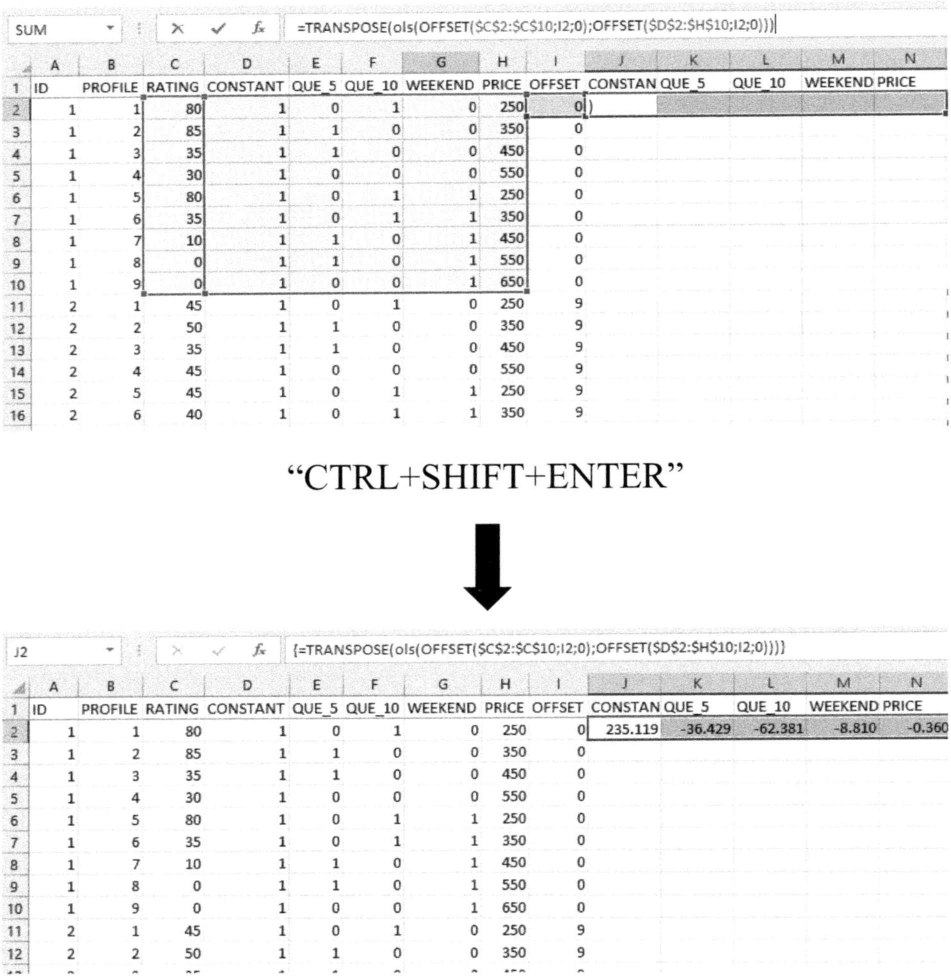

252 Conjoint analysis for pricing decisions

Figure 14.4 Implementation of the user-defined function by Veka (2011) to estimate parameters of a multiple regression model in the spreadsheet.

Step 2: Set a "status quo" profile alternative and calculate u_i^*

In this analysis we use the same *status quo* profile for all respondents, as done in Kohli and Mahajan (1991). The *status quo* combination is set to:

- 10 minutes' waiting time.
- Weekend.
- Price: NOK 350.

Conjoint analysis for pricing decisions   253

Figure 14.5 Illustration of how the spreadsheet shall look like after the estimation is completed.

Figure 14.6 Implementation of the SUMPRODUCT function to calculate predicted utilities.

This is easily implemented in Excel using an IF(AND()) statement and then the AVERAGEIF function, as illustrated in Figure 14.8. This results in calculations of u_i^*, that is, predicted utilities for all respondents for a fixed combination of all the attributes going into the conjoint model.

Step 3: Calculate reservation prices for all consumers

The calculation of the reservation price was given in Equation (14.5) as:

$$PRICE = \frac{u_i(p)}{\beta_{4,i}}$$

254 Conjoint analysis for pricing decisions

O2				=SUMPRODUCT(J2:N2;D2:H2)										
	A	B	C	D	E	F	G	H	I	J	K	L	M	N	O
1	ID	PROFILE	RATING	CONSTANT	QUE_5	QUE_10	WEEKEND	PRICE	OFFSET	CONSTAN	QUE_5	QUE_10	WEEKEND	PRICE	u
2	1	1	80	1	0	1	0	250	0	235.119	-36.429	-62.381	-8.810	-0.360	82.857
3	1	2	85	1	1	0	0	350	0	235.119	-36.429	-62.381	-8.810	-0.360	72.857
4	1	3	35	1	1	0	0	450	0	235.119	-36.429	-62.381	-8.810	-0.360	36.905
5	1	4	30	1	0	0	0	550	0	235.119	-36.429	-62.381	-8.810	-0.360	37.381
6	1	5	80	1	0	1	1	250	0	235.119	-36.429	-62.381	-8.810	-0.360	74.048
7	1	6	35	1	0	1	1	350	0	235.119	-36.429	-62.381	-8.810	-0.360	38.095
8	1	7	10	1	1	0	1	450	0	235.119	-36.429	-62.381	-8.810	-0.360	28.095
9	1	8	0	1	1	0	1	550	0	235.119	-36.429	-62.381	-8.810	-0.360	-7.857
10	1	9	0	1	0	0	1	650	0	235.119	-36.429	-62.381	-8.810	-0.360	-7.381
11	2	1	45	1	0	1	0	250	9	103.214	-16.071	-34.286	7.143	-0.107	42.143
12	2	2	50	1	1	0	0	350	9	103.214	-16.071	-34.286	7.143	-0.107	49.643
13	2	3	35	1	1	0	0	450	9	103.214	-16.071	-34.286	7.143	-0.107	38.929
14	2	4	45	1	0	0	0	550	9	103.214	-16.071	-34.286	7.143	-0.107	44.286
15	2	5	45	1	0	1	1	250	9	103.214	-16.071	-34.286	7.143	-0.107	49.286
16	2	6	40	1	0	1	1	350	9	103.214	-16.071	-34.286	7.143	-0.107	38.571
17	2	7	50	1	1	0	1	450	9	103.214	-16.071	-34.286	7.143	-0.107	46.071
18	2	8	35	1	1	0	1	550	9	103.214	-16.071	-34.286	7.143	-0.107	35.357
19	2	9	40	1	0	0	1	650	9	103.214	-16.071	-34.286	7.143	-0.107	40.714
20	3	1	40	1	0	1	0	250	18	24.643	19.286	12.143	31.429	-0.021	31.429
21	3	2	35	1	1	0	0	350	18	24.643	19.286	12.143	31.429	-0.021	36.429
22	3	3	30	1	1	0	0	450	18	24.643	19.286	12.143	31.429	-0.021	34.286
23	3	4	10	1	0	0	0	550	18	24.643	19.286	12.143	31.429	-0.021	12.857
24	3	5	55	1	0	1	1	250	18	24.643	19.286	12.143	31.429	-0.021	62.857
25	3	6	60	1	0	1	1	350	18	24.643	19.286	12.143	31.429	-0.021	60.714
26	3	7	75	1	1	0	1	450	18	24.643	19.286	12.143	31.429	-0.021	65.714
27	3	8	60	1	1	0	1	550	18	24.643	19.286	12.143	31.429	-0.021	63.571
28	3	9	45	1	0	0	1	650	18	24.643	19.286	12.143	31.429	-0.021	42.143

Figure 14.7 Illustration of how the spreadsheet shall look like after completing step 1 of the implementation.

=IF(AND(F2=1;G2=1;H2=350);O2;"NA")											
E	F	G	H	I	J	K	L	M	N	O	P
QUE_5	QUE_10	WEEKEND	PRICE	OFFSET	CONSTAN	QUE_5	QUE_10	WEEKEND	PRICE	u	u*-step-1
0	1	0	250	0	235.119	-36.429	-62.381	-8.810	-0.360	82.857	=IF(AND(F2=1;G2=1;H2=350);O2;"NA")
1	0	0	350	0	235.119	-36.429	-62.381	-8.810	-0.360	72.857	NA
1	0	0	450	0	235.119	-36.429	-62.381	-8.810	-0.360	36.905	NA
0	0	0	550	0	235.119	-36.429	-62.381	-8.810	-0.360	37.381	NA
0	1	1	250	0	235.119	-36.429	-62.381	-8.810	-0.360	74.048	NA
0	1	1	350	0	235.119	-36.429	-62.381	-8.810	-0.360	38.095	38.0952381

↓

SUM				=AVERAGEIF($A$2:$A$5383;A2;$P$2:$P$5383)									
	A	B	C	D	E	F	G	H	I	J	K	L	M	N	O	P	Q
1	ID	PROFILE	RATING	CONSTANT	QUE_5	QUE_10	WEEKEND	PRICE	OFFSET	CONSTAN	QUE_5	QUE_10	WEEKEND	PRICE	u	u*-step-1	u*
2	1	1	80	1	0	1	0	250	0	235.119	-36.429	-62.381	-8.810	-0.360	82.857	NA	=AVERAGEIF($A$2:$A$5383;A2;$P$2:$P$5383)
3	1	2	85	1	1	0	0	350	0	235.119	-36.429	-62.381	-8.810	-0.360	72.857	NA	
4	1	3	35	1	1	0	0	450	0	235.119	-36.429	-62.381	-8.810	-0.360	36.905	NA	
5	1	4	30	1	0	0	0	550	0	235.119	-36.429	-62.381	-8.810	-0.360	37.381	NA	
6	1	5	80	1	0	1	1	250	0	235.119	-36.429	-62.381	-8.810	-0.360	74.048	NA	
7	1	6	35	1	0	1	1	350	0	235.119	-36.429	-62.381	-8.810	-0.360	38.095	38.0952381	
8	1	7	10	1	1	0	1	450	0	235.119	-36.429	-62.381	-8.810	-0.360	28.095	NA	
9	1	8	0	1	1	0	1	550	0	235.119	-36.429	-62.381	-8.810	-0.360	-7.857	NA	

Figure 14.8 Implementation of the "status quo" alternative in Excel.

Conjoint analysis for pricing decisions 255

We have $\beta_{4,i}$, which is the coefficient for the price variable in the regression model. However, we don't have $u_i(p)$. That is, the contribution of price to individual i's utility. We do know that this can be found by the relation presented in Equation (14.4):

$$u_i(p) \; u_i^* - u_{it|\sim p}$$

We also know that $u_{it|\sim p}$ is the utility of alternative t (a given profile) where the utility due to price is not included. This is simply calculated as $u - \beta_{4,i} Price$. The implementation of $u_{it|\sim p}$, $u_i(p)$, and the reservation price in Excel is shown in Figure 14.9 below:

If implementing all these steps correctly, the reservation prices for each profile per respondent should appear in column T as illustrated in Figure 14.10.

Step 4: Estimate mean and variance of the normal density of reservation prices

Conjoint reservation prices can only be estimated in the price range we have used in the questionnaire. The calculations done in the previous step reveal reservation prices outside this range. Hence, we need to do some modifications to the calculations and this essentially boils down to properly estimating the normal distribution from truncated

H	I	J	K	L	M	N	O	P	Q	R
PRICE	OFFSET	CONSTAN	QUE_5	QUE_10	WEEKEND	PRICE	u	u*-step-1	u*	u_itp
250	0	235.119	-36.429	-62.381	-8.810	-0.360	82.857	NA		38.10 =O2-N2*H2
350	0	235.119	-36.429	-62.381	-8.810	-0.360	72.857	NA		38.10
450	0	235.119	-36.429	-62.381	-8.810	-0.360	36.905	NA		38.10
550	0	235.119	-36.429	-62.381	-8.810	-0.360	37.381	NA		38.10
250	0	235.119	-36.429	-62.381	-8.810	-0.360	74.048	NA		38.10

↓

H	I	J	K	L	M	N	O	P	Q	R	S
PRICE	OFFSET	CONSTAN	QUE_5	QUE_10	WEEKEND	PRICE	u	u*-step-1	u*	u_itp	u_ip
250	0	235.119	-36.429	-62.381	-8.810	-0.360	82.857	NA		38.10	172.74 =Q2-R2
350	0	235.119	-36.429	-62.381	-8.810	-0.360	72.857	NA		38.10	198.69
450	0	235.119	-36.429	-62.381	-8.810	-0.360	36.905	NA		38.10	198.69
550	0	235.119	-36.429	-62.381	-8.810	-0.360	37.381	NA		38.10	235.12
250	0	235.119	-36.429	-62.381	-8.810	-0.360	74.048	NA		38.10	163.93

↓

H	I	J	K	L	M	N	O	P	Q	R	S	T
PRICE	OFFSET	CONSTAN	QUE_5	QUE_10	WEEKEND	PRICE	u	u*-step-1	u*	u_itp	u_ip	RP
250	0	235.119	-36.429	-62.381	-8.810	-0.360	82.857	NA		38.10	172.74	-134.64 =S2/N2
350	0	235.119	-36.429	-62.381	-8.810	-0.360	72.857	NA		38.10	198.69	-160.60
450	0	235.119	-36.429	-62.381	-8.810	-0.360	36.905	NA		38.10	198.69	-160.60
550	0	235.119	-36.429	-62.381	-8.810	-0.360	37.381	NA		38.10	235.12	-197.02
250	0	235.119	-36.429	-62.381	-8.810	-0.360	74.048	NA		38.10	163.93	-125.83

Figure 14.9 Implementation of $u_{it|\sim p}$, $u_i(p)$, and the reservation prices in Excel.

256 Conjoint analysis for pricing decisions

Figure 14.10 Illustration of how the spreadsheet shall look like after completing step 3 of the implementation.

Figure 14.11 The use of IF(OR()) function in Excel to get reservation prices within a specific range.

data. The procedure described here is presented in Kohli and Mahajan (1991) and the references therein. We implement all the calculations of this step in Excel separately in sub-steps 4.1–4.5 below.

Sub-step 4.1: Calculate $\bar{p}_t$ and; the average and the standard deviation of the reservation price observations between p_{min} and p_{max}

Before doing this calculation, we must prepare the dataset somewhat. We start by creating a new variable containing the reservation prices, only if it is within the range of NOK 250–650 (RP_R). This is done using a simple IF(OR()) statement in Excel as shown in Figure 14.11.

In this formula, the text "OR" is returned if the reservation price is outside the given range. Then, as we shall calculate the average and standard deviation of the reservation prices (within the given range) for each product/service type, we should create a column where the unique profiles we have in our questionnaire are returned. In our scenario, we have six unique profiles, of which one of these (Profile 6 in the table below) is the status quo combination (Waiting time: 10 minutes, Price: NOK 350, Weekend):

Profile	Queue	Weekend
1	1	0
2	5	0
3	10	0
4	1	1
5	5	1
6	10	1

Conjoint analysis for pricing decisions   257

```
=IF(AND(E2=1;G2=0);2;IF(AND(F2=1;G2=0);3;IF(AND(E2=1;G2=1);5;IF(AND(F2=1;G2=1);6;IF(G2=0;1;IF(G2=1;4))))))
```

E	F	G	H	V	W	X	Y	Z	AA	AB	AC	AD	AE
QUE_5	QUE_10	WEEKEND	PRICE	UNIQUE-PROFILE									
1	0	1	0	250	=IF(AND(E2=1;G2=0);2;IF(AND(F2=1;G2=0);3;IF(AND(E2=1;G2=1);5;IF(AND(F2=1;G2=1);6;IF(G2=0;1;IF(G2=1;4))))))								
1	1	0	0	350	2								
1	1	0	0	450	2								
1	0	0	0	550	1								
1	0	1	1	250	6								
1	0	1	1	350	6								

Figure 14.12 The use of the IF(AND()) function in Excel to create the Profile variable.

V	W	X	Y	Z	AA	AB	AC	AD	A
UNIQUE-PROFILE									
3		PROFILE	QUE	WEEKEND	$\bar{p}_t$	s_t	q_{1t}	q_{2t}	$F(z_t,$
2		1	1	0	=AVERAGEIF($V$2:$V$5383;X3;$U$2:$U$5383)				
2		2	5	0	409.4	91.5	0.17	0.13	
1		3	10	0	353.4	83.5	0.27	0.04	
6		4	1	1	433.2	95.1	0.13	0.17	
6		5	5	1	427.3	87.8	0.09	0.13	
5		6	10	1	350.0		0.00	0.00	

Figure 14.13 The calculation of $\bar{p}_t$ in Excel.

The PROFILE variable could be created in many ways, but one possible approach is to use the following IF(AND()) statement (note that column I:U is hidden in this screenshot) as illustrated in Figure 14.12.

The actual calculation of $\bar{p}_t$ and s_t is most efficiently done using the =AVERAGEIF() function and an IF statement combined with the =STEDDEV() function in Excel. These functions calculate the average and the standard deviation if a certain criterion is met and the implementation is illustrated in Figure 14.13 and Figure 14.14.

The standard deviation is an array formula and you therefore need to hit *ctrl+shift+enter* to make it work properly,

Sub-step 4.2: Calculate q_{1t} and q_{2t}; the fraction of consumers with reservation prices below p_{min} and above p_{max} respectively.

These quantities can be calculated using a combination of =COUNTIFS and =COUNTIF as shown in Figure 14.15.

Sub-step 4.3: Calculate $Z_{t,min}$ and $Z_{t,max}$; the standard normal value at q_{1t} and $1 - q_2$, respectively.

The Excel function to obtain these quantities is =NORM.S.INV() as illustrated in Figure 14.16.

258 Conjoint analysis for pricing decisions

	U	V	W	X	Y	Z	AA	AB	AC	AD
	RP_R	UNIQUE-PROFILE								
	374.50	3		PROFILE	QUE	WEEKEND	$\bar{p}_t$	s_t	q_{1t}	q_{2t} F(:
	446.69	2		1	1	0	430.0	=STDEV.S(IF($V$2:$V$5383=X3;IF(		
	446.69	2		2	5	0	409.4	$U$2:$U$5383>250;IF($U$2:		
	548.01	1		3	10	0	353.4	$U$5383<650;$U$2:$U$5383))))		
	350.00	6		4	1	1	433.2	95.1	0.13	0.17
	350.00	6		5	5	1	427.3	87.8	0.09	0.13
	422.19	5		6	10	1	350.0		0.00	0.00
	422.19	5								
	523.51	4								
	283.33	3								
	453.33	2								
	453.33	2								
	603.33	1								
	350.00	6								
	350.00	6								
	520.00	5								

Figure 14.14 The calculation of s_t in Excel.

	T	U	V	W	X	Y	Z	AA	AB	AC	AD	AE	AF	
	RP	RP_R	UNIQUE-PROFILE											
4	374.50	374.50	3		PROFILE	QUE	WEEKEND	$\bar{p}_t$	s_t	q_{1t}	q_{2t}	$F(z_{t,min})$	$F(z_{t,max})$	z.
0	446.69	446.69	2		1	1	0	430.0	103.5	=COUNTIFS($V$2:$V$5383;$X3;$T$2:$T$5383;				
0	446.69	446.69	2		2	5	0	409.4	91.5	"<250")/COUNTIF($V$2:$V$5383;X3)				
2	548.01	548.01	1		3	10	0	353.4	83.5	0.27	0.04	0.27	0.96	
3	350.00	350.00	6		4	1	1	433.2	95.1	0.13	0.17	0.13	0.83	
3	350.00	350.00	6		5	5	1	427.3	87.8	0.09	0.13	0.09	0.87	
9	422.19	422.19	5		6	10	1	350.0		0.00	0.00			
9	422.19	422.19	5											
1	523.51	523.51	4											
6	283.33	283.33	3											
7	453.33	453.33	2											

	T	U	V	W	X	Y	Z	AA	AB	AC	AD	AE	AF	AG	
	RP	RP_R	UNIQUE-PROFILE												
4	374.50	374.50	3		PROFILE	QUE	WEEKEND	$\bar{p}_t$	s_t	q_{1t}	q_{2t}	$F(z_{t,min})$	$F(z_{t,max})$	$z_{t,min}$	z_t
0	446.69	446.69	2		1	1	0	430.0	103.5		0.18	=COUNTIFS($V$2:$V$5383;$X3;$T$2:$T$5383;		
0	446.69	446.69	2		2	5	0	409.4	91.5		0.17	">650")/COUNTIF($V$2:$V$5383;X3)		
2	548.01	548.01	1		3	10	0	353.4	83.5	0.27	0.04	0.27	0.96	-0.60
3	350.00	350.00	6		4	1	1	433.2	95.1	0.13	0.17	0.13	0.83	-1.11
3	350.00	350.00	6		5	5	1	427.3	87.8	0.09	0.13	0.09	0.87	-1.32
9	422.19	422.19	5		6	10	1	350.0		0.00	0.00			
9	422.19	422.19	5											
1	523.51	523.51	4											
6	283.33	283.33	3											
7	453.33	453.33	2											

Figure 14.15 The calculations of q_{1t} and q_{2t} in Excel.

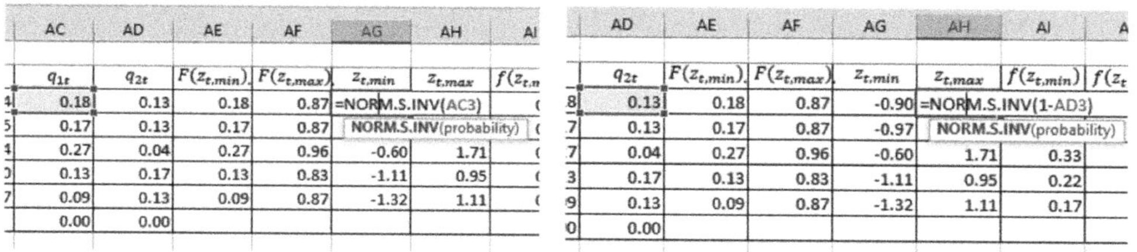

Conjoint analysis for pricing decisions 259

Figure 14.16 The calculations of $z_{t,min}$ and $z_{t,max}$ in Excel.

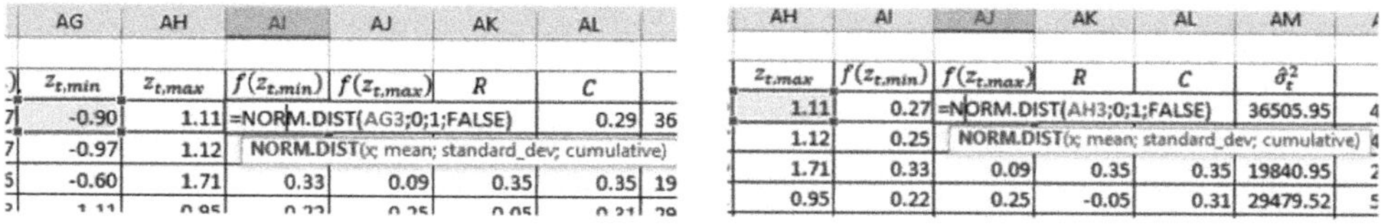

Figure 14.17 Calculations of $f(Z_{t,min})$ and $f(Z_{t,max})$ in Excel.

Sub-step 4.4: Calculate $R = \dfrac{f(z_{t,min}) - f(z_{t,max})}{F(z_{t,max}) - F(z_{t,min})}$

In this formula, $f(z_{t,min})$ and $f(z_{t,max})$ are the probability density function, which yield the probability of seeing a value less than $z_{t,min}$ and larger than $z_{t,max}$, respectively. We can easily calculate these numbers using the =NORM.DIST() function in Excel. As the NORM.S.INV returns the standard normal cumulative distribution (mean = 0, and standard deviation = 1), we need to specify the same mean (0) and standard deviation (1) in the =NORM.DIST function. Figure 14.17 shows the implementation.

Further, $F(z_{t,max})$ and $F(z_{t,min})$ are the cumulative proportions under the normal density curve at $z_{t,max}$ and $z_{t,in}$. Hence, $F(z_{t,mn}) = q_{1t}$ and $F(z_{t,max}) = 1 - q_{2t}$.

Once we have these values we can quickly estimate R as done in Figure 14.18.

Sub-step 4.5: Calculate $C = 1 + \dfrac{z_{t,min} f(z_{t,min}) - z_{t,max} f(z_{t,max})}{F(z_{t,max}) - F(z_{t,min})}$

All the quantities going into the estimation of C are already described in the previous steps. Implementing this calculation in Excel is therefore straightforward as illustrated in Figure 14.19.

We now have all the metrics we need to estimate the means and variances for each profile for the untruncated normal distribution presented in Equation (14.6) and Equation (14.7). Figure 14.20 illustrates the implementation in Excel (variance in upper panel and mean in lower panel).

When these estimates are available, step 5 can be implemented.

260 Conjoint analysis for pricing decisions

AE	AF	AG	AH	AI	AJ	AK	AL
$F(z_{t,min})$	$F(z_{t,max})$	$z_{t,min}$	$z_{t,max}$	$f(z_{t,min})$	$f(z_{t,max})$	R	C
0.18	0.87	-0.90	1.11	0.27	0.22	=(AI3-AJ3)/((AF3-AE3))	
0.17	0.87	-0.97	1.12	0.25	0.21	0.05	0.31	26
0.27	0.96	-0.60	1.71	0.33	0.09	0.35	0.35	19
0.13	0.83	-1.11	0.95	0.22	0.25	-0.05	0.31	29
0.09	0.87	-1.32	1.11	0.17	0.22	-0.06	0.40	19

Figure 14.18 Calculations of R in Excel.

AC	AD	AE	AF	AG	AH	AI	AJ	AK	AL	AM	AN	AO	AP
q_{1t}	q_{2t}	$F(z_{t,min})$	$F(z_{t,max})$	$z_{t,min}$	$z_{t,max}$	$f(z_{t,min})$	$f(z_{t,max})$	R	C	$\hat{\sigma}_t^2$	$\hat{\mu}_t$		
0.18	0.13	0.18	0.87	-0.90	1.11	0.27	0.22	0.07	=1+(((AG3*AI3)-(AH3*AJ3))/((1-AD3)-AC3))-AK3^2				
0.17	0.13	0.17	0.87	-0.97	1.12	0.25	0.21	0.05	0.31	26684.18	497.90		
0.27	0.04	0.27	0.96	-0.60	1.71	0.33	0.09	0.35	0.35	19840.95	246.36		

Figure 14.19 Calculations of C in Excel.

AB	AC	AD	AE	AF	AG	AH	AI	AJ	AK	AL	AM	AN
s_t	q_{1t}	q_{2t}	$F(z_{t,min})$	$F(z_{t,max})$	$z_{t,min}$	$z_{t,max}$	$f(z_{t,min})$	$f(z_{t,max})$	R	C	$\hat{\sigma}_t^2$	$\hat{\mu}_t$
103.5	0.18	0.13	0.18	0.87	-0.90	1.11	0.27	0.22	0.07	0.29	=(AB3^2)/AL3	
91.5	0.17	0.13	0.17	0.87	-0.97	1.12	0.25	0.21	0.05	0.31	26716.02	400.51
83.5	0.27	0.04	0.27	0.96	-0.60	1.71	0.33	0.09	0.35	0.35	19889.82	303.58
95.1	0.13	0.17	0.13	0.83	-1.11	0.95	0.22	0.25	-0.05	0.31	29550.73	442.58
87.8	0.09	0.13	0.09	0.87	-1.32	1.11	0.17	0.22	-0.06	0.40	19205	436.01
	0.00	0.00										

AA	AB	AC	AD	AE	AF	AG	AH	AI	AJ	AK	AL	AM	AN	AO
$\bar{p}_t$	s_t	q_{1t}	q_{2t}	$F(z_{t,min})$	$F(z_{t,max})$	$z_{t,min}$	$z_{t,max}$	$f(z_{t,min})$	$f(z_{t,max})$	R	C	$\hat{\sigma}_t^2$	$\hat{\mu}_t$	
430.0	103.5	0.18	0.13	0.18	0.87	-0.90	1.11	0.27	0.22	0.07	0.29	36596.31	=AA3-AK3*SQRT(AM3)	
409.4	91.5	0.17	0.13	0.17	0.87	-0.97	1.12	0.25	0.21	0.05	0.31	26716.02	400.51	
353.4	83.5	0.27	0.04	0.27	0.96	-0.60	1.71	0.33	0.09	0.35	0.35	19889.82	303.58	
433.2	95.1	0.13	0.17	0.13	0.83	-1.11	0.95	0.22	0.25	-0.05	0.31	29550.73	442.58	
427.3	87.8	0.09	0.13	0.09	0.87	-1.32	1.11	0.17	0.22	-0.06	0.40	19205	436.01	
350.0			0.00	0.00										

Figure 14.20 The calculations of the means and variances in Excel.

Step 5: Create the price–response functions and optimize prices

To create the price–response functions, we need the estimates of the mean and variance (standard deviation) calculated in step 4. These are presented together with the unique profile numbers and the corresponding values of the attributes in a table like this:

Conjoint analysis for pricing decisions 261

Profile	Queue	Period	$\hat{\sigma}_t^2$	$\hat{\sigma}_t$	$\hat{\mu}_t$
1	1 Min	Midweek	36,596.3	191.3	415.9
2	5 Min	Midweek	26,716.0	163.5	400.5
3	10 Min	Midweek	19,889.0	141.0	303.6
4	1 Min	Weekend	29,550.7	171.9	442.6
5	5 Min	Weekend	19,205.0	138.6	436.0
6	10 Min	Weekend	0.0	0.0	350.0

Then the spreadsheet must be organized for the non-linear optimization. This involves defining a cell with the price–response function $(d(p))$, defining the objective cell (the total profit) and defining a cell containing the decision variable (the price). An example of how this can be done is presented in Figure 14.21 (the screenshot to the right shows the formulas).

An initial value of the decision variable is simply set to NOK 400. Moreover, the price–response function for the target market can be adjusted by multiplying $d(p)$ by m, where m is the size of the target market. In the example above, m is set to 1 (this will not affect the results as it is just a constant). We shall now ask Excel to maximize the profit (Z) by changing the price. To do this, we use the solver add-in (see the Appendix for Chapter 6 on how to install this add-in). For example, let us optimize the midweek price with a waiting time of one minute using the solver. The setup for running this optimization is presented in Figure 14.22.

The objective cell is the total profit and given in cell J19. The decision variable is the price and is given in cell J9. Once the solving method is chosen (GRG non-linear) the problem can be solved by hitting Solve. The result is provided right awayas illustrated in Figure 14.23.

That is, the profit-maximizing price during the midweek, for a waiting time of one minute in the main lifts is NOK 339.78. At this price, we serve a total of 65.5% of the total market, meaning that 34.5% of the skiers have a reservation price below this. The exact same procedure shall be used to find the profit-maximizing prices for the other profiles.

	I	J	K		I	J	K
		Q=1 min				Q=1 min	
		MW	WE			MW	WE
Mean		415.897	442.581	Mean		=G4	=G7
Std.dev		191.302	171.903	Std.dev		=F4	=F7
Optimal price		400.000	400.000	Optimal price		400	400
vc		0.000	0.000	vc		0	0
m (target market)		1.000	1.000	m (target market)		1	1
H(p)		0.467	0.402	H(p)		=NORM.DIST(J9;J5;J6;TRUE)	=NORM.DIST(K9;K5;K6;TRUE)
d(p) - fraction		0.533	0.598	d(p) - fraction		=(1-J14)	=(1-K14)
d(p) - total		0.533	0.598	d(p) - total		=J15*J11	=K15*K11
Z		213.246	239.127	Z		=(J9-J10)*J16	=(K9-K10)*K16

Figure 14.21 Setup for the optimization problem in Excel.

262 Conjoint analysis for pricing decisions

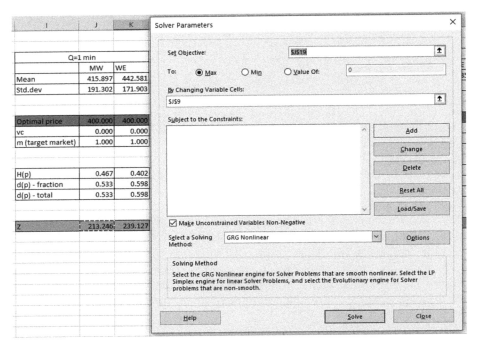

Figure 14.22 Solving the optimization problem in Excel.

	Q=1 min
	MW
Mean	415.897
Std.dev	191.302
Optimal price	339.778
vc	0.000
m (target market)	1.000
H(p)	0.345
d(p) - fraction	0.655
d(p) - total	0.655
Z	222.435

Figure 14.23 The result of the optimization problem.

14.4 Summary

- Conjoint analysis is about revealing customers' preferences for product or service attributes by having them choose between various options.
- One advantage of this method is that it avoids a direct focus on price.
- There are two main methods within the conjoint framework: (1) Rating-based, and (2) choice-based.
- The choice-based method has some advantages compared to the rating-based method, but the design and techniques used to estimate price–response functions from choice-based data are generally more complex.
- The chapter shows in a step-by-step manner how price–response functions can be estimated from rating-based conjoint data. The data used stems from a Norwegian ski resort.

14.5 Problems

1. Replicate the analyses presented in the main text of this chapter. Either use your own data or the data accompanying Chapter 14.

Acknowledgment

Gudbrand Lien has contributed to the content of this chapter.

Notes

1 There are two main methods within the conjoint framework: (1) Rating-based, and (2) choice-based. The choice-based method has some advantages compared to the rating-based method, but the design of the former (choice-based) method is far more complex due to the difficulties of generating choice sets. We therefore choose to focus on the rating-based method here and refer interested readers to Rao (2014).
2 Equation (14.1) reads like this in Kohli and Mahajan (1991): $u_{it|\sim p} + u_i(p) \geq u_i^* + \epsilon$, where ϵ is a small positive number, which is assumed to be selected by the user in any application of the model. In the application of this chapter we set ϵ to 0.
3 We modify the function slightly by including the subscript t to make it clear that we do the optimization with respect to product or service alternative t.
4 In recent versions of Excel, it is possible to use the LINEST function to obtain the same result. However, for the benefit of readers who do not have access to this function, the user-defined VBA function is valuable.

Chapter 15

Acceptance, ethics, and the law

The various pricing analyses and optimal solutions considered in previous chapters have a few things in common: (1) They assume that the prices we charge now will not affect future customer behavior; (2) they do not consider ethical aspects; and (3) they ignore the law. However, it is extremely important that you are aware of these aspects. This chapter aims to raise your awareness about these issues within the field of pricing. Specifically, the following topics will be covered:

- Customer acceptance;
  - Price presentation;
  - Fairness.
- Ethical constraints.
- Legal issues.

15.1 Customer acceptance

Pricing theory asserts that a firm's objective is to maximize profits and, consequently, prevailing prices do not influence future customer behavior. However, customers are not super-rational beings, but are influenced by, among other things, reference prices and perceptions of fairness. Their past and present experiences may induce them to change their future behavior. A pricing strategy that ignores customer reactions is thus bound to fail as the following two examples illustrate.

Praktiker AG discounts itself out of business

Praktiker AG was a leading do-it-yourself retail chain operating in several European countries. In its initial days of operation, the company launched a long-lasting campaign slogan: "20% Discount on everything except pet food." Subsequently, it ran this campaign every other month. This always brought a lot of customers into the store when the campaign was on. However, in 2013 after running a "30% Off everything campaign," the company went out of business.

J.C. Penney's not so welcome pricing strategy

At the beginning of 2012, American department store chain J.C. Penney introduced what it called its "Fair and square every day" pricing strategy. The plan stemmed from the company's realization that three-quarters of everything sold at its department stores was typically sold at a 50% discount from the list price. Instead of using deep discount sales to attract customers, the chain embarked on simply offering three prices: (1) "Everyday;" (2) "Month-long value" (theme sales such as back-to-school related products in August); and (3) "Best prices" (clearance). In addition, prices that ended in "99" would now end in "0" and price tags listed just one price (instead of including the *de rigueur* "Previously sold at a higher price" convention). Within weeks of the campaign, the stock price of J.C. Penney dipped, and one business reporter wrote: "Not only did Penney's plain pricing structure fail to attract fair-minded shoppers – it 'repelled' them."

Both Praktiker and J.C. Penney had one thing in common: They did not correctly evaluate customers' reactions to their pricing strategies. Studies on purchasing behavior from the standpoint of psychology and behavioral economics show that people evaluate outcomes by comparing them to their reference point. For Praktiker, long-running and predictable discounts meant that the reference price was the discounted price, and customers would have perceived regular prices of items in the store to be an overcharge. Similarly, J.C. Penney's plain price strategy eliminated the usual discounted price that the customers were used to seeing. We will further explore these examples in this chapter. Several factors, some of which may seem irrelevant, can influence customer response to price. Phillips (2005, p. 304) mentions the following:

- How the price is presented and packaged.
- How much profit the customer believes the merchant will realize.
- How this price compares to past prices and anticipated future prices.
- Prices the customer believes are being charged to other customers.

All these aspects can influence customer responses and are usually not accounted for in the price–response models of firms. Broadly speaking, there are two main categories of behavior not conforming to the rational decision-making model as it relates to customer response to non-product related issues: (1) Price presentation and (2) fairness.

Price presentation

Digit-ending: The most famous example of a price presentation issue is the digit-ending phenomenon (Phillips, 2005). That is, buyers tend to overweight the leading digits when comparing prices. A reduction in price from $20.00 to $19.99 is perceived to be a greater saving than a reduction from $19.99 to $19.93. From the customer's viewpoint, prices ending in "0" are more representative of the true price of a product than prices ending in "99." However, for the firm, the reverse is true because prices ending in "99" are perceived to be lower than they actually are. Therefore, this may be one of the factors that explain why J.C. Penney's new pricing strategy was initially unsuccessful. A pair of sneakers sold for $49.99 before implementation of the pricing strategy would now be sold for $50.00, the former price seen as being in the 40s range, whereas the latter in the 50s range and thus more expensive. An illustration of digit-ending pricing approach is given in Figure 15.1.

Sales price: Customers will respond differently to a price if is presented as a sales price rather than a regular list price or a surcharge (Phillips, 2005). Two examples of sales price presentations are given in Figure 15.2.

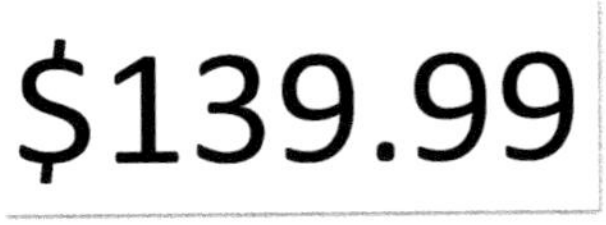

$139.99

Figure 15.1 An example of the digit-ending pricing approach.

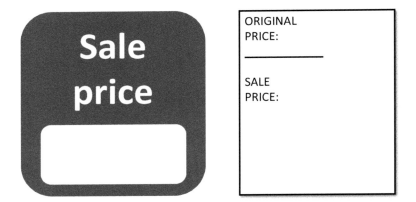

Figure 15.2 Two examples of sales price presentations.

Hiding-the-price and bounded rationality: For some products it can be extremely difficult to figure out what the real price of the product is, or it can be difficult to compare the price of similar products because they differ in some of the characteristics that are hard to evaluate. Examples include loans and electronics. The price of a loan can be presented in many ways: Payment per month, payment per year, total interest, annual percentage rate, total interest payments, and so forth. The lender can sometimes choose (although there are restrictions on this in many countries) how to present the price of the loan. The lender will then try to make the price look attractive from the customer's point of view. Another example is products where it is hard to know exactly what attributes contribute to the price. Take a TV, for example. Two TVs with almost identical specifications can have very different prices. To evaluate what is the "best price" in this case, the consumer will need to have good knowledge of all the technical characteristics. Most consumers do not have such detailed knowledge of all products and therefore make so-called mental shortcuts (Phillips, 2005). Such mental shortcuts are not in line with the principles of economic rationality, where the consumer is assumed to make his or her choices based on complete information about the product and competing products. Herbert Simon (1972) introduced the concept of bounded rationality to describe how consumers make decisions in a complex and rapidly changing environment. The implications of the fact that most consumers do not strictly follow economic theory are important when it comes to price management.

Asymmetric evaluation: In their seminal paper on prospect theory, Kahneman and Tversky (1979) make important propositions about the value function for consumers.

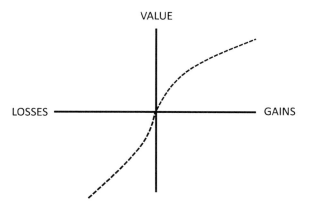

Figure 15.3 An example of a hypothetical value function. Source: Kahneman and Tversky (1979, p. 279).

First, they state that the value function is defined on the deviations from the reference point. Second, it is generally concave for gains and convex for losses. Third, it is steeper for losses than for gains. An example of such a value function is given in Figure 15.3.

In practical terms, prospect theory implies that customers evaluate stated prices as changes from a reference price. Reverting to the example of Praktiker, let us consider that today is the first day of August, a month where the chain's stores do not offer a discount. A customer walks in and finds that a hammer costs €10, but a day before its price was €8 resulting from the 20% discount every other month. From the customer's perspective, the reference price will most likely be the discounted price of €8. Therefore, the current price implies a loss of €2. From the value function in Figure 15.3, it is apparent that losses are treated more seriously than equivalent gains because the value function is steeper in the loss domain (for example, the value of a loss of 2 will be greater than the value of a gain of 2). So as not to feel ripped off, the customer may wait until prices return to the reference price in the next month. If many customers were to exhibit this behavior, it would lead to depressed sales in the months when there are no discounts: One can start understanding how Praktiker ran into difficulties. The value function also explains various framing effects and why firms adopt different methods to describe prices. Thaler (1980), for example, considers the early stages of credit card usage in the U.S.A., where a number of stores charged credit card users higher prices because of the additional costs incurred in processing credit card transactions. The reference point in this case depends on whether you frame the price as a "cash discount" or a "credit card surcharge." Preference for the former, Thaler notes, makes sense if consumers view the cash discount as an opportunity cost of using the credit card, but the surcharge as an out-of-pocket cost. The same explanation can be advanced for why grocery stores will refer to lower prices charged to clubcard members as "loyalty discounts" and not a surcharge to non-members.

Mental accounting: Thaler (1980) states that consumer decision-making in many instances mimics "naïve accounting." For any price evaluation, the consumer classifies it as either a gain or a loss relative to some reference price. The consumer may quickly combine several gains and several losses, or a combination of gains and losses before storing the final figure in their mind. However, when thinking about gains and losses, consumers do not combine these but consider them separately, weighting losses more than gains, as illustrated previously by the value function in prospect theory. Mental accounting has important implications for pricing. For example, consider a retailer who has slow-moving inventory of one brand of vacuum cleaners and another slightly less expensive but popular brand. If the higher-priced brand costs NOK 4,000 and the other brand sells at NOK 3,400, the retailer may announce a sale of both brands at NOK 3,000, which yields a lower but positive profit margin for both brands. This scenario is a common occurrence and can be explained by mental accounting. The retailer expects to move a large quantity of the previously higher-priced vacuum cleaner because customers will perceive that there is a greater gain from purchasing the higher-priced vacuum cleaner at the discounted price. What the customers do not know was that the seller was having a hard time selling these vacuums and that perhaps their reference point, which was the previous price, may have always been an over-valuation.

Other framing issues: Should a gym bill its customers monthly, or annually? Should the local football team sell season tickets, or tickets for each game? Apart from aspects to do with the time value of money, these questions are simply related to presentation. The nominal amount of money collected through a payment of NOK 500 per month is precisely equal to an annual amount of NOK 6,000. However, laboratory and field experiments in psychology and behavioral economics show that the frequency of billing, time of purchase and whether products are bundled or sold separately influence how consumers behave and the total revenues that the firm earns. Gourville and Soman (2002), for example, found that health club users who were billed annually used the club facilities more in the first half of the year, then their use declined drastically in the second half, compared with club users who were billed monthly. This suggests that a clever pricing implementation where above-capacity memberships maintained in the latter part of the year could increase revenue, much like how airlines use overbooking to maximize revenues.

Fairness

Psychological research shows that fairness affects a wide range of human emotion, attitude, and behavior. Therefore, it is important that the firm evaluates the consequences of various pricing strategies and how fairness affects these. In this section, we shall consider the principle of dual entitlement and interpersonal fairness and discuss some of their implications for pricing.

Dual entitlement

In many industries, it has been observed that sellers are reluctant to raise prices to ration off excess demand. Clearly, such a move would have increased revenues and thus profits. Kahneman et al. (1986) proposed that consumer judgements of seller fairness could explain the observed phenomenon. A few years later, Urbany et al. (1989) found empirical support for this prediction that unjustified price increases are perceived as unfair, whereas price increases emanating from increases in costs are justified. This theory, referred to as dual entitlement, contends that firms are entitled to a "reasonable" profit and consumers are entitled to a "reasonable" price. If a firm is seen to be increasing prices to an unreasonable level, it risks being shunned by consumers. Therefore, it is very important for a firm that is facing rising costs to signal this reason as the basis of any price increment so that consumers do not mistakenly assume that the principal consideration was profit.

Interpersonal fairness

To illustrate interpersonal fairness, Bazerman, White and Loewenstein (1995) present the following case relating to the price of labor:

> "You are graduating with a Ph.D. from a good [institution]. After a few interviews, a university that you were very interested in makes you an offer of an assistant professorship at $40,000 a year. The offer is not negotiable. You like the people. You like the job. You like the location. However, right before you are about to accept the offer, you find out that the same university is offering another new assistant professor $42,000. You do not see any characteristics that make the other individual more qualified than you. Would you still accept the offer?"

They remark that many people would be bothered by the differences even if they thought that this situation was not indicative of how the university would treat them in the future. Indeed, one of the major theories of social preferences within the last two decades is Fehr and Schmidt's (1999) inequality aversion model. The model contends that individuals dislike inequality and are willing to punish themselves and others to avoid it. Experimental studies, for example, by Capizzani et al. (2017), back up predictions from the model, showing that individuals are bothered by inequality whether this leads to an advantageous allocation to them or not (that is, even the individual who would be earning $42,000 in the example above would be bothered knowing that a similarly qualified individual hired at the same time is earning a lower amount). For firms that engage in price differentiaton, this is a pertinent issue because if consumers cannot find an acceptable basis for charging two different prices for the same product, then they may shun the firm in the future.

15.2 Ethical constraints

An important aspect to pricing strategy is the firm's obligation to uphold the highest ethical standards. Even though the law may be in place to regulate some practices, such as price fixing, it is impossible to rely on courts to enforce all suspected instances, due to both resource limitations and the difficulty proving that such acts were intentional and clearly violated the law. However, from an economic point of view, integrity and moral values are not just desirable characteristics for the firm but have real consequences in terms of its long-term viability. This is due to reputation, and a firm that is perceived to engage in unethical and dishonest behavior will be shunned by customers. As the American investor Warren Buffet noted: "[I]t takes 20 years to build a reputation and five minutes to ruin it." Therefore, it is important for the firm to consistently maintain high ethical standards because only one instance of unethical behavior may be enough to ruin the business. In this section, we will consider five pricing practices where a gray area exists between ethics and the law, and for which firms may act in an unethical manner.

Price fixing

This refers to an agreement between firms to sell a product at a fixed price, or control supply such that a given price level is maintained. In many countries, most forms of price fixing are illegal, but they may be difficult to detect or prosecute. The ultimate losers, however, are consumers and society since price-fixing both restricts output and increases the price of the product.

Bid rigging

Construction firms are an example of organizations whose business entails soliciting building or renovation projects from other firms, individuals, governments, etc. Thus, they are required to price the projects beforehand, and in many cases submit a bid that will be evaluated by the contracting entity. Bid rigging is a form of price fixing where the contract is promised to one party, even though for the sake of appearance, several other parties also present a bid. Like price fixing, bid rigging results in non-optimal allocation and use of resources because other bidders may exist who would, for the same level of quality, complete the contract at a lower cost. This therefore causes economic harm to the contracting entity and society at large. It may seem surprising that an entity seeking bids will want to harm itself, but this should be evaluated in the context of the principal–agent problem. The managers of a firm, for example, are agents of the owners (shareholders) and may not always work in the best interest of those owners. This therefore requires some incentive or monitoring mechanism for the firm to curtail the principal–agent problem.

Price differentiation

Price differentiation, covered in Chapter 2, can be used by the firm to extract a higher profit at the expense of consumers. This could arise, for example, if the firm hides lower-priced products from customers with a higher willingness to pay, or the conventional form whereby the firm segments the market and sells the product at different prices to the different segments. While some instances of price differentiation can be viewed as ethical, for example half-price fares for senior citizens, the practice allows the firm to engage in unethical behavior for short-run gains. A *Wall Street Journal* article dated August 23, 2012 outlined a pricing strategy by the online travel firm Orbitz Worldwide Inc., where it intentionally showed Apple Mac users costlier travel options than Microsoft Windows users. This was based on statistics that indicated that Mac users spend as much as 30% more a night on hotels. While Orbitz's action did not violate any laws, it was viewed as highly unethical and resulted in an enormous public relations backlash for the firm.

Price skimming

Price skimming attempts to extract the maximum profit possible at each step of the demand curve. It refers to the practice of introducing a new product and selling it at a higher price, and successively lowering the price over time to attract new customers who were not willing or able to purchase the product at the higher price. While the practice is not illegal, it offers an avenue to engage in unethical behavior by exploiting "impatient" consumers who are attracted by the latest release. One sector where price skimming is rampant is the technology industry, where software and gadgets are usually updated on an annual basis. Once an update occurs and is introduced to the market, there is a price drop for the older versions.

Price gouging

Price gouging can be understood in the context of a street vendor raising the price of umbrellas when there is a downpour. Firms can and do take advantage by raising prices when there is a shortage, or if a certain product has no close substitutes and is not available elsewhere. In such cases, the prices are in excess of production costs and a reasonable profit margin for the firm, and therefore the question that arises is whether such price increases are justified or unethical. Following Hurricane Harvey in September 2017, *Business Insider Nordic* reported incidents of price gouging in parts of Texas where a gallon of gas went for as high as $20 and a case of water for $99, more than five times the normal price for each. It would be difficult to claim that such margins are not unethical, especially since consumers in this instance also faced the misfortune of dealing with the aftermath of the hurricane.

15.3 Legal issues

Pricing laws are designed to protect consumers from unscrupulous dealings by firms. This may range from deceptive pricing where one price is advertised and consumers end up paying a higher price, to price fixing, which we covered in the previous section. Pricing laws may differ among countries, but, as we shall see, there is a large overlap in what practices are considered lawful and what are not. It is important that you understand the law both as a consumer and a business enterprise to know your rights and obligations.

Pricing laws

Most countries have laws and regulations that govern pricing. Because the laws may relate to minor aspects, such as accidentally displaying two prices for the same product, to large collusion arrangements between big corporations, there will be several enforcement agencies at different levels that have authority to ensure adherence to the laws. In the U.S.A., each state has its own laws and regulations relating to the pricing of products. The Director of Weights and Measures is generally tasked with enforcement on behalf of their state. However, for violations of the US antitrust law, which is intended to promote fair competition, the Federal Trade Commission, US Department of Justice, state governments, and private parties may proceed to the courts for enforcement. The

European competition law and the Competition and Consumer Act are, respectively, the legislations used in the European Union and Australia.

Price misrepresentation

This practice is illegal in most countries and mainly relates to charging an amount greater than the advertised, displayed, or quoted price for a product. However, it can be interpreted broadly to include any pricing actions that mislead customers. In the U.K., for example, when announcing a special offer price, sellers are required to announce that there is limited stock or availability for the product if they anticipate that demand will outstrip supply. Otherwise the offer price is considered as misleading. Another form of price misrepresentation can occur if a seller uses *comparative pricing* deceptively. This involves comparing the sale price of a product to an inflated former price, for example, when using "was, now" advertising.

Price marking of goods

Advances in electronic commerce have meant that a large percentage of transactions are online. Therefore, whether online or offline, the law in many countries requires that sellers explicitly display the selling price of goods. In the European Union, this should be inclusive of value added tax, whereas in the U.S.A., because of different tax jurisdictions and the confusion that the same product may be priced differently depending on the jurisdiction, the norm is to display the price net of tax.

Predatory pricing

This occurs when a firm with significant resources reduces the price of a product to drive out competition from the market. The practice lowers competition and violates the competition laws of many countries.

Unit pricing code

Retailers in several countries are required by law to display both the product price and a unit price for certain grocery items to allow customers to compare the price and value of similar types of products. For example, the price of a 750-milliliter carton of milk would normally display the price and what this price translates to for a liter. Similarly, a 500-gram bag of sugar will display both the quoted price and the price for a kilogram.

Payment surcharges

The total amount paid for a product can differ if there are surcharges imposed on certain methods of payment. In recent periods, however, several governments have banned imposing surcharges on consumers for credit card, debit card, and charge card payments, or when using e-payment services such as PayPal.

15.4 Summary

- Customers are influenced by many factors in addition to the price level itself. Examples are: Reference prices, perceptions of fairness, how the price is presented, how much the customer believes the merchant will realize, past and expected future prices, prices charged to other customers, and more.
- Prospect theory can be used to understand how customers value price changes from a reference point.
- Customers' perceived fairness should be taken into consideration before implementing a pricing decision. The principles of dual entitlement and interpersonal fairness can be used to understand the implications of (un)fairness on pricing.
- Ethical and legal considerations are always important in any pricing strategy. Most countries have laws and regulations governing pricing and the consequences of violating these can be severe.

15.5 Problems

1. Purple Bricks is a real estate agent based in the U.K.. In 2018, it ran a series of commercials emphasizing that it did not charge commissions, like most other real estate agents, when it handles purchases and sales of properties on behalf of its clients. However, the Advertising Standards Authority, the regulator, ruled the commercials were "misleading" and demanded that the firm make it explicit that they charge clients a flat fee whether their properties are bought or sold. From the client's perspective, paying a commission or a fee represents a monetary outflow. Discuss why Purple Bricks would not want the comparison between fees and commissions to be seen simply as a matter of framing.
2. Discuss some implications of the prospect theory for pricing. Using the value function, explain why grocery stores will refer to lower prices charged to clubcard members as "loyalty discounts" and not a surcharge to non-members.
3. Describe two ways a retailer may use mental accounting to maximize profits.
4. Are consumers affected by fairness? Discuss giving examples.
5. List five areas where there may exist ambiguity between ethics and the law.
6. A firm that acts in an unethical manner may hurt itself in the long run. Evaluate this statement.

Acknowledgment

This chapter is written by Andrew Musau.

Bibliography

Akter, S. & Wamba, S. F. (2016). Big data analytics in E-commerce: A systematic review and agenda for future research. *Electronic Markets*, 26(2), 173–194.

Andreyeva, T., Long, M. W. & Brownell, K. D. (2010). The impact of food prices on consumption: A systematic review of research on the price elasticity of demand for food. *American Journal of Public Health*, 100(2), 216–222.

Barton, D. & Court, D. (2012). Making advanced analytics work for you. *Harvard Business Review*, 90(10), 78–83.

Bazerman, M. H., White, S. B. & Loewenstein, G. F. (1995). Perceptions of fairness in interpersonal and individual choice situations. *Psychological Science*, 4, 39–43.

Belobaba P. P. (1987). Air travel demand and airline seat inventory management. PhD dissertation. Flight Transportation Laboratory, Massachusetts Institute of Technology, Cambridge, MA.

Berman, B. (2005). Applying yield management pricing to your service business. *Business Horizons*, 48(2), 169–179.

Beyer, M. A. & Laney, D. (2012). *The importance of 'Big Data': A definition*. Technical report, Gartner.

Blumenschein, K., Blomquist, G. C., Johannesson, M., Horn, N. & Freeman, P. (2008). Eliciting willingness to pay without bias: Evidence from a field experiment. *Economic Journal*, 118(1), 114–137.

Bodea, T. & Ferguson, M. (2014). *Segmentation, revenue management, and pricing analytics*. Routledge, New York.

Breidert, C., Hahsler, M. & Reutterer, T. (2006). A review of methods for measuring willingness-to-pay. *Innovative Marketing*, 2(4), 8–32.

Camerer, C. (2003). *Behavioral game theory: Experiments in strategic interaction*. Princeton University Press, New Jersey.

Capizzani, M., Mittone, L., Musau, A. & Vaccaro, A. (2017). Anticipated communication in the ultimatum game. *Games*, 8(3), 29.

Combris, P., Lecocq S. & Visser M. (1997). Estimation of a hedonic price equation for Bordeaux wine: Does quality matter? *The Economic Journal*, 107, 390–402.

Dunse, N. & Jones, C. (1998). A hedonic price model of office rents. *Journal of Property Valuation and Investment*, 16(3), 297–312.

Erevelles, S., Fukawa, N. & Swayne, L. (2016). Big Data consumer analytics and the transformation of marketing. *Journal of Business Research*, 69(2), 897–904.

Falk, M. (2008). A hedonic price model for ski lift tickets. *Tourism Management*, 29(6), 1172–1184.

Fehr, E. & Schmidt, K.M. (1999). A theory of fairness, competition and cooperation. *Quarterly Journal of Economics*, 114, 817–868.

Glennerster, R. & Takavarasha, K. (2013). *Running randomized evaluations: A practical guide*. Princeton University Press.

Gourville, J. & Soman, D. (2002). Pricing and the psychology of consumption. *Harvard Business Review* (September), 90–96.

Gradín, C. (2012). Poverty among minorities in the United States: Explaining the racial poverty gap for Blacks and Latinos. *Applied Economics*, 44(29), 3793–3804. https://doi.org/10.1080/00036846.2011.581219.

Greiner, B. (2004). An online recruitment system for economic experiments. In *Forschung und wissenschaftliches Rechnen*. (K. Kremer and V. Macho, Eds.). Göttingen: Ges. für Wiss. Datenverarbeitung, 79–93.

Griliches, Z. (1961). Hedonic price indexes for automobiles: An econometric analysis of quality change. Reprinted in *Price indexes and quality change: Studies in new methods of measurement*. (Griliches, Ed.). Cambridge, Mass: Harvard University Press, 55–87.

Havranek, T., Irsova, Z. & Janda K. (2012). Demand for gasoline is more price-inelastic than commonly thought. *Energy Economics*, 34 (1), 201–207.

Haugom, E., Malasevska, I. & Lien, G. (2020). Optimal pricing of alpine ski passes in the case of crowdedness and reduced skiing capacity. *Empirical Economics*, 1–19. https://doi.org/10.1007/s00181-020-01872-w

Holmes, D. E. (2017). *Big Data – A very short introduction*. Oxford University Press, Oxford.

Kahneman, D. & Tversky, A. (1979). Prospect theory: An analysis of decision under risk. *Econometrica*, 47(2), 263–291.

Kahneman, D., Knetsch, J. L. & Thaler, R. H. (1986). Fairness as a constraint on profit seeking: Entitlements in the market. *American Economic Review*, 76, 728–741.

Ketkar, K. (1992). Hazardous waste sites and property values in the state of New Jersey. *Applied Economics*, 24, 647–659.

Kohli, R. & Mahajan, V. (1991). A reservation-price model for optimal pricing of multiattribute products in conjoint analysis. *Journal of Marketing Research*, 28(3), 347–354.

Lancaster, K. J. (1966). A new approach to consumer theory. *Journal of Political Economy*, 74(2), 132–157.

Laney, D. (2001). 3D Data Management: Controlling Data Volume, Velocity and Variety. Meta Group, available at: www.bibsonomy.org/bibtex/742811cb00b303261f79a98e9b80bf49. Accessed; March 15, 2020.

LaValle, S., Lesser, E., Shockley, R., Hopkins, M. S. & Kruschwitz, N. (2011). Big Data, analytics and the path from insights to value. *MIT Sloan Management Review*, 52(2), 21–32.

Lohr, S. (2012, February 11). The age of Big Data. *The New York Times*.

Marn, M. V. & Rosiello, R. L. (1992). Managing price, gaining profit. *Harward Business Review*, 84–94.

McGill J. I. & van Ryzin G. J. (1999). Revenue management: Research overview and prospects. *Transportation Science*, 33(2), 233–256.

Miller, K. M., Hofstetter, R., Krohmer, H. & Zhang, Z. J. (2011). How should consumers' willingness to pay be measured? An empirical comparison of state-of-the-art approaches. *Journal of Marketing Research*, 48(1), 172–184.

Mills, S., Lucas, S., Irakliotis, L., Ruppa, M., Carlson, T. & Perlowitz, B. (2012). *Demystifying Big Data: A practical guide to transforming the business of government*. TechAmerica Foundation, Washington. Available at http://breakinggov.com/documents/demystifying-big-data-a-practical-guide-to-transforming-the-bus/ Retrieved March 15, 2020.

Mok, H. M. K., Chan, P. P. K. & Cho, Y. S. (1995). A hedonic price model for private properties in Hong Kong. *Journal of Real Estate Finance and Economics*, 10(1), 37–48.

Nagle, T. T., Hogan, J. E. & Zale, J. (2011). *The strategy and tactics of pricing a guide to growing more profitably*. Prentice Hall, New Jersey.

Pindyck, R. S. & Rubinfeld, D. L. (2018). *Microeconomics* (Global ed., The Pearson series in economics). Pearson, Harlow.

Phillips, R. L. (2005). *Pricing and revenue optimization*. Stanford University Press, California.

Ramakrishnan, R., Özer, O. & Phillips, R., (Ed.). (2012). Chapter 25. *Markdown management* (pp. 620–654). Oxford University Press.

Rao, V. R. (2014). *Applied conjoint analysis*. Springer-Verlag, Berlin Heidelberg.

Richardson, H. W., Vipond, J. & Furbey, R. A. (1974). Determinants of urban house prices. *Urban Studies*, 11, 189–199.

Rosen, S. (1974). Hedonic prices and implicit markets: Product differentiation in pure competition. *Journal of Political Economy*, 82(1), 34–55.

Talluri K. T. & van Ryzin G. J. (2004). *The theory and practice of revenue management*. Kluwer, Boston.

Thaler, R. (1980). Toward a positive theory of consumer choice. *Journal of Economic Behavior and Organization*, 1, 39–60.

Tomkins, J., Topham, N., Twomey, J. & Ward, R. 1998. Noise versus access: The impact of an airport in an urban property market. *Urban Studies*, 35(2): 243–258.

Urbany, J. E., Madden, T. J. & Dickson P. R. (1989). All's not fair in pricing: An initial look at the dual entitlement principle. *Marketing Letters*, 1(1), 17–25.

Veka, S. (2011, September 4). A more flexible OLS function easily created as a user defined function in VBA. STSVAVE. https://stsvave.wordpress.com/2011/09/ Retrieved March 15, 2020.

Price elasticity of demand. In Wikipedia. https://en.wikipedia.org/wiki/Price_elasticity_of_demand Retrieved March 15, 2020.

Index

accuracy, 206–207
adjusted R square, 90
airline, 7, 69, 178–181, 268
amusement park, 43, 128, 178
analytics: Big Data, 188, 192, 212; business, 191; modern data, 193
approximate market price, 96–97
arbitrage, 45, 116
arc elasticity, 68
asymmetric evaluation, 266
auction, 37

bid, 270
bid rigging, 270
binomial, 75
booking control, 180
booking limit, 180–183
bounded rationality, 266
break even, 49–60
budget lines, 13–16

cancellations, 178
cannibalization, 45, 123, 129, 159–160
case study, 128
centroids, 199
channel, 5, 41–42, 129, 190
competition, 31–32, 45, 125, 271–272
conditional probability, 200, 211
conjoint analysis, 245
conjoint method, 245
consumer behavior, 12, 74
consumer choice, 13, 125
consumer preferences, 12
consumer surplus, 19–21, 38–40
contribution margin, 44, 51, 54, 105, 112, 118, 124
cost-plus pricing, 7
costs, 21–23
cumulative distribution, 249, 259
cumulative probability, 183, 185
customer acceptance, 264–265

customer commitment, 108
customer-driven pricing, 7

data analysis tools, 103
data analytics techniques, 192–193
data mining, 191
data set, 172–174, 189–190, 204–205
data sources, 191
data table, 226–227, 235
data visualization, 136
decisionvariable, 105, 112, 146, 149–151, 162–163, 207, 261
decision problem, 13, 27
decision rule, 110
demand curve, 3, 14, 31–32, 66–68, 70, 271
demand function, 44
demand shifting, 121–124, 129, 147–151
dependent variable, 66, 90, 140, 147, 170, 172–175, 246, 249
descriptive statistics, 134, 174, 232
deterministic changes, 235
deterministic markdown management, 162
differentiation. *See* price differentiation
digit-ending, 152, 265–266
discounts, 72, 74, 80, 86
discrete data, 72
discrete choice modelling, 83
discrete price–response function, 3–4, 18, 71–72
discrete probability distribution, 221–223
diversion, 148–149, 151
downward sloping, 32, 133
dual entitlement, 268
dummy variable, 131
Dutch auction, 37
dynamic: markdown, 163–165; optimization, 5; pricing, 164, 190, 192; weather forecasts, 212–213

e-commerce, 6, 189, 192
empirical estimation of price–response functions, 82

EMSR, 184–186
estimation of price–response functions, 137
Euclidean distance, 195–199, 203–204, 207–209
Excel's solver, 98, 144, 146, 150
expected: demand, 82, 152; profit, 228; revenue, 179
expected value, 224, 234
exponential function, 94

F9 key, 222, 225, 233
fairness, 268–269
false negative, 206
false positive, 206
fare class, 180–186
fares, 178–179, 270
fashion goods, 154–155
first degree price differentiation, 37
fixed costs, 22
forecasting, 85, 212
FREQUENCY function, 228, 229, 235
frequency table, 219, 227–229
frequent buyers, 5

game theory, 32
gender: price differentiaton, 38, 41
Giffen goods, 104
global: price–response, 74
groups: price-differentiation, 37–38, 41, 180

histogram, 227–228, 230, 236–237, 239
historical data, 84, 125, 191, 193, 200, 220, 224
hotel industry, 44, 108
hotel room prices, 170–172, 175–176
hotel rooms, 170, 174, 176
hotels, 108, 178–179, 270
hypothesis, 91
hypothetical bias, 85, 87
hypothetical experiment, 83
hypothetical methods, 85
hypothetical value function, 267

incremental costs, 21, 23, 107–108, 120, 156
incremental fixed costs, 23–24, 29–30
independent variable, 66, 71, 89–90, 140, 147, 170, 172–176, 246, 249, 251
indifference curve, 13–19
inferior, 42
integers, 222
intercept, 71, 240–241, 249
INTERCEPT function, 89
inverse of the price–response function, 116
investment, 56

iso-utility curves, 14

judgement, 152
judgement expert, 83
jurisdiction, 272

key characteristics, 129, 134–135
k-Means clustering, 199
k-nearest neighbor algorithm, 193, 198

least squares, 89, 170
lift ratio, 201
lift ticket prices, 172–173, 246
linear function, 89, 92
linear price–response function, 71–74
linear programming, 114
linear regression, 71, 89–90, 93
Littlewood's rule, 182
local parts of the price/demand relationship, 77
logit, 75
logit model, 79, 94–99
logit price–response function, 94–99
long-run effect, 69

margin. See contribution margin
marginal costs, 23–24
marginal opportunity cost, 114–115
marginal revenue, 25–30
marginal utility, 38
markdown optimization, 154–167
markdowns, 154–155
market basket, 14–15, 17, 193, 199
market demand, 3, 14
market price, 96
market structures, 31
market-based pricing, 7
market-basket analysis, 193
MAX function, 228
maximize objective function, 146
maximum willingness to pay, 19–20, 70
mental accounting, 267–268
MIN and MAX functions, 228
minimize objective function, 95
monopolistic competition, 31
monopoly, 32
Monte Carlo simulation, 218
multinomial logit model, 125
multiple regression, 172, 249–252

nesting booking control, 180
non-linear price–response, 100
non-linear optimization, 99, 108
non-linear programming, 114
non-linear shape, 139

non-negative demand, 108
non-negativity constraints, 112
non-smooth cost functions, 30
NORM.INV function, 224
normal distribution, 224–226, 234, 238–239
normalize, 197

oligopoly, 31
opportunity cost, 112
optimization model, 105, 112, 117, 120, 123
outlets, 42

PERCENTILE.INC function, 207
percentiles, 207
perfect competition, 31–32
PivotTable, 134–137, 139
point elasticity of demand, 67
Poisson distribution, 237
population, 84
Power Query, 212–213
predicted values, 91–94, 97, 140–143
preference functions, 246–249
price changes: break-even analysis, 50
price differentiation, 36–45, 116, 119–120, 129, 137, 270
price elasticity, 66–70, 91
price management, 4–5
price optimization: basic, 105–108; capacity contraints, 108–111; case study, 146–151; Excel, 108–109, 111–112
price presentation, 265–266
price sensitivity, 64
price–demand relationship, 12, 84–85
price–response function, 3–4, 67, 74–75; willingness to pay, 76–77
price–response functions, 78–79; estimation, 88; functional forms, 75; markdown optimization, 156–158; simulation, 237–240; simulation and willingness to pay, 237–240; survey questions, 86–87; theoretical foundation, 12–21
pricing analytics, 5–7, 189–190, 192, 212
pricing process, 6–7
PRO cube, 6, 41–42
probability density function, 259
probability distribution: discrete, 221; uniform, 222
production levels, 25
product versions: segmentation based on, 41
profit function, 2
promotions, 199, 219
prospect theory, 266–268
protection levels, 181
P-value, 93

quantitative techniques, 6
quantity demanded, 3, 16–20, 38
quantity discounts, 38

RAND function, 221–225
RANDBETWEEN function, 221–223
random numbers: simulation, 218–219
random sample, 84
random values: centroid, 207
reference prices, 264
regional pricing, 44
regression: Excel, 89–91, 93, 140, 175
regression analysis, 170
reservation price, 36–37, 40, 70–71, 74–75, 202, 207, 247–249, 253, 255–257
revenue management, 178–186
runout price, 110–111

sample, 84, 129, 131, 134–135, 197, 221–224, 226, 235, 249, 251
sample size, 131
sampling, 234, 237–238
satiating price, 72–73, 76
scatter plot, 95, 97, 139, 143, 147, 194
second degree price differentiation, 37
segmentation, 36
self-selection price differentiation, 44
senior citizens, 38, 270
service providers, 7, 108, 147
shadow price, 112, 114
short-run price elasticity, 69
significance, 91
simple bivariate regression, 147
simulation, 218–242
single-period price, optimal, 156
SLOPE function, 89
slope of: bivariate regression model, 140, 147, 149; price-response function, 66, 69, 241; TC function, 23–25; Z (profit), 106
solver add-in, 98, 261
sporting events, 41–42, 108, 128
squared deviations, 95, 140, 143
S-shaped price-response function, 78
standard deviation, 75, 183, 185, 197, 224
strategic pricing, 5, 11
summary statistics, 135, 230
SUMPRODUCT function, 251
superior variants, 42
supervised methods, 193
supply constraint, 111

tactical pricing, 5
target variable, 205
third degree price differentiation, 37–38
time-based price differentiation, 44, 119

total contribution margin, 50–51, 54, 115, 119
total costs, 12, 21, 22, 24
total profit, 2
total revenue, 49
training data, 203–204
transaction data, 189, 192, 201, 209–211
t-value, 176
two-class model, 182
two-period markdown model, 156–158

uniform probability distribution, 222
uniform willingness-to-pay distribution, 70
unsupervised methods, 193
utility contribution of price, 247
utility maximization
utility maximization problem, 13
utility of goods, 169

validation set, 198
value-based pricing, 7
variable pricing, 119–121, 128, 147, 154–155
variable unit costs, 2

variance, 248, 255, 259–260
VLOOKUP function, 163–164, 204–205, 223–224, 235
volume, 2
volume changes, 64

waiting time, 245–246, 252, 256, 261
weather forecast, 192, 212–213
weather sensors, 189
web retailers, 44
What-if-Analysis, 226
wholesale dealers, 37
willingness to pay, 19–21, 39, 41, 42–43, 45, 74–75, 83, 85–88, 119, 154, 156–157, 159, 181, 237–241, 243, 248, 270
  definition, 70
worst case scenario, 232

x-variable, 66

yield management, 179
y-variable, 66

z-score, 197–198, 208